"This thoroughly researched and clearly written book should be a welcome addition to all college, school, and public libraries.

"Popular accounts of the Phoenicians are rarely coherent and comprehensive. Sanford Holst's survey of the rise and fall of the Phoenicians is a splendid exception. He traces their history from the rise of Phoenician shipbuilders in the fourth millennium BC until the fall of Carthage to the Romans in 146 BC, at the end of the Third Punic War. Throughout the book Holst makes insightful use of the latest archaeological evidence from land and beneath the sea, as well as the testimony of ancient writers. He even shows the survival of Phoenician traditions in modern Lebanon.

"Despite its scholarly underpinnings, the book presents an engaging narrative that clearly explains the salient points without getting bogged down in details of interest only to specialists. The author's clear prose should make the story attractive even to beginning students of the ancient world. The book's many illustrations and maps add to its appeal.

"I learned a great deal from it and know that others will, too."

David Northrup
Professor of History
Boston College

"A well written, historically accurate book about a great civilization which has been by-passed by the annals of history. I have given many copies to my friends and they have found it equally enjoyable."

Judge James Kaddo

"There are few history books so compelling as to leave you wanting to read more. I thoroughly enjoyed every moment of it. Mr. Holst has done a phenomenal job in writing as well as researching the Phoenicians. I have read other books about Phoenicians in the past and was never really impressed. This one has a special way of pulling everything together so that their accomplishments make sense."

Dany Chalhoub

ALSO BY SANFORD HOLST

Sworn in Secret

PHOENICIANS

Lebanon's Epic Heritage

Second Edition

SANFORD HOLST

foreword by
Antoine Khoury Harb, Ph.D.

SANTORINI BOOKS

Santorini Publishing
14622 Ventura Boulevard, #800
Los Angeles, California 91403

Second Edition
Printing: December 2021

Excerpt used with permission: Lichtheim, Miriam.
Ancient Egyptian Literature Vol II. ©1976 The Re-
gents of the University of California.

Publisher's Cataloging-in-Publication Data

Holst, Sanford.
   Phoenicians : Lebanon's epic heritage / by Sanford
 Holst ; foreword by Antoine Khoury Harb. – 2nd ed.
   p. cm.
   Includes bibliographical references and index.
   Library of Congress Control Number: 2021930532
   ISBN 978-1-945199-04-2

   1. Phoenicians. 2. Phoenicia – Civilization. 3. Phoenician
 antiquities. 4. Lebanon – Antiquities, Phoenician.   I. Title.

DS81.H65 2021   930'.04926

ACKNOWLEDGMENTS

Special thanks to

Joumana Medlej in Beirut and London, friend, confidante, advisor and proof of why the Phoenicians worshiped their women.

Dr. Antoine Khoury Harb in Kaslik, Lebanon, respected educator, historian and archaeologist, passionate about the heritage of his people.

Zack Anton in Beirut, media entrepreneur and devoted supporter of the Lebanese people.

Judge James Kaddo, Chairman of the Lebanese American Foundation and a well-respected leader in the Lebanese community.

Amira Matar in Los Angeles, whose tireless efforts on behalf of expatriates and the people of Lebanon have value beyond measure.

I also acknowledge and thank the following people, who took time amid their important duties to share with me some of their considerable expertise in areas essential to this research. Their contributions enabled me to amend the earlier drafts of this manuscript and made it a much stronger representation of the events that took place. The responsibility for any error which might remain is solely my own.

Dr. Suzy Hakimian, curator of the Beirut National Museum, Lebanon.

Dr. Helene Sader, head of the Department of History and Archaeology, American University of Beirut, Lebanon.

Antonia Kanaan, Lebanese historical site advisor and guide, who studied under noted archaeologist Dr. Maurice Dunand.

Dr. Ahmed Abdel Fattah, General Director of Museums and Antiquities of Alexandria, Egypt.

Dr. Mervat Seif el Din, General Director of the Graeco-Roman Museum, Alexandria, Egypt.

Dr. Alaa Ashmawy, Professor of Engineering, University of South Florida, United States.

Dr. Christos Doumas, Director of the Excavations at Akrotiri, Santorini, Greece.

Dr. Nota Dimopoulou, Director of the Iraklion Archaeological Museum, Crete, Greece.

Dr. Reuben Grima, curator of World Heritage Sites, Malta.

In addition I thank the heavenly Author who actually writes all books and causes us to bring these works into the world when the time is right.

FOREWORD

by Antoine Khoury Harb, Ph.D.

A very important aspect of Phoenician/Lebanese heritage or "patrimoine" is its expansion into the world. We are today exactly the way we were thousands of years ago. Is there any other nation on earth that has more citizens outside the motherland than within its borders? It is unique! Going back in time, we can understand the reasons for this. Geographic reasons: Lebanon is the result of a dialog between mountain and sea. This dualism is a geographic reason without which one cannot understand the Lebanese.

If you are not aware of your origins, you are uprooted. Whereas if you know your family—your father, your aunt, your siblings, especially if there is reason to be proud of them—then you care! Plus, when you know there is a heritage going back thousands of years that is constant in our history, we can say, "This is mine." I am a resultant of my history. When I know myself, I gain confidence.

Also, beyond the cultural, moral, or spiritual heritage, there is the level of physical heritage: the land. Even before the concept of state existed, Lebanon had both its borders and its name. That is a notion of belonging which no one can question.

A Lebanese person knows his right, his history, and his role in the civilization. It is the Phoenicians' commerce that opened civilizations to each other in a peaceful way! Commerce is a peaceful dialog between people, and a dialog of cultures. You get to know the other; and the more you know each other, the closer people come together.

Let me conclude by quoting Charles Corm, "the bard of the Phoenicians," who wrote these lines:

> Si je rappelle aux miens nos aïeux phéniciens,
> C'est qu'ils n'étaient alors, au fronton de l'histoire,
> Avant de devenir musulmans ou chrétiens,
> Qu'un même peuple uni dans une même gloire.

Which means:

> If I remind my own of our Phoenician forefathers,
> It is because we were, at the gate of history,
> Before becoming Muslims or Christians,
> A single people united in the same glory.

A.K.H.
Beirut, Lebanon
January 21, 2005

Introduction

by Sanford Holst

The Phoenician and Greek people shared many intimate experiences during their long history together. That included an intriguing event documented in Homer's *Iliad*. In his eloquent verses Homer told of a silver bowl crafted by the Phoenicians which was so valuable it was a worthy prize for an athletic competition between the greatest of the Greeks gathered at Troy.[1]

> Achilles, the son of Peleus, then offered prizes for speed in running: a mixing-bowl beautifully wrought, of pure silver. It would hold six measures, and far exceeded all others in the whole world for beauty; it was the work of cunning artificers in Sidon, and had been brought into port by Phoenicians from beyond the sea....
>
> Homer, *Iliad* 23.740

Believe it or not, 150 years ago it was thought those early Greeks and Phoenicians were only mythical and never existed. Even the

Trojan War was said to have never happened. That is how history was taught in schools and colleges.

But then new discoveries began to take place. And they have continued to take place right up to the present time. Fascinating archaeological findings have been filling in missing pieces of ancient Mediterranean history and giving us a more vivid picture of the epic events which shaped those ancient societies. But Greek history and Phoenician history have been updated unevenly, resulting in problems for those who read and work in the field of ancient history.

This is how it happened.

In those early days it was said that a widespread Dark Age existed before the brilliant emergence of Classical Greece. That period of darkness began around 1200 BC when the Sea Peoples laid waste to much of the ancient Mediterranean. After that, the Greeks were thought to have retained only a few imaginative legends about gods and noble individuals competing in some mythical Minoan kingdom and Trojan War.

The people of Phoenicia—the land now known as Lebanon—were assumed to have had their cities destroyed by the Sea Peoples as well. So it was believed that Phoenician society began after 1200 BC.

Then came a series of archaeological discoveries which disproved those notions about the Greeks and Phoenicians. The ancient city of Troy was uncovered by Heinrich Schliemann in 1873. This indicated the Trojan War was not just mythology but actual history.[2] He then unearthed the city of Mycenae in 1876, demonstrating the Mycenaean Greeks and their society likewise existed. In 1900, Sir Arthur Evans excavated the palace of Knossos at Crete, proving the rich and art-filled Minoan civilization also was real.

Among the Phoenician cities, similar discoveries took place when Ernest Renan performed excavations at Byblos in 1860, revealing its long history. Pierre Montet added to that work in 1921, and Maurice Dunand continued it from 1925 to 1975. At other ancient sites in Lebanon archaeological efforts yielded a wealth of historical findings, especially the work of Patricia Bikai at Tyre in 1973. These excavations showed in great detail that the Sea Peoples caused no destruction at Phoenician cities in 1200 BC. The rich Phoenician sea-trading society was clearly continuous before, during and after that time.

As a result of all these discoveries, historians have updated their writings on Greek history to acknowledge the Minoans and Mycenaean Greeks who lived before 1200 BC.

Yet those same historians have been slow to acknowledge the existence of Phoenician society before 1200 BC. To remedy that situation, this book presents a treasure-trove of detailed Phoenician history from its earliest days in Byblos to the aftermath of the Punic Wars. The well-documented Phoenician involvement in epic events before and after 1200 BC significantly affected the lives and wars of the Greeks, Romans, Egyptians and members of other societies.

It is important to note that this process of assembling the history of the Phoenician people and their society has been going forward on two fronts. One is the traditional presentation of academic papers that I and others have produced, as well as the field reports written by experienced archaeologists. These will necessarily continue for many years until the full range of Phoenician history has been explored with appropriate annotations and citations.

As a companion to that process, the current volume you now hold is the broad flow of this epic story painted in bold strokes. It is well known that there are often several opinions on what actually happened during each event in history. In scholarly papers one is apt to identify those various opinions, with the pro and con of each, and then conclude with support for one opinion. Yet to cover three thousand years of history and hundreds of significant events in one volume using that approach would require perhaps two thousand pages, and that is too large a scope for the present work.

Therefore, the approach used here is to simply present the explanation of each event that is best supported by all available historical, archaeological and scientific data. This is a much more understandable rendition of the events which have occurred, and is reasonable in scope. However, it is certainly not perfect. For that reason full disclosure of sources are made in citations so that those interested in probing deeper have the means to do so.

In recent years genetic research has added a new dimension to our understanding of these ancient societies. With regard to the Phoenicians, Pierre Zalloua and Spencer Wells conducted a genetic analysis of DNA samples collected in Lebanon and other locations around the Mediterranean. They identified components of the Y-chromosome that they believe give a good indication of where the Phoenician people established their colonies and conducted their trade. These genetic markers are still found in some of the people living there today.

One of the conclusions they noted was that the people carrying these genetic markers had lived in and around the land we know as Lebanon for at least 12,000 years.[3] That is consistent with the historical and archaeological records which indicate the Phoenicians arose on the shores and mountains of Lebanon, rather than arriving from some distant place as had been considered in the past.

What you see here is an eye-opening journey through the fascinating and critically important days of the ancient Mediterranean. It encompasses exotic lands and islands, intriguingly different societies, great leaders, epic battles, and an up-close view of resilient people from the shores of Lebanon who sailed across white-capped seas to affect the events of history.

These stirring experiences are part of our heritage. This is the world from which the West arose.

S.H.
Los Angeles
February 12, 2021

CONTENTS

*In the wish to get the best
information that I could
on these matters, I made
a voyage to Tyre in
Phoenicia. . . .*

*Herodotus
The Histories 2:44*

Fig. 1   *Phoenician coins*

CHAPTER 1

AN OFFERING AT THE TEMPLE

Hiram was not yet king of the Phoenician city of Tyre when his people were confronted by an imminent threat to their survival. King David of Israel had sent out troops to extend his authority northward, and they marched from victory to victory until they reached Tyre in the land known today as Lebanon. While destiny hovered over the anticipated battlefield along the Mediterranean coast, Hiram saw his father Abibaal craft a path toward peaceful resolution of the crisis. Rich gifts were offered to the Hebrew king, and the impending devastation was avoided. Hiram learned this lesson well.

Shortly thereafter his father passed away, and at nineteen years of age Hiram came to wear Tyre's crown.[4] As fortune would have it, David died eight years later in 970 BC and left to his son Solomon the crown of the Jewish people. These young kings acted quickly to establish good relations, and then set out on a monumental undertaking in Jerusalem. They began to raise a great temple to God, as worshipped by the Jewish people.

This building of Solomon's Temple was a moment of such importance to the Hebrews that their scribes meticulously recorded each step of the process. Their writings revealed much about how these two societies dealt with the people around them, and how ancient Mediterranean societies wove the material of civilization, one thread at a time. It is true that documents from antiquity, particularly those which contain articles of faith, need to be compared with other sources to see which parts are historically accurate. But since we know Solomon's Temple existed and other aspects of building it have proven to be reasonably accurate, then letters such as the following may actually have been exchanged.[5]

Every successive generation of Jewish scribes kept and copied these words, allowing their experiences to come down to us today as part of the Tanakh, also known as the Old Testament.

> And Hiram king of Tyre sent his servants unto Solomon; for he had heard that they had anointed him king in the room of his father; for Hiram was ever a lover [great admirer] of David.
>
> And Solomon sent to Hiram, saying, "Thou knowest how that David my father could not build an house unto the name of the LORD his God for the wars which were about him on every side, until the LORD put them under the soles of his feet. But now the LORD my God hath given me rest on every side, so that there is neither adversary nor evil occurrent. And, behold, I purpose to build an house unto the name of the LORD my God, as the LORD spake unto David my father, saying, Thy son, whom I will set upon thy throne in thy room, he shall build an house unto my name. Now therefore command thou that they hew me cedar trees out of Lebanon; and my servants shall be with thy servants; and unto thee will I give hire for thy servants according to all that thou shalt appoint; for thou knowest that there is not among us any that can skill to hew timber like unto the Sidonians."
>
> And it came to pass, when Hiram heard the words of Solomon, that he rejoiced greatly, and said, "Blessed be the LORD this day, which hath given unto David a wise son over this great people."
>
> And Hiram sent to Solomon, saying, "I have considered the things which thou sentest to me for; and I will do all thy desire concerning timber of cedar, and con-

cerning timber of fir. My servants shall bring them down from Lebanon unto the sea; and I will convey them by sea in floats unto the place that thou shalt appoint me, and will cause them to be discharged there, and thou shalt receive them; and thou shalt accomplish my desire, in giving food for my household."

So Hiram gave Solomon cedar trees and fir trees according to all his desire. And Solomon gave Hiram twenty thousand measures of wheat for food to his household, and twenty measures of pure oil; thus gave Solomon to Hiram year by year. And the LORD gave Solomon

Fig. 2   The Western Wall of Mount Moriah in Jerusalem

wisdom, as he promised him; and there was peace between Hiram and Solomon; and they two made a league
together.

1 Kings 5:1-12

In due course the great Temple of Solomon stood on Mount Moriah above the city of Jerusalem, built upon a foundation of large,
perfectly-cut rectangular stones. It was written that "they brought
great stones, costly stones, and hewed stones, to lay the foundation of
the house." [6] Above this was arrayed massive timbers of cedar and
works of gold and brass.

Solomon's Temple would stand for 379 years, then a second temple was built upon the foundations of the first. In 586 years more, that
second temple fell, and adversaries erased all traces of the massive
stone foundation. By so doing, they caused the magnificent Temple
of Solomon to pass into the realm of legend and imagination, growing in importance as a symbol and talisman for several groups of
people around the world as the centuries passed.

Many other mysteries and legendary events likewise began to fill
the ancient Mediterranean's history and lore, attracting the curiosity
and attention of young and old over the years. The Great Pyramid of
Egypt has attracted its share of wonder and exploration, as have the
curious events of the Mesopotamian epic of Gilgamesh. Later, the
Minoans seemed to appear from nowhere, followed by the equally
perplexing Sea Peoples. Etruscans evolved and disappeared in Italy,
as did the Mycenaeans in Greece. The Eleusinian Mysteries became
popularly practiced, and their secrets were faithfully kept. The
secretive society of Pythagoras combined math and mysteries.
Wondrous feats were performed by Alexander the Great, Hannibal
Barca, Scipio Africanus and others.

The ancient Mediterranean has a seemingly endless mixture of
mysteries and lore that still fascinates us today. These relics from
those early days appear like brightly-colored jewels below the surface
of deep waters, giving us glimpses of things enticing, yet remain just
out of reach. Into this fascinating world sailed the Phoenicians, who
for many centuries explored the lands where all these things took
place and traded with the people who lived there. By coming to
know the Phoenicians and their personal involvement with other

societies, we acquire a fresh view of great leaders, pivotal events and elusive mysteries, making them more understandable and sometimes even more fascinating than before.

King Hiram of Tyre contributed to the fabric of the ancient Mediterranean not only through his role in building Solomon's Temple, but by casting the net of Phoenician colonies farther than before. He began by expanding the two ports of Tyre with landfill and stoneworks around the harbors.[7] Then he sent his cedar ships and experienced captains out across the sea to increase the volume of profitable trade and establish new outposts. This work was vigorously continued by his successors, and continued until Phoenician colonies covered the Mediterranean Sea from shore to shore, and across many islands in between. These colonies even spilled out onto the Atlantic coastlines of Europe and Africa. They grew into a pulsing network of activity whose crown jewel was the legendary city of Carthage on the coast of North Africa.

One of the early Phoenician colonies, established long before Hiram's time, covered the southeastern part of Cyprus, the large island just 120 miles off the Phoenician coast. It encompassed a number of outposts, but in particular it included the small city of Kition, a good port that gave these sea traders access to the rich copper deposits of the Cypriot mountains. This metal was an essential ingredient for the making of bronze, so transporting and trading ingots of copper was an early staple of Phoenician commerce.

During the summer of 2004 I flew to Larnaca in Cyprus, the city that now covers much of this old Phoenician colony, to examine the intriguing remains of that ancient port. Many people from Turkey and Greece had come to different parts of Cyprus in antiquity, but it is clear that in the 13th century BC there was a small Phoenician temple and sacred garden in northern Kition, to which was added a grand temple to the Phoenician goddess just after 1200 BC.[8] I found these sites to be a quarter-mile northwest of the Larnaca Archaeological Museum, and still in surprisingly good condition.

One of the most remarkable attributes of this grand temple in Kition was the massive stones that made up its foundation, which are still in place today. Carefully hewn to perfectly square corners and edges, these large rectangular blocks were roughly nine feet long, six feet high, and six feet thick. Carvings on one side of the stones may have included images of ships at sea, but are difficult to make out now due to erosion. That is understandable, since the temple is from the same time period as Solomon's Temple, and even slightly older.

Fig. 3   Phoenician temple at Kition, Cyprus

Perhaps even more striking is how much the Phoenician temple at Kition resembles the description by Hebrew scribes of the great temple and other buildings raised on Mount Moriah.

> All these were of costly stones, according to the measures of hewed stones, sawed with saws, within and without, even from the foundation unto the coping, and so on the outside toward the great court. And the foundation was of costly stones, even great stones, stones of ten cubits, and stones of eight cubits.
>
> I Kings 7:9-10

The great foundation stones of Solomon's Temple have been removed and their traces completely erased. It is therefore quite possible that this temple in Kition—crafted by Phoenician artisans employing the same methods used on Mount Moriah—is as close as we will ever come to seeing how the Temple of Solomon looked when it stood above the city of Jerusalem.

These great temples in Jerusalem and Cyprus are but one glimpse of how the Phoenician people were involved in events both famous and mysterious across the ancient Mediterranean world. There would also be rich trade, alliances, alphabets, arts, gold, silver, cedar boats and much more. There were kings and queens, war and peace, full-blooded men and women, fertility rites, ancient documents and epics, tears and laughter, spiced food and wine—all adorning their adventures on the irresistibly alluring shores of the Mediterranean Sea.

It is into those early days that we now go.

CHAPTER 2

IN THE BEGINNING

It was a truly beautiful place, overgrown with oleander and other tall bushes bearing bright flowers in shades of yellow and red. Divided by stands of tall cedar trees and broad meadows of wild grass flecked with tiny white flowers, the low tableland which would be known as Byblos must have looked like a paradise on earth.

In these early days around 6000 BC most of the lands bordering the clear blue Mediterranean Sea were clothed with verdant growth and virgin wilderness. It was much cooler and wetter than would be the case in later years, and the foot of man had not fallen heavily upon the land. Fruits and wild grain were abundant on the hills overlooking the sun-dappled waters which lapped the sandy shore. Glossy-coated animals of various shapes and sizes, as well as birds bedecked with bright-hued feathers, fed themselves easily among the woods and brought forth their young in profusion each spring.

Narrow footpaths meandered across green meadows and among the tall trees. These were the only signs that revealed the presence of men, women and their offspring. Small tribes followed the ancient custom of migrating from place to place as the food and game around them became scarce, because it was always plentiful over the next hill. But changes were coming.

The richness of the land brought forth an ever-increasing population despite an occasional outbreak of disease, natural disaster, or onset of fighting among roving tribes seeking the best land. The relatively new practice of harvesting wild grains in autumn and sowing them on the fertile soil in spring enabled a growing number of people to thrive in one place instead of constantly moving in search of food for themselves and their animals. Small towns began to appear, some of which would rise, flourish and then fade away. Other towns would persevere, grow strong, and echo through the lore of the people in these lands for thousands of years.

Among the latter was the young habitation of Byblos on the eastern shore of the Mediterranean Sea.[9] Migrating tribes had passed by this place since time immemorial. Yet now that some were seeking a place to settle, they could find no better home. Though wildly overgrown with dense vegetation, the rolling land was fairly flat and stood perhaps seventy-five feet above the sea and the surrounding lowlands, making it easily defendable. But the riches of the land went far beyond that.

Just inland from this young settlement, the Lebanon Mountains rose to incredible heights. The highlands above Byblos were part of a long range of peaks, which extended roughly forty miles to the north and the same distance to the south along the seacoast. Known to early travelers and dwellers as the cedar forest on the white mountains, this Lebanon range eventually bequeathed its name on the narrow strip of land that rested between it and the shore, and on the broader plain to the east. All came to be known as Lebanon.

High atop the snow-capped peaks of this mountain range that rose to ten thousand feet, ice slowly melted in the sunlight and sent rivulets of frigid water down the slopes. These became streams that fed dense tangles of roots at the feet of tall, straight and massive cedars, which thrived at these high altitudes. As those streams of cold water flowed downhill, they merged into rivers that passed through more forests where juniper, pine and oaks mingled with the cedars in a mélange of competing pine needles and leaves. The thick woods grew right down to the small Byblos plateau by the sea.

And the sweet water came also. Underground streams fed a natural well in the middle of the small table of land, making life possible there throughout the year. So roaming people settled down beside

Fig. 4　Cedars at Bcharré in the Lebanon Mountains

the well. They cleared the land and planted it with a rustic form of wheat. They built oval homes with local stones and the plentiful wood. Their labors and simple life created a village, and then a small town. Though they could not know it, their modest community would one day grow to have vast riches, great honors, deep secrets, great anguish, deep-seated determination, and finally peaceful joy as the cavalcade of its destiny marched through the cobble-stoned streets.

For this community had another bequest of good fortune that would firmly shape its fate and thrust it into a place alongside the great societies of the world. As one walked to the end of the promontory at the westernmost edge of the plateau at Byblos, it was possible to look down a steep slope that plunged twenty-five yards to the clear Mediterranean waters. To the right was a natural harbor, which cut into the shore just north of the tableland. To the left was another natural harbor which edged into the lowland to the south of the plateau. Though travel upon the sea was still in its infancy in these times, the day would come when the two harbors of Byblos would transship much of the wealth of the civilized world.

The pattern this community established—building upon a promontory with two adjacent harbors—was something their descendants would repeat in many other places over the centuries. And these people who built them would become known by a name inextricably linked to lush images of exotic foreign trade, for they were the Phoenicians.

But those days were yet to come. In these early times the people of Byblos contented themselves with their simple life on the lower edge of the Lebanon Mountains. They lived on a daily diet of grains, wild berries, lamb, a few fishes from the sea, and the occasional rabbit or other game found on the forested slopes. As time went on, the game upon the land decreased, but the bounty of the sea was found to be never-ending. So they took to the sea and became fishermen.

Fishing at first was a straightforward affair. One simply waded into the shallows of the sea and used a long, sharp stick to spear the silvery catch. But this required a great deal of patience, and sometimes the elusive quarry would move quickly right or left and make good an escape. In time, two short, sharp sticks were lashed near the end of the spear—one aimed diagonally to the left and the other to the right. This created a three-pointed stick called a trident and gave the advantage clearly to the fisherman. As simple hooks and woven nets became popular—and strong enough to hold their catch—fishing became a full-time livelihood. Still, the bigger and more plentiful schools of fish were in the deeper waters, and some new discovery was needed.

It had long been known that one could sit on a log, or several logs tied together, and paddle from island to island near the shore when the Mediterranean was quiet and no storms were brewing. The enterprising fishermen of Byblos, and surely other fishermen as well, discovered that one could dig out a hollow on one side of the log and use it as a place to sit with a spear, line or net.[10] With this "dugout," they could paddle to where the dense schools of fish swam in deeper waters and multiply their catch.

Fig. 5 Byblos home foundations from 4500 BC

Fig. 6 Steps up to Byblos from the old harbor

As centuries rolled by, they used the plentiful wood of Byblos—especially the huge, durable cedar logs—to build larger, multiple-person dugouts. To allow more men to come aboard and to store even larger catches of fish, they added boards of wood to the sides of the dugout. The higher sides also kept out the salty water when the sea turned suddenly windy or stormy, and provided support for large oars instead of the smaller hand-held paddles. This latter innovation allowed several men to row strongly and take their boat quickly across long distances in pursuit of schools of fish. That proved to be a godsend because it reduced the number of days when they would come home with no catch, the bane of fishermen everywhere. By 4500 BC, the people of Byblos were sending many of these small fishing boats in every direction across the clear blue waters.

Each day, as the heat of midday set in, they rowed their boats ashore at the two harbors, and pulled them up onto the sand above the high-water mark. With the help of their sons or daughters on board, the fishermen off-loaded their catch and bore baskets brimming with slippery produce up the short slope to the top of the plateau. There they were greeted by the sounds of domestic animals bleating in their pens and children playing outside the rustic huts of the growing town, which now numbered in the hundreds of homes gathered around the deep well. Many of those homes can still be seen there, unearthed after all these years.[11] The floors of pounded powder and soil are still intact and are surrounded by low walls of stone which once were much higher. The wood which would have formed the upper structure and roof is now long gone, but when people were living there the tiny homes would have held up a small sea of rooftops spanning the distance from the well to the cliff-edge above the sea.

The fishermen carried their wet loads past the women who were drawing water from the well, tending the small fields of wheat, and minding the myriad tasks that kept the town alive. When the ships had been emptied, a light noonday meal was set out. Afterwards came the traditional cleaning of fish, mending of fishing gear, and preparation of the evening's supper. As the sun set low over the vast sea and cast its orange-red light on the scattered clouds above, a few words of thanks were said to Mother Nature, and the dinner was eaten with gusto. Then the fermented beverages would come out, women would catch up on the events of the day, men would repeat adventures that got better with each telling, and young couples would quietly steal away to find a place where they could be alone for the evening. Life was good in this rustic, fruitful land.

Of course Byblos was not the only place where people chose to give up the nomadic life in favor of villages and towns around the Mediterranean. One of those early towns was the ancient city of Jericho in what is now called Palestine. It was about 160 miles south of Byblos near the Dead Sea, and happened to come into existence much

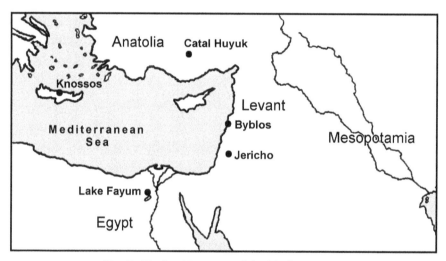

Fig. 7   *Early cities around the Mediterranean*

earlier. Jericho's major claim to fame was its great walls and the well-known story of its destruction. By 7000 BC those massive stone walls were twelve feet high and over six feet thick.[12] They were augmented by a circular stone tower and a deep, wide ditch. If not the first walled city, it was at least one of the most spectacular of its time. The need for such protection unfortunately underscored the fear in which people in the Jordan Valley lived due to the roving tribes who threatened their existence.

The fall of Jericho about six thousand years later was likewise spectacular, as chronicled in the Old Testament of the Bible.

So the people shouted when the priests blew with the trumpets: and it came to pass, when the people heard the sound of the trumpet, and the people shouted with a great shout, that the wall fell down flat, so that the people went up into the city, every man straight before him, and they took the city. And they utterly destroyed all that was in the city, both man and woman, young and old, and ox, and sheep, and ass, with the edge of the sword.

And they burnt the city with fire, and all that was therein: only the silver, and the gold, and the vessels of brass and of iron, they put into the treasury of the house of the LORD.

Joshua 6:20-21, 24

In the other direction from Byblos, about 260 miles to the northwest in Anatolia, another city existed that was already well established by 6000 BC. It was known as Çatal Hüyük. Nestled at a 3,000-foot altitude in the high plains of what is now Turkey, it was about sixty-five miles north of the Mediterranean Sea and cut off from those waters by a ridge of steep mountains. Nevertheless it became a thriving metropolis with a remarkably high degree of civilization. Since metals had not yet come into use, the people of this city did a brisk business selling obsidian, a volcanic glass which was ideal for making sharp tools. It was found locally in abundant supply and was greatly in demand almost everywhere.

One of the most notable aspects of Çatal Hüyük's society was that it could afford enough leisure to sponsor the arts.[13] In fact, the people of this city created the earliest known paintings on man-made walls. Among these were images of red and black bulls placed on walls of fine white plaster. These people also painted representations of the goddess of fertility, showing her as a young girl, as a mother giving birth, and then as an older woman.

Çatal Hüyük flourished for many centuries and produced many of Anatolia's contributions to civilized life. Eventually, however, it faded from view.

Far to the west, roughly five hundred miles from Byblos, another settlement was created during this time at Knossos on Crete. This was the southernmost island in a collection of mainland and isles which would one day be known as Greece. The village of Knossos would eventually grow to become a significant city and then the crown jewel of the Minoan civilization, but at this time it was just a small agricultural community. Its residents quietly pursued their special interest in raising almonds on this picturesque hilltop located about three miles from the sea.

To the east of Byblos other settlements appeared beside the north-ernmost headwaters of the Tigris and Euphrates Rivers. While this ore-rich region was credited with starting the metal-working age by shaping copper into tools, it had formed only scattered villages by the early sixth millennium. Then after 4500 BC significant urban areas begin to appear hundreds of miles downriver in the land that would become famous as Mesopotamia.

Even Egypt, whose great Nile River emptied into the southern part of the Mediterranean, emerged at a relatively slow pace. Des-tined to produce many marvels, a great civilization, and a special relationship with the Phoenicians, it began as a pastoral land with grassy fields covering a wide region. Unfortunately, the significant warming that was felt all over the world in those formative days was particularly disastrous for Egypt. The broad grasslands dried up, and the nomadic people who depended upon them were forced to retreat to the life-saving waters of the Nile.

This legendary river flowed deep and wide all the way to where the Nile Delta began, near the present-day location of Cairo. There it fanned out into seven major branches, each of which found their way to the sea. Those seven branches and the multitude of small channels that split off from them made up the marshy delta land. This broad area attracted a large number of refugees from the former pastures that had turned to sand.

Traces of habitation have been found in the delta dating from this time, but no notable towns have yet emerged. Unfortunately, the annual flooding of the Nile regularly inundated and buried the whole area. During the rest of the year it was still muddy enough that subsidence would cause homes—and in later years whole towns—to descend into the mud and disappear. This was not helped by the fact that homes in the delta at that time were made from bundles of reeds, rush mats, palm thatch, and woven twigs mixed with dried mud. This was not exactly the wherewithal to withstand the test of time.

The other haven in Egypt as the fields dried out was Lake Fayum, a pleasant oasis about forty miles southwest of where the Nile met the delta. It was not until about 4500 BC that evidence of town life began to take shape on the northern banks of the lake. The most significant aspect of life here was not just that people raised grain and stored it in underground granaries, but that they also began to weave a crude form of linen. In time the linen of Egypt would become one of the finest in the world.

Returning to Byblos, we see again the small plateau with its twin harbors from which diligent fishermen set sail on the coastal waters. As they pursued their daily catches, it was only natural that they put into port at neighboring fishing villages from time to time to escape inclement weather or to make repairs. As was the custom, they would use these visits to also trade a few of their fresh fish for objects of value: a bit of colorful cloth for their wives, or some wine for the dinner table.

At some later date, when a new dress was needed or the table wine ran dry, it was not a haphazard visit but rather a purposeful one that took them to the neighboring village, and the desired trades were made. Nor were the people of Byblos the only ones engaged in this. Any fisherman had the same opportunity to make calls at neighboring villages and make a trade for what he might need or desire.

However there was one thing that set the people of Byblos apart, and it made all the difference. They had the huge, straight logs of cedar from hillsides above their town. And those logs were readily hewn into aromatic and highly durable timber for building boats and homes. It was true that this cedar was only of modest interest when their sailing trips took them northward, since many other types of evergreen and hardwood were available on the well-watered hills in that direction. But when they sailed to the south, where the low hills had dried out and were becoming covered with drifting sand, the response to their visits was completely different. The huge pieces of lumber hewn from cedar logs caused a measure of excitement, and large amounts of goods were offered in trade.

This eventually became a profitable sideline for the fishermen of this cedar-blessed town, but it also presented them with a daunting amount of work. Felling trees, dragging the huge logs downhill, and then hewing them into lumber required different skills and disciplines. It was not at all like their main trade of sailing, knowing the likely movements of fish, and patient trawling to pull in a good catch. No doubt there were some at Byblos who specialized in the culling of wood and the building or repairing of boats, but they would not have been great in number in these early years. Cedar weathered so magnificently and the local population grew so slowly that there would rarely have been a need to commission a new boat.

All of these considerations naturally led to the next reasonable step in their trade: building boats for others. Some fishermen in other villages, particularly in the wood-poor south, certainly would have traded for lumber and tried to build their own boats. Yet as we have already seen, this required a different set of skills than most people possessed. Moreover it would have been quite expensive to buy those materials log by log, even before all the work began. It was much easier to trade something they had in surplus or could make easily— cloths, olive oil, wine, jewelry, handicrafts or anything else of value— in exchange for a boat, and leave the boatbuilding to those who did it for a living.

The people of Byblos, with their virtually unlimited supply of majestic cedars, became those boatbuilders. And they raised this skill to an incredible level of virtuosity. It is almost stunning to consider, so many years later, what beautiful works of art these watercraft were. Shipwrecks preserved at the bottom of the Mediterranean Sea near places like Uluburun on the southern coast of Anatolia reveal the intricate shape and construction of these vessels in the many centuries BC.[14]

Good fortune brought me to Tyre in Lebanon just as the harbor's boatmaster was finishing a handmade vessel of Phoenician design that he had created using these same ancient methods. Until you have seen such a boat for yourself and run the palm of your hand over the smooth, seamless pieces of finely linked wood, it is hard to appreciate what a miracle these creations actually were. And when built by a master boatwright, each one was a consummate work of art.[15]

Fig. 8   Newly built boat in Tyre of Phoenician design

At Byblos the small number of boats built for others and the modest trade transacted on the way back from fishing trips at this time were simply sidelines for the villagers. To earn their living, they worked the sea and were, for the most part, content to be fishermen.

But a few clearly were not content. They enjoyed the bits of luxury that came from trade, and yearned for more. These may well have been the younger men at first, skilled at sailing the sea from the time they were youths helping in the fishing boats, but perhaps not enamored of being covered in fish oil after a day's work. Some of the men may have wanted to attract the eye and heart of an appealing maiden, and realized that a small container of exotic perfume from a distant land was more of an inducement than two very nice fish.

Whatever the reason, a handful of these questing spirits was enough to crew one or two boats dedicated to trade, and to launch an activity that had a dramatic impact on everyone in the community. This course of action gave rise to Phoenician society in the years that followed. Yet it was not without serious obstacles.

The first challenge they faced was the one encountered by all traders through the ages: getting provisioned for their voyage. As in most fishing villages, the assets of value were fairly evenly distributed among the families, with the only things of real value being their modest fishing boats and small houses. Up to 3200 BC the stone-and-wood houses at Byblos were all fairly similar in size and shape, though some may have been better furnished than others. And while their boats were no longer simple dugouts, at this early stage they would have progressed to no more than a few wide boards on each side and room for a small crew. It is likely that two or three families at a time would get together and commission a small boat to be built, promising to pay for it with a percentage of their daily catch for a set amount of time, or until an agreed-upon quantity of fish had been delivered. The two or three husbands, possibly with one or more teenage children aboard, would take the boat out and row to good fishing waters, then bring back their catch and share the proceeds among themselves and with their benefactor. Then, when the boat was paid off, all the proceeds were their own.

Provisioning an expedition for purposes of trade was quite similar in some ways, but much more difficult in others. The first thing required was the boat. But having one built in return for promises of future payment immediately ran into difficulties. Unlike fishing, which was a drudgingly repetitive though fairly reliable business, trade was highly variable. The erstwhile traders might go a long time in search of a buyer who wanted what they had to trade, and then the offer might be so low as to make the trade not worthwhile. So the risk of not getting repaid for the boat was already somewhat higher.

Not only that, these fishermen were fairly much limited to a half-day travel from their home port since they brought their catch home each day. If they had no catch at all, they might have gone farther and spent the night at some village or under the stars, and then sped home the next day. But that would have been the exception rather than the rule. This meant they basically traveled the same coasts and depths over and over. They knew each rock, each shoal, every reef, and every movement of current within their limited range. The risk of a fishing vessel crashing on a rock was almost nonexistent. But for traders who had to search out new markets not already being covered by the fishermen, it was necessary to go beyond that roughly half-day limit.

Those farther waters were not completely unknown, since each generation no doubt had some adventurous members who had to go see what was there so they could say they had done it. And sometimes a fishing boat would be caught in a storm and be blown as far as Cyprus, with two days' travel required to get home using the limited rowing power available in those days. But beyond the half-day limit of travel, the rocks, shoals and reefs were not known. Until those obstacles were mapped, boats would be lost.

The other "higher risk" and cost involved with outfitting a fledgling merchant boat was the need to load it with cargo for trade—something the fishing boats did not require. To put lumber aboard, a grizzled woodworker in the village had to take time away from his other work to fell and hew the giant cedars. To put some cloth among the trading goods, several women together had to take time from tending their crops and caring for their families to weave and dye the material. For olive oil, the family tending an orchard of olive trees had to give up much of their harvest and take turns with grandparents, parents and children pressing the dark fruit to make extra oil that could go into the cargo. Clearly, the neophyte traders could not afford to pay the small fortune required to purchase all these goods for their venture. As a result, each of these providers had to accept some of the risk. In return for putting their wares aboard the vessel they received a promise of excellent profits when the voyage was completed. But if the boat sailed over the horizon and sank, all was lost.

The imponderable risk and rich investment needed for such trading ventures required a new arrangement than the "trust me, I will pay you back" approach used for launching fishing vessels. All of the investors—the boatbuilder, woodcutter, weavers, olive pressers, captain, crew, and others putting things of value into the enterprise—were at risk and would have needed to meet and make the major decisions that affected the proposed trip. Those choices would include a limit on how long the trip was to last, the distance to go, the acceptable items to receive in trade, the risks to take, and many other issues. All of the terms would have to be acceptable to the whole group, otherwise any skittish members would pull out. To steer all of

this to successful resolution and launch, the partners would reasonably choose one among them to be the senior partner. That person's
role was mainly to monitor the progress and decide when an issue
was important enough to call the group together.

Once the cargo was finally set and the captain had his firm in-
structions, the trading boat and its crew could finally set sail. In their
ensuing adventures they entered many strange lands, each with its
own exotic customs, quixotic languages, romantic encounters and
near escapes. When all was said and done, however, the element of
overriding importance was that the boats returned. And their glittering cargoes were more than enough to satisfy those who were at risk.
So the next vessel was sent out. And the next....

True, some traders and boats did not return. They were victims to
unseen rocks, sudden storms, pirates and the occasional local war-
lord. But those losses were much less than the gains, so the traders
persisted. And a new way of life grew among the people of Byblos.

All of this would be echoed thousands of years later when the
great European trading companies came to be formed. In England,
for example, the moneyed investors in trading voyages sat as a board
of directors for the venture, and the leading partner—who resolved
smaller issues and brought the larger ones to the board—was designated as the managing director. These practices and terms are still in
use today.

In Byblos, these ad hoc arrangements eventually became a tradition. The way these individuals shared the wealth, made decisions,
and treated each other contributed strongly to the foundation of the
Phoenicians' vibrant society. But a few more pieces were still needed.

In 3200 BC the inhabitants of this plateau were still growers of
grain—though less so than they had been when the village was first
started—and they were fishermen pulling in the bounty of the
waters. But now they were also sea traders learning to move easily
and profitably among the people of other lands. As a result, the
village was beginning to struggle with forces pulling its citizens in
different directions and it faced a growing crisis.

While wrestling with this, one of the trading vessels from the village ventured farther to the south than their boats had ever gone
before. Whether this was by agreement to take an extremely risky
voyage or whether it was a headstrong captain who took matters into

his own hands, we may never know. However it happened, the expedition came to the mouth of the Nile River. This was a land that the local inhabitants called Kemet, but later became known as Egypt. It would not be too much of an exaggeration to say that the people of Byblos—and possibly the rest of the world as well—would never be the same.

CHAPTER 3

GOLDEN SANDS

The Byblos traders found an opportunity in Egypt which was about to make their greatest dreams possible. By 3200 BC, these people of the Nile had changed considerably from their days as a small, well-established community along the shore of Lake Fayum. In the fertile delta they had multiplied significantly as refugees from the expanding deserts swelled their ranks. Up river, many more of the up-rooted people had come to the narrow strips of fertile land on each side of the deep and wide watercourse which flowed all year long. Boisterous cities sprang up along the Nile and across the delta, led by strong rulers, administrators and local priests.

When the traders from Byblos arrived, they apparently did not penetrate very far into these strange surroundings. This was not due to lack of courage, but rather to caution and lack of local piloting experience. The muddy waters that oozed out of the marshlands of the Nile Delta were treacherous with sandbars under the surface of the silt-filled water. The traders' sea-going wooden boats with their fairly deep draught and low keels were built for the open waters, not for conditions such as these. In those places where good passage could be found up one of the major branches of the waterway, they might have reached the first large town, but not much farther. The open sea would have been kept at their back as an escape route, ready in case someone wanted to take their cargo without paying. In this land as in others they had visited, they were hopelessly outnumbered, and had lost other trading ships before. They learned caution the hard way.

The Egyptians were not constrained by those concerns since this was their homeland and they already knew whom they could trust and where to be watchful. Also, the quirky ways of the river had become second nature to them, and their riverboats were of a different design.

Lacking wood, they ingeniously tied bundles of papyrus reeds together to form floating pontoons.[16] They then lashed together whatever number of bundles were needed to make a raft or boat of the size and shape they wanted. Besides being cheap and quick to build, these craft had flat bottoms which made them ideal for traveling on a river where shifting sandbars might appear at any time. Most such obstructions passed directly beneath the reed-bundle boats without even being noticed. So the visitors from Byblos found the Nile branches to be awash with reed boats of all sizes and descriptions. Modest four-bundle dinghies, each with a single man paddling, would have had to make way for large craft belonging to the local ruler which were laden with heavy bales of goods and propelled by many powerful rowers.

Yet while the river branches became busier the farther one went upstream, the opposite was true as one drifted downstream toward the sea. As the placid river waters gave way to the choppy waves of the Mediterranean, all the advantages of the reed boats now turned into disadvantages. Their shallow draught and high flotation caused them to be tossed on the surface of the waves like a cork. The flat bottoms and lack of a keel meant that each side-wind pushed them sideways and off their course. And the structural integrity of the reeds and ropes could be forced past their limit if caught in a stormy sea, resulting in the scattering of many reeds across the waves and the loss of all cargo.

As a result, reed-boat fishing in the sea was a fair-weather sport only, and the exhausting work needed to overcome these deficiencies meant they stayed close to shore and did not go very far. The traders from Byblos had the completely opposite experience in their deep, heavy wooden boats. After a trade of their cedar and olive oil for

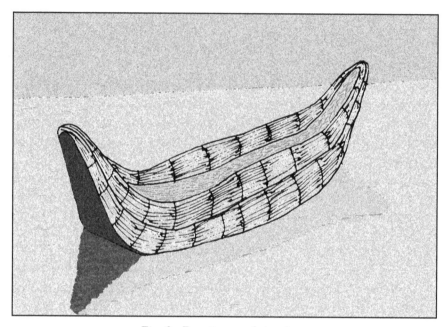

Fig. 9   Egyptian reed riverboat

linen and other rare goods, they gratefully escaped the claustropho-
bic confines of the river and burst past the last of the reed boats as
they entered the deep blue sea.

    Later, as they continued to return for profitable visits to this exotic
land, word spread that the strange traders in boats of wood chose not
to venture upriver, so potential dealers had to come to the delta to
trade with them. The solid beams of cedar that they had sold on
previous trips were also calling cards like no other in this land that
was virtually bereft of wood.

    The local palm trees had soft, pithy cores that were totally unsuit-
able for building. The small acacia trees could produce boards—but
no more than three feet in length.[17] As a result, a wealthy Egyptian
aspiring to build a great house could make no stronger declaration of
his or her vaunted position than to have a few massive pieces of
aromatic cedar used in the design to span the top of a wide doorway
or serve as ceiling rafters in a grand hallway, leaving the wood
exposed for all to see. Visitors to the house could only grind their
teeth with envy, because unless they could outbid other buyers when

the next boat came from Byblos, nothing to match it could be found in the land of the Nile.

So it was that word traveled far up the Nile about this magnificent wood, and wheels were set in motion. Excited talk of cedar passed the village of Tamit on the Damietta branch of the great river. It went past the gathering place of all the branches that made up the delta, beyond which was only the single, broad river. It went past the twists and turns of the watercourse, past the place that would later be the Valley of the Kings, and past the town of Naqada near the place where opulent Luxor would one day stand. At last, after a five-hundred mile journey up the Nile from the sea, word came to Nekhen, the town which would also bear the Greek name of *Hierakonpolis*, meaning "City of the Falcon."

The leaders of Hierakonpolis, like those of many other towns along the Nile, were anxious to elevate themselves and their town above their neighbors. Hearing word of the remarkable occurrences down in the delta, they seem to have decided upon a bold move. They would take advantage of these strangers' remarkably large beams of wood to expand their sanctuary dedicated to Horus, the falcon-god, and make it into the greatest temple anyone in Egypt had ever seen.

To launch this plan they reasonably followed the practice that became well-established in later years, and sent a priest of the temple to buy the large beams they desired. Provisioned with a quantity of gold and list of requirements, the priest would have set out for the neighborhood of Tamit where trading ships might be found.

When the priest and the traders from Byblos finally met and began to negotiate, it is likely that the exchange almost fell through from the start. It was too preposterous. The commission from Hierakonpolis consisted of four extremely massive cedars. Instead of the usual pieces of wood in the trader's cargo, which were perhaps a dozen feet long and a few inches thick, this order was for cylindrical pieces roughly forty feet long and three feet in diameter![18] A smaller fifth piece may also have been used as a crossbar. The request was staggering. But the exchange offered this time was not a modest amount of linen or grain. With a quantity of gold as deposit, and more to come when the gigantic cedars were delivered, it was a temptation they could not refuse.

When the traders returned to Byblos, they and their partners must have realized there was no way they could deliver on the Egyptian commission. Not by themselves. A town meeting would have been needed, and the traders' predicament laid out. The question was whether the entire town could take on the task and bear the staggering cost and risk—against a prince's ransom in return. No doubt the issue was hotly debated, though we will probably never know the details of it. But at some point, the rich rewards carried the day.

To secure such gigantic cedars they could not draw from the forest near the town. The biggest and best were many miles up the thickly overgrown mountainside, and a large crew had to be sent to retrieve them. Once found, the giants had to be felled carefully so they would not be damaged, and then trimmed of their branches. Each needed to be cut to comparable length with the others, then slowly dragged many miles down the mountain—again, without being damaged.

At least four large boats had to be commandeered, whether owned by fishermen or traders. The most physically fit men were needed to row the boats with their heavy loads. The most experienced captains had to take the helms to bring the valuable cargo through.

There were many other decisions to be made as well, with the whole town sitting as the board of partners on the venture. The loss of food and other daily necessities from giving up these resources would have to be borne by all. The bounty, if it came, would be shared by all. But much remained to be done.

The voyage would be exceedingly long. While a lightly laden boat with a favorable wind and good rowers might get through in seven days, these five boats would each be towing one of the giant cedars in the water behind them. Not only was such a load a chore to pull, but it was also difficult to control, as wind and current would want to keep sending the load to one side or the other. To keep their precious cargo off the rocks the ships' crews would have to travel in deep water, but also put in to shore with great care each night for food and rest. At least fourteen consecutive days of backbreaking work would be required to see it through.

So more boats had to be commandeered, and outfitted with the remaining older men, youths, and capable women to organize food, camps and provisions for the venture. Being unburdened by giant cedars and having only smaller boats left, they would be able to move more quickly than the lumbering cargo vessels. They could go ahead each day to build a camp for the coming night, at a place where the cargo boats could put into shore without damage.

And so the remarkable voyage was launched. By some miracle, the massive cedars survived the hundreds of miles of travel across the sea. The exchange was made at the mouth of the Nile, and the spectacular products of nature from a distant mountain were towed by the Egyptians five hundred miles up the river.

We know this effort was successful because in 1985 archaeologist Michael Hoffman conducted an excavation at Hierakonpolis in the hope of finding a well-preserved house among the hundreds or thousands that were buried under the sand at this ancient city.[19] What he found instead was the oldest temple yet discovered in Egypt. It was extraordinarily unique because—in a land virtually devoid of wood—it had a magnificent façade made up of four huge cedar columns. The crossbar would have been used to hold the columns in place. In a time and place when almost every building was a one-story mud-brick affair, the façade of this majestic temple soared three stories high. It must have been clearly visible to every-

Fig. 10   At Hierakonpolis, the holes in foreground held cedar columns

one who passed by on the Nile, towering above the other rooftops. And what they saw was thick, beautiful columns of wood, which no one from any other town could emulate. This temple dedicated to Horus, the falcon-god, would come to play a major role in the birth of Egypt as a single, unified country, setting her feet on a path to greatness.

The people of Byblos likewise profited greatly from this enormously risky adventure. They returned home with more wealth than they had ever imagined. In the process of accomplishing this, they also seem to have experienced a deep catharsis that opened their eyes to a fresh new view of the world. It was a world of luxurious trade, a world of many boats upon the sea, a world in which they were free to travel vast distances and to do remarkable things. In the town meetings held after they returned, their euphoria and profits were shared by all, and their new life began.

They commissioned larger boats. They courted the huge population in Egypt. They brought to those people whatever was desired, in exchange for things of great value. They began to sail far up and down the Mediterranean coast to pass along whatever they had received in trade, and double its value again.

The bringing of these cedars to Egypt and all the consequences it produced had changed them forever. At the town meeting after their return to Byblos, they had walked into the gathering hall as fishermen, traders and harvesters, but they walked out as Phoenicians.

These events revealed two principles of Phoenician society which would be seen over and over again in the centuries which followed. These, and the other principal characteristics of Phoenician society which re-occurred on a regular basis during their long history, gradually became apparent during the forty-five years of study in which I came to know them.

The first principle was highly visible to the outside world: international trade in the form of sea-based exchange of goods. In fact, to most people this encompassed the entirety of what was known about these remarkable people. They were the famous sea-traders of the ancient Mediterranean, and they built excellent boats of cedar with which to transact their trade. From this early beginning their trade and boats would indeed grow to be truly worthy of the world's notice and respect.

Less well-known but tremendously important to the Phoenician people was the second principle—creating powerful partnerships among themselves and with others. Among themselves, the pooling of their resources allowed them to accomplish together what they could not do alone. The spreading of risk and the strength gained by united action paid such handsome rewards that it would become a driving force behind all they accomplished in the years to come. It joined them together into a true society, rather than being a group of followers dominated by a strong leader. That they were such a society would be their lasting strength and hallmark.

The second half of this principle—creating powerful partnerships outside their group—was also essential to their existence, but in a different way. The outside partnership in this case was with the wealthy and populous Egyptians who became the huge "flywheel" in the Phoenicians' young trading business, allowing it to grow and expand. The small amounts earned by trading with other villages up and down the coast were good, but it was the tremendous gains from supplying the demanding cities of Egypt that thrust the Phoenicians into the first rank of all traders in those days.

The Phoenician society had come into existence, and much of its shape and character was already in place, even in these early times. The seeds had been planted which would grow into the first of their great empires.

The people of Byblos had been gradually distinguishing themselves from their neighbors and creating their own society, but now the pace increased significantly. Nowhere was this seen more dramatically than at the town of Ugarit, about ninety miles north on the Mediterranean coast.

Both towns had come from the same ethnic stock of nomadic people known as Canaanites. Ugarit was apparently settled at an earlier date while conducting land-based trade with Mesopotamia. They originally had similar customs, and shared the same worship of Mother Nature. Both of them were located on the seacoast and both of them were traders. But one of them looked inland, and the other to the sea. When Ugarit eventually sought to become a player in sea trade, the two towns became competitors.

While they shared these external similarities, both of them had changed so much internally that they were becoming two separate cultures. Ugarit and some of its neighbors came to be regarded as the exemplars of Canaanite society, just as Byblos became the standard bearer of the divergent Phoenician society.

One of the major reasons for this digression was the towering Lebanon Mountains, which loomed immediately behind Byblos and cut it off from most of the land powers and land battles which raged across the inland areas. Less harried, the people of Byblos were able to be much more the masters of their own fate. They retained their reverence for Mother Nature, as represented by figurine images of a pregnant woman, and the fertility rites held each spring. But along with this, the people of Byblos developed a peace-loving disposition and learned to excel in the use of negotiation and diplomacy to defuse confrontations instead of going to war.

Ugarit had no such protection. Similar to many other towns in the region, it was kneaded like dough by the war parties who came at them from all directions. All the land between Anatolia and Egypt was traditionally called Canaan, and all the people in that area were considered Canaanites. Yet two specific groups among them developed their own distinct societies which made them clearly recognizable and distinct from others — the Hebrews and the Phoenicians.

This was quite similar to the situation that later developed in Europe. Eventually everyone in Europe came to be called European. Yet some would be members of British society, while others were members of French, German and other societies. The fact that they were all called Europeans did not erase their distinct societies.

The same was true in Canaan. All of the people who lived here were called Canaanites. But just as clearly, there were several distinct societies within this land. The Phoenicians and Hebrews were two of them.

That should not be too surprising because this area, which covered the whole eastern shore of the Mediterranean, stood at the crossroads of the ancient world. To the north was Anatolia where cities such as Çatal Hüyük scattered the seeds of civilization southward into Mesopotamia and down through Canaan. Even farther to the north were the wild forests of Europe from whence ferocious tribes descended on the "civilized" lands and infused them with fresh blood and energy, albeit with a temporary rash of destruction as well.

To the east of Canaan was the land bridge which passed between the treacherous mountains and deserts to bring many good and not-so-good things from Mesopotamia. Inventions and wealth came across this land bridge, but armies also came marching from Assyria, Babylonia and Persia.

To the south of Canaan lay Egypt and the Arabian lands. These were likewise sources of commerce and discoveries, but also, from time to time, of marching armies and mounted troops.

Even in times of relative peace there was an ongoing ebb and flow of people between these outside areas and Canaan. This was brought on by drought and warlords in those outlying lands, causing many people to flee into Canaan. But drought sometimes also drove people out of this land and into Egypt. Over time, the people and culture of different parts of Canaan evolved to reflect all these changes that stormed through the crossroads.

Ugarit and many other Canaanites adopted the male gods of the warlike people who set upon them, and brought those attributes into their lives. Worship of Mother Nature fell into the background of their practices, or were banished completely into the darkness of obscurity.

The chief god of the Canaanite pantheon was acknowledged as El, called the father of men. The lesser deities were Baal, the god of fertility; Asherah, the consort of Baal; Yam, the god of the sea; and Mot, the god of death. Interestingly, the Hebrews, who later lived among the Canaanites after the time of their founding by Abraham, also called their god El, and used *yam* as their word for "sea," and *mot* as their word for "death." Hebrew culture was heavily influenced by the Canaanites in the early days even while it was developing its own robust and unique set of characteristics.

One of the appealing aspects of Canaanite religious ceremonies which attracted many followers was that it involved large amounts of alcoholic beverages and sexual promiscuity. In some ways the proceedings resembled a drunken orgy, with priests joining the worshippers in sharing an excess of drink and sexuality. This actually was in keeping with the larger picture of their belief that Baal was the god of fertility. It was believed that to persuade him to shed rain on their crops, they shed semen, since the two were seen as similar in much of the ancient world. Regardless of whether or not the crops benefited, there can be little doubt that these practices at least filled the meeting halls.

Asherah, sometimes also called Anat or Astarte, was the goddess who once commanded all this and more, before El and Baal were raised above her. She was relegated to the role of consort to Baal, and was described as aggressive and active in war. She was commonly depicted with a helmet, a battle axe and a spear.

The Phoenicians were far different. They remained true to their belief in Mother Nature as the source of all things. They revered her as *Baalat Gebal*, which meant "Our Lady of Byblos." When a male god was added later, it was as a consort to her. She always remained first in the hearts of the Phoenician people, and honor was accorded to women in their society, in association with her.

It is perhaps also worthy of mention that the Phoenicians and Canaanites held their beliefs long before the birth of Abraham, Jesus or Muhammad. Therefore the religions to which those revered individuals gave rise did not yet exist. As a result, the people of these times simply did the best they could in trying to live a good life. It also meant there was no conflict among those particular religions at that time. On the matter of religion, the Phoenicians were at peace.

The difference between the Phoenician and Canaanite cultures was just as wide or even wider on the subject of war. The Phoenicians had no deity of war, and did not glorify it in any way. They were not weak by any means—they dominated trade upon the seas and dealt with the greatest powers of their times. But war was not their chosen way. This was one of the things that made their society truly different, if not entirely unique: to be incredibly successful while holding unwaveringly to peaceful beliefs.

In fact, it was this peaceful nature that caused the people of Byblos to blur the line between themselves and their neighbors. Being successful at trade had taught them to be highly skilled "readers" of people. Through this finely honed skill, they became aware that war-like people tended to attack those who were different from themselves. History unfortunately verified this observation a great many times. In reasonable response to this observation, the Phoenicians sought to make themselves as much like the people around them as possible. And so it was that even though the gap between themselves and the Canaanites around them continued to grow wider over time, the Phoenicians resolutely referred to themselves—publicly at least—as Canaanites. They also wore articles of dress similar to the Canaanites around them, and gave many of their children Canaanite names. They would later follow this same "blending in" practice with the Egyptians, Assyrians, Persians and others. But in the beginning, it was the Canaanites whose warriors concerned them, and it was with the Canaanites that they outwardly blended.

Throughout all the centuries and all the changes in their outward affiliations, it is interesting to note that their core principles and practices—regarding trade, group decisions, peace, Mother Nature, and all the other things which made them Phoenician—never changed. The principles and practices they had in 3200 BC were still essentially the same in 320 BC.

Yet despite everything else, Byblos and Ugarit did share one thing which was highly significant: proximity to the sea. As a result they both had designs on expanding their sea trade. This put the two towns on a collision course.

The crucial difference in this competition proved to be the trade with Egypt. From the moment cedar of Lebanon was introduced to the land of the Nile—and especially after the tremendous breakthrough at Hierakonpolis—the Egyptians were hooked on trade with Byblos. The land of the Nile was a huge customer whose demand for trade goods propelled the Phoenicians upward for many centuries. The only factor that at times acted in restraint of this trade was the conflicts—and sometimes open warfare—which broke out among Egyptian cities from time to time.

Ugarit did not have access to the treasured cedar, though it did have other less-desirable woods available. And it was located well north of Byblos, putting it that much farther from the largest customer for trade goods in the Mediterranean.

So as fortune would have it, the nod went to Byblos—and the Phoenician people began their ascent. These peaceful people, the ones who revered women and made each member of the community a partner in their success, were the ones upon whom fate smiled.

Ugarit stayed small for now, but did not go away. It is said that every dog has its day. And in time, when the tables of fortune turned, there would be a new reckoning: one in which the continued existence of the Phoenician people would hang in the balance. Until then, Ugarit lay back in its doghouse ninety miles up the coast, where it watched and waited.

CHAPTER 4

A NATURAL WOMAN

Egypt, the demanding customer which enabled all these changes to happen in Byblos, was going through some dramatic changes of its own in those days. More people came to the banks of the Nile, a surplus of food was created, a strong birthrate prevailed, and the cities swelled like mushrooms. As each of these cities reached outward, the competition between them accelerated, often accompanied by open warfare. Small kingdoms called *nomes* were created as powerful and ambitious city leaders consolidated their control over increasingly greater areas. Then the nomes began to attack each other up and down the Nile, creating constantly shifting borders.

In time, a large kingdom emerged in the north, which covered all the nomes of the delta and ruled its many cities from Buto, just east of the Rosetta branch of the river. South of the delta, where the Nile was a single, broad river, a second kingdom arose whose rule was in dispute between the competing cities of Naqada and Hierakonpolis. The tremendous amount of power amassed in these northern and southern kingdoms found its outlet through bloodshed and instability—not just between the two kingdoms, but between cities within the kingdoms. It pushed all of Egypt to the edge of a violent upheaval. Yet troubled times often create great leaders, and so it was in this land of black soil beside the great river.

In the city of Hierakonpolis, built around the venerable temple of Horus whose massive cedar pillars were still visible high above the rooftops, a leader named King Narmer emerged. He presented himself to the townspeople in that large, oval courtyard of the temple surrounded by high walls and flanked by the imposing entrance to the inner sanctum. There he declared that he would lead them to victory. This was promised in front of the gleaming gold-and-copper statue of Horus, the falcon-god that rested in the place of honor atop a tall pole in the courtyard. Narmer apparently benefitted from the custom of the people of Hierakonpolis that the man who ruled from the house of Horus had the right to lead them. He used this leverage to gather all the fighting men of that city, and of their dependent cities, and led them on a campaign of conquest.

Fig. 11   Scorpion's macehead

Of course Narmer was not the first to dream of sweeping all of Egypt into one great kingdom. A shadowy figure known as King Scorpion had very nearly accomplished the same feat. Leading an army from Naqada, which lay only fifty-five miles downriver from the ancient temple of Horus, Scorpion seemed to have won great victories in the delta and wore the red crown of the north, all of which was documented on the remains of a ceremonial macehead created in those times. But he fell short of his goal in two important ways: Scorpion was apparently never able to subdue his neighbors in the south—most notably Hierakonpolis; and the cities of the north eventually slipped away.

Even worse, it appears that the angry northerners used their strategic position in the delta to punish Scorpion's people by inhibiting and even cutting their lines of trade. The delta stood solidly between the river cities and the Phoenicians, whose flow of ships brought essential sea trade. In addition, most land caravans from the Levant and Mesopotamia crossed the Sinai desert and ended their parched journey at the delta. While it would be possible for a caravan to bypass the delta and come directly to the broad Nile, this could be done only with greater difficulty.

So in setting out on his campaign, Narmer was able to hold out two strong inducements to his followers: they would gain the worldly economic benefits of unrestricted trade, as well as the spiritual benefits of a quest blessed by their patron god Horus.

Leading a vigorous and well-prepared army down the Nile, he conquered Naqada and brought all of the south into his hands. Then he began the long campaign farther downriver that plunged deeply into the delta. He must have learned from his predecessor's experiences, for there was no escape from his campaign. This was not a partial victory from which some might later slip away—this march was ruthless and thorough. When he finally captured the northern capital city of Buto, his conquest was complete. He became the first king to rule a unified Egypt, and was father of the first dynasty.

A magnificent piece of artwork known as Narmer's Palette was discovered at Hierakonpolis, and it shed some light on these times. It documented his many accomplishments in beautiful detail. Carved artistically on both sides of a flat piece of greenish slate about two feet high, the first side depicted Narmer wearing the tall white crown

Fig. 12 Narmer's Palette

of the southern king and personally subduing his enemies. On the other side, he appeared wearing the short red crown of the northern king as he surveyed ten defeated enemies who had been decapitated. By wearing both crowns, he was recognized as ruler of both upper and lower Egypt.

An exceptionally intriguing marking also appeared at the top of both sides of the palette, which would be repeated in one way or another by all Egyptian pharaohs to follow. It showed the hiero-glyphic characters of Narmer's name, and enclosed them inside the outline of a building. The building was identified by its four large pillars, and it had an image of Horus the falcon-god sitting on top of it. This was the visible representation of his right to rule and his claim of authority: "Narmer rules from the house of Horus," referring to the temple in Hierakonpolis. This image was called a *serekh*, and it became a binding tradition that only the king or queen who ruled all of Egypt could have his or her name so enclosed. In time, this depiction was replaced by a simple oval-and-knot surrounding the pharaoh's name and was called a *cartouche*.

King Narmer did more than conquer and unify Egypt, though that would certainly have been enough. He also kept his promise to open the restricted trade lines and allow goods of all kinds to flow into Egypt. This opening of trade was outstanding news for the Phoenicians, who gladly put more boats into the water to ferry additional loads of cargo in and out of the delta by sea. Yet such temporary upswings had happened before. If Narmer faded as his predecessors had done, all the gains would fall away. It was critical for Egypt, and also for the Phoenicians, that his son and heir likewise be successful, and that a dynasty begin which would carry on what had been started.

But when Narmer died, the festering resentment of the defeated northerners burst forth, and Egypt teetered on the verge of revolt and civil war. Yet just as Narmer had chosen well in war, he had chosen well in marriage. His wife, Neith-hotep, stepped in and began working to preserve the empire for their son. While her husband had been content to rule by force and had been highly successful with the sword, Neith-hotep used imagination and reconciliation to get her way.

She used the fact that she was from an influential northern family, and her husband Narmer was a great leader from the south. With that background, she presented her son as the personification of union between north and south. It was reasonably argued that her concerns, and those of her son, encompassed the people of both lands. Preserving the empire became her devotion, if not her obsession, and she proved to be masterful at it. The golden dynasties of Egypt may owe as much to her as to Narmer for their creation.

Not too surprisingly, her military-minded husband had named their son *Aha*, which meant "the fighter." Now that the young man had become king, Aha was the name that appeared inside his serekh with the falcon of Horus on top. It was his official or "Horus" name. Every pharaoh who came after him would likewise have a Horus name.

Yet in the interest of reconciling the people of north and south and holding the fresh empire together, Neith-hotep created a second name for her son, calling him *Menes*, which meant "established." To show this, the serekh with his Horus name was followed by images of the goddesses of Upper and Lower Egypt, and then his new name. The goddess of Lower Egypt was Wadjet and her symbol resembled a cobra sitting on a bowl. The goddess of Upper Egypt was Nekhbet, and her symbol of a vulture was likewise shown sitting on a bowl. The king's second name, preceded by these symbols, became known as his *nbty* name, which meant "two ladies" (referring to the two goddesses). The pharaohs who followed Aha Menes also had *nbty* names, signifying their commitment to reconciliation and unity. An exquisite example of this is a square of ivory later found in Neith-hotep's tomb which was intricately carved with Aha's serekh followed by the two goddesses and the name Menes.

Fig. 13 Ivory label showing Aha–Menes in upper right

Another important step was needed to blur the lines of division and strengthen the ties of unification, and that was to create a new royal city for Egypt that was neither north nor south. The place chosen for this new capital was the border between the two lands, where the single Nile split into the seven branches of the delta. The great city of Memphis, built largely of white stone, was created at that exact place. Herodotus, the noted Greek historian, described the event this way:

> The priest said that [Menes] was the first king of Egypt, and that it was he who raised the dyke which protects Memphis from the inundations of the Nile. Before his time the river flowed entirely along the sandy range of hills which skirts Egypt on the side of Libya. He, however, by banking up the river at the bend which it forms about a hundred furlongs south of Memphis, laid the ancient channel dry, while he dug a new course for the stream half-way between the two lines of hills. To this day, the elbow which the Nile forms at the point where it is forced aside into the new channel is guarded with the greatest care by the Persians, and strengthened every year; for if the river were to burst out of this place, and pour over the mound, there would be danger of Memphis being completely overwhelmed by the flood. [Menes], the first king, having thus, by turning the river, made the tract where it used to run, dry land, proceeded in the first place to build the city now called Memphis, which lies in the narrow part of Egypt; after which he further excavated a lake outside the town, to the north and west, communicating with the river, which was itself the eastern boundary. Besides these works, he also, the priests said, built the temple of Vulcan which stands within the city, a vast edifice, very worthy of mention.
>
> Herodotus 2:99

Curiously, although Narmer was the first king and was recognized as such on the early lists of Egypt's kings, later lists do not show his name but instead begin with Menes. There are two possible reasons for this. First, the conquered north could well have harbored great bitterness over the ruthless way Narmer established his empire and, when a later dynasty gained power, the Northerners chose to recognize his son as the first king by using the rationale that he was the first to bear blood from north and south. The second explanation is much more direct: The later king lists used the *nbty* name for each king. Menes was the first to have such a name, so hundreds of years later when scribes compiled these lists, they naturally began with him. But whatever the reason, it was clear Narmer created, then Neith-hotep and Aha Menes preserved, this mantle of greatness for Egypt which many pharaohs have worn.

The bountiful trade created by King Narmer was likewise preserved by his successors, and the fortunes of the Phoenicians grew in similar measure.

If the people of Byblos had any doubts about giving themselves over to sea trade, the Egyptian demands gave them no time to consider it. Shipbuilding became a full-time occupation for many people, and their detailed, laborious woodworking put vessel after vessel of beautiful cedar on the waters. There was a fair degree of urgency, because if the Phoenicians could not supply all the Egyptian demands, the door would be left open for others to enter, and that was unthinkable. It was not just the ongoing euphoria of seeing the value of their cargo multiply every time they touched port that proved so attractive, it was the quality of life those valuables could buy.

Up to this time they had accrued a reasonably good life atop their low plateau by the sea. As sea trade largely—though not completely—replaced their planting and fishing, they had been able to gradually improve their homes and set aside open space for places of worship. Now, with Egypt unified and all its cities open to trade, growth at Byblos virtually exploded.

Archaeological excavations have shown that the small, oval homes of one or two rooms were replaced by rectangular, multi-room houses of two different designs.[20] Widely prevalent were the new townhouses, which were large and roomy but shared a common wall with their neighbors. The other design that grew in popularity but consumed more resources to build was the small villa, a single home divided into three parts. In these homes it became traditional for the main door to open into the middle third of the residence, which was generally a common room for dining and family activities. On the left side were several doorways leading into small private rooms in the left third, and on the right were more doorways leading to small rooms in that third. In a world where a one-room hut was prevalent and many people lived without any permanent shelter at all, this was incredible luxury. With the new wealth from Egyptian trade being shared among the families of the town, these townhouses and small villas rapidly became the standard residences in Byblos.

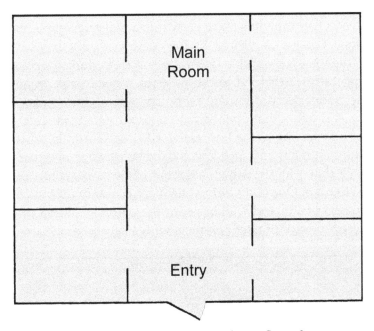

Fig. 14 Traditional Lebanese house floor plan

Nor did their bounty end there. The homes became furnished with bits of finery collected from their voyages and trades: not just linen, gold and artwork from Egypt, but also ebony from the Sudan, lapis-lazuli from the land beyond Mesopotamia, and objects of copper from Cyprus. Doubtless the homes were also adorned with tasteful furniture expertly carved and finished using the many woods available locally, though these have not come down to us.

With this growing affluence came a certain amount of civic pride, causing the fish-cleaning and grain-processing workshops to be moved to the outskirts of the residential area. Large areas that had been tilled fields and productive orchards were made into parklands and public buildings. In a short span of time, Byblos became a young city—and was well on its way to being the most influential seaport on the Mediterranean. Keeping close to its roots as lovers of nature and the land, they set aside a space at the center of the city for remembrance of Mother Nature, whom they knew as Baalat Gebal, Our Lady of Byblos. A surrounding enclosure set these grounds apart as a sacred garden, and on the grounds was built a house for Our Lady which was quite similar to the villas in which they lived themselves. Over time this place grew into a majestic temple made of large stone blocks. A visitor to the temple would have entered through the massive wooden doorway, and then walked up a broad, sweeping staircase that led to the spacious inner rooms. In addition to many artworks decorating these chambers, there were large windows and doors that opened onto outdoor verandas. This gave a light and airy feeling to the impressive edifice. Returning downstairs to stand in the main entrance, one looked southward over the fresh-water well that was the other "essential of life." Together, the well and the House of Our Lady formed the very center of the city.

Stepping outside and walking east, the pathway skirted the well and entered a grove of trees complete with a sacred pool. Continuing

Fig. 15   Baalat Gebal temple in Byblos

through the grove to the other side revealed another enclosure. Passing through its gate, one encountered a small building that was the home of many other deities. With the passage of years, this would likewise become a building of large stone blocks and be known as the L-shaped temple. It became the residence for several male gods. This grand structure was emblematic of the openness of the Phoenician people. They were willing to acknowledge and respect the religions of other people and to allow their worship. But this never replaced their deep feeling for Mother Nature and the beauty of their land.

It is worthy of mention once again that this was a time long before the birth of modern religions. All the people of this time simply did the best they could in regard to divine worship, until further guidance should come along. In the beginning they turned to the worship of God's creation, which they saw in the form of nature around them.

Looking back, it can be seen that worship of Mother Nature was widely practiced in Europe for more than ten thousand years. This was attested by the myriad small figurines representing women with enhanced sexual characteristics, which were associated with the origin of life. These small figures of stone, ivory and clay have been found in a wide variety of places, and the goddess they represented

Fig. 16   L-shaped temple in Byblos

was revered by many cultures.

In Anatolia and the Near East this phenomenon was also widely prevalent. At the time Byblos was founded, Çatal Hüyük was already representing Mother Nature as the source of fertility, showing her in beautiful paintings and artwork. This potent image of a woman as the source of good things in life was likewise celebrated among the early Canaanites all the way south to the border with Egypt. The Canaanites thereafter turned away from this to male-oriented beliefs, but the Phoenicians stayed loyal to this initial vision.

As mentioned earlier, the first two principles of Phoenician society were international trade and the creating of partnerships. Now we come to the third, which was that these people respected their women. The honor and deference they accorded to Mother Nature seemed to carry over to all of the women in their community.

This enabled them to gain the full benefit of women's abilities in the conduct of their community-wide enterprises and civic affairs. In later years when they commissioned works of art, we see women participating fully in the activities of the city and being presented in a confident and respected manner. In keeping with this basic tenet, the Phoenicians' devotion to Our Lady continued for all of their long existence.

Since Our Lady was the first deity to appear among the Phoenicians, she was clothed in all the attributes of the land—she was Mother Nature, the mistress of animals, the protector of women and children, and the one who brought forth the bounty of the earth for her people.

One concession the Phoenicians made to the male-oriented beliefs of their neighbors was that they added a male god as consort to Our Lady. This male god then gained a major, if somewhat unenviable, role in the fertility rites practiced each spring. Since the Phoenicians' traditional practices were quite ancient, they were based on the changes in the land and the seasons that had been part of human existence since time immemorial. To personify the seasons, the male god—who was given several names—died each winter and was burned in effigy. He was then re-born in the spring through the love of Our Lady. This re-birth and subsequent re-marriage was the basis for their uninhibited spring rituals, which rivaled those of the Canaanites in food, drink and sexual release.

The male god was first known as Adonis or, more properly, as 'Adon which meant "lord" since he was the consort of Our Lady. Over time he was promoted to co-equal status with the female goddess and given the name Baal, which meant Our Lord. An early manifestation of this name showed him as Baal Shamem, which meant "Lord of the Heavens," placing his realm not on the earth but in the sky above. He was the master of storms, which was of great concern to the fishermen among this local society at the time of his appearance. Storms were the major cause of loss of life on ships at sea. Being on good terms with this god was deemed prudent to fend off storms so the fishing could be done, and to survive storms when they struck suddenly without warning.

In the next stage of their life—when sea trade emerged as their skill, art and source of well-being—the Phoenicians did not create gods for every purpose as most other cultures did in those days. Instead they went in a unique direction, which gave some insight into their life, society and character.

Since they were people who traveled to many strange lands, each with its own language, customs, gods and beliefs, the Phoenicians were faced with basic decisions on how to conduct themselves. What demeanor and image should they present to these many different kinds of people with whom they would associate and hopefully accomplish beneficial trades? Without question, the people of most societies had their own distinctive image. The Egyptians generally presented themselves to others as somewhat imperious and larger-than-life. This was accomplished through displays of massive statues, gleaming objects of gold, dictatorial terms, and a large army ready to move at any time. As a general rule, they seemed to pride themselves on standing apart from—and above—the others around them.

In a completely different comportment, caravan drivers brought their donkeys (and later would bring camels) into each town on their route, and then stood in the marketplace wearing their distinctive clothing of the desert. They practiced a cajoling and sometimes in-your-face bargaining culture, and then retired to their tents outside of town. Although living with much less pomp and circumstance than the Egyptians, these people likewise held themselves separate from those around them.

The Phoenicians followed a completely different course. Privately it is clear that they maintained their own individual culture. But as noted earlier, they outwardly tried to blend in with the different people they encountered. It became one of their most recognizable characteristics that they would arrive in each new land professing great admiration for the local culture, including the local gods. There is much evidence that with the leading Egyptians and especially the pharaoh, they were effusive in their praise and their admiration of the individual and the society as a whole.

With the Egyptians this approach proved so successful that the Phoenicians were treated more or less as cousins—people who lived elsewhere but were part of the family. Not only were their cedars, other woods and resins so critical to the Egyptians' preservation of mummies, building of temples and furnishing of palaces, but their blending-in mannerisms made the presence of Phoenicians readily accepted in these highly sensitive areas.

This relationship became so widely and deeply established that it even found expression in the Egyptians' traditions and religious myths. In the legend of Isis and Osiris, for example, the people of Byblos were quite naturally and easily included. This reflected how well-known and accepted the Phoenicians were in these intimate building blocks of Egyptian culture and beliefs. In the version of the story recorded by Plutarch—the noted Greek biographer—the god Osiris was king of Egypt and, with his wife Isis, had an epic confrontation with his jealous brother Seth. It began when Seth killed his brother Osiris by sealing him into an air-tight box and throwing it into the Nile River.

> Isis on [hearing] the news, sheared off one of her tresses, and put on a mourning robe, whence the city, even to the present day has the name of "Copto" (*I beat the breast*).... She learnt by inquiry that the chest had been washed up by the sea at a place called Byblus [Byblos], and that the surf had gently laid it under an *Erica* tree. This *Erica*, a most lovely plant, growing up very large in a very short time had enfolded, embraced and concealed the coffer

within itself. The king of the place being astonished at the size of the plant, and having cut away the clump that concealed the coffer from sight, set the latter up as a pillar to support his roof. They tell how Isis having learnt all this by the divine breath of fame, came to Byblus, and sitting down by the side of a spring all dejected and weeping spoke not a word to any other persons, but saluted and made friends of the maid servants of the queen, by dressing their hair for them, and infusing into their bodies a wonderful perfume out of herself; when the queen saw her maids again, she felt a longing to see the stranger, whose hair and whose body breathed of ambrosial perfume; and so she was sent for, [and] becoming intimate with the queen, was made nurse of her infant. The king's name they say was Malacander, herself some call Astarte, others Sooses, others Neinanoë, who is the same with the Greek Athenais.

Isis is said to have suckled the child by putting, instead of her nipple, her finger into his mouth, and by night she singed away the mortal parts of his body. She turned herself into a swallow and flew around the pillar until the queen watched her, and cried out when she saw her child all on fire, and so took away the boy's immortality. Then the goddess, manifesting herself, asked for the pillar of the roof, and having removed it with the greatest ease, she cut away the *Erica* that surrounded it. This plant she wrapped up in a linen cloth, pouring perfume over it, and gave it in charge of the king; and to this day the people of Byblus venerate the wood, which is preserved in the temple of Isis.[21]

Plutarch
Morals

Osiris, according to legend, went on to become god of the dead and dwelt in the underworld. His son Horus defeated Seth and became god of the living and protector of the pharaohs.

This was a remarkable degree of acceptance for the Phoenicians to have earned. And it apparently came to them not only by being respectful of the Egyptians' customs and religious beliefs while in the land of the Nile, but also by maintaining this same posture at home. In Byblos the L-shaped temple and the succeeding one built on the same site was sometimes called the Egyptian temple because so many votive offerings dedicated to Egyptian deities were found there. The Phoenicians also allowed—and even encouraged—Our Lady of Byblos to be called Hathor, the Egyptian goddess of love, dance and beauty.

Yet this deep respect for the beliefs of others was not solely altruistic. It had an extremely practical side as well. Religion was—and still is—one of the major reasons for fighting in the Middle East. It provided an easy excuse for ambitious leaders to attack a neighboring city and disgorge all its wealth to themselves and their people. Not only did this make the leaders wealthier and more popular, it increased the size of their realm and drew attention away from internal problems, such as the drastic difference between the sumptuous lifestyle of most nobles and the meager hand-to-mouth existence of many of their people.

If the people of Byblos had been military-minded citizens in the mold of the Spartans or Romans, they could have stuck out their chins and accentuated their differences without caring what anyone thought. But that was not their way. Not only were they peaceful by preference, they were also small in number compared to their neighbors. They therefore had to defend themselves by means other than force of arms. Having respect for the religions of those around them was one of those defenses.

They were able to do this through a remarkable insight. Being keen observers of so many different societies, they seemed to come to the realization that everyone was worshiping God by different names; but it was always God they worshiped. If they did not always understand why others insisted on using certain names and attributes, then they could at least respect those beliefs. To the Phoenicians, God was God, by whatever name one wanted to use. Beyond that, they followed their own practices and begrudged no one else theirs.

Other people such as the Egyptians therefore had the perception that while the Phoenicians had some practices of their own, they also showed reverence toward the Egyptian deities. When Egyptians visited Byblos, they were able to see visible signs of this as they were ushered from the temple of "Our Lady, Hathor" to the temple where other familiar deities were readily available for the visitors' worship. At the same time, young Phoenician traders who were outward bound for the Nile with a load of cargo were able to become familiar with the names and characteristics of the different Egyptian deities before leaving home on their voyage. Without this preparation, any claim of "reverence for Egyptian beliefs" would have been immediately exposed the moment young traders stepped off the boat and revealed their ignorance by violating a local custom. That the Phoenicians' preparation was quite thorough is attested by the warmth with which they were included into Egyptian legend and mythology.

If the Egyptians were their only neighbors and customers, that would be the whole story. Much closer to home, however, were the Canaanites who inhabited Ugarit and many other nearby cities. To keep alive the "reverence for others' religion" concept, the Phoenicians allowed—and again, encouraged—Our Lady of Byblos to be called Asherah, Anat and Astarte, which were the various names of the leading Canaanite goddess. With their male god Baal it was even easier. Since the major deity of the Canaanites was called Baal, El or Baal-with-an-adjective-attached, the similarity of names made for a ready connection.

Cultural connections with the Canaanites around them were also easily accomplished since both peoples had come from the same stock. They maintained similar clothing and language, and even called themselves fellow Canaanites. Implicit in all of this was the message, "Do not attack us, brother!"

Since many people seem to get tangled in arguments over who was a Canaanite, the earlier point is worth repeating here. Everyone in Canaan was called "Canaanite," just as everyone in Europe is called European. But there are different countries in Europe and they have different societies. In similar manner, there were several distinct societies in Canaan. Clearly, the Phoenicians were one such society. The Hebrews were another. The Phoenicians were not the same as the Hebrews, Egyptians, Ugaritic people or any of the other groups around them.

Yet the Phoenician traders did their best to blend in with each of these other societies. They developed this skill into a high art. One might say they became the chameleons of the ancient world—able to change their "color" to match the surroundings wherever they went.

The physical manner in which they supported their reverence-for-other-religions was also quite fascinating. They made no graven images as objects of worship. By comparison, the Egyptians created towering stone images of gods with human bodies and animal heads. Some Canaanites made golden calves and other objects of worship. The Phoenicians simply placed a stone marker to designate a location as a holy place.

This marker or stele was a small obelisk. They referred to it as a *maṣṣebah*. The obelisk stood on a square stone base and its four sides tapered slightly as they went upward. Near the top the sides quickly tapered toward the center, creating a small pyramid shape atop the stone. The Egyptians would one day build huge obelisks of this same shape and put them in public places. The Washington monument in Washington, D.C., is a similar obelisk, albeit a very large one.

As used by the Phoenicians, these were small markers only a few feet high. They were put in any place of worship, whether it was a natural stone grotto in the side of a hill, a single room in a house, or the middle of a large temple. It should be noted, however, that the stone object was not a deity. It simply marked a place where God resided. It was believed that by going near one of these markers, a person went into the presence of God, and one's prayers would be heard.

One significant benefit these markers had over graven images was that one obelisk fairly much looked like any other. True, the stone base upon which it stood might be inscribed with a dedication by the donor, but nothing about its appearance differentiated it in any way. In its presence one could comfortably offer a prayer to God by any name one chose to use.

A special honor was reserved for Our Lady. While she might have an obelisk placed for her in a room or cave, her normal place in large edifices such as a temple was identified by an empty throne. Set in the place of honor, this throne served the same purpose as the obelisk: It designated the place where she resided and where she would hear one's prayers. No graven image of her was made with Levantine hairstyle or Egyptian headdress to dictate who resided there. One could refer to the seated goddess as Our Lady, Hathor, Astarte, or any other name with equal ease.

In all of these things we see two more essential principles of Phoenician society revealed to us over and over during the course of many centuries. Religious tolerance, the fourth principle, played a tremendous role in their relations with people, and in their long survival. The incredible number of wars that have been fought for religious reasons throughout history is staggering. And each of those came with loss of life and destruction of property. The Phoenicians realized this at an early date and incorporated this tolerance into their lives.

Walking hand-in-hand with this was the next principle: peaceful resolution of differences. Religious differences were peacefully resolved through tolerance, as we have just seen. When war parties arrived outside their city, rich gifts were offered and peace was obtained, as we saw with King David. Although the specific methods used in dealing with the many differences among people might change, the underlying principle was always constant: They wanted to do it peacefully.

As noted earlier, this was not an altruistic desire for peace. It was an eminently reasonable one. The societies around them devoted much of their focus and energies preparing for war and surging into battle in an attempt to satisfy their desires. Then those societies eventually fell to some foe more powerful than themselves. The Phoenicians instead devoted themselves to building their international trade and gradually raised the level of prosperity for their whole society. They managed to survive for three thousand years while others were cut down on bloody battlefields and disappeared.

These two principles of religious tolerance and peaceful resolution of differences proved to be extremely valuable.

Yet it is clear that not all battles were fought between different cultural or religious groups. Sometimes simple greed was the motivation, and they urgently needed to address that serious problem as well.

CHAPTER 5

GO FORTH AND MULTIPLY

The burgeoning sea trade gradually raised the Phoenicians higher and higher above their neighbors in terms of the good things they could afford. Although they tried not to be ostentatious with their wealth in public, the growing size of their homes and the finery within them were enticing bait for the feral raiding parties that roamed the Canaanite countryside. So as one of their protections, the people of Byblos built a thick wall around their city.

It covered the three sides that faced the surrounding land and left only the seaward side uncovered. They relied upon the short cliffs on that side to provide a natural defense facing the water. A huge wooden gate was erected in the broad stone wall to separate this flourishing city from the major north-south road just outside the solid ramparts. That busy thoroughfare was a primary route for travelers on foot or on beasts of burden making their way up and down the Mediterranean coast, because there was only a limited amount of land between the Lebanese Mountains and the shore.

Important visitors making a grand entrance into Byblos through the main gate first traversed the sacred grove between the two large and impressive temples dedicated to Our Lady and to the other gods, arriving at the life-giving fountain. Continuing on, they passed

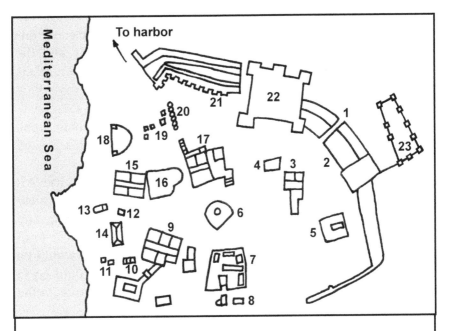

Byblos Landmarks

1. Remains of the City Gate stand between two ancient stone ramparts.
2. Primitive wall built before 2500 BC, this is the oldest fortification on the site.
3. Foundation of the L-shaped Temple erected in 2700 BC.
4. Sacred pool between the L-shaped Temple and Baalat Gebal.
5. Obelisk Temple originally built on top of the L-shaped Temple; was moved by archaeologists to its present position.
6. Ancient well is reached by stone steps which spiral down to the water.
7. Enclosure and houses from 3200-3000 BC.
8. Foundations of three houses from 3800-3000 BC.
9. The Trading House.

10-13. House foundations from 4500-3200 BC.
14. Modern house retained by archaeologists for use during excavations.
15. Villa from third millenium BC.
16. Rock quarry.
17. Baalat Gebal Temple dedicated to Our Lady of Byblos; rebuilt and modified many times.
18. Reconstructed Roman theater, was moved from its original site between City Gate and L-shaped Temple.
19. Royal tombs dating to second millennium BC.
20. A line of Roman columns.
21. Ramparts and city walls of the third and second millennia BC.
22. Crusader castle.
23. Persian castle.

Fig. 17 Ancient Byblos

clusters of townhouses and finally came to the large building that had become the beating heart of this city: the trading house.

Despite its name, this house was not where public trading happened. Those events took place in hundreds of marketplaces scattered across lands from Egypt in the south to Anatolia and the Aegean Sea far to the north and west. One of those active markets was located just outside the city walls of Byblos. This was where peddlers came from towns and villages farther inland—some even coming considerable distances by caravan—bringing their wool, copper, olive oil, and even fine products from Mesopotamia packed on the backs of donkeys.

Only the results of all those trades came to the trading house. After each sea voyage this was where the captain's report ultimately was deposited, showing the results of all trades and noting any exceptional events. The rich cargo itself was held at the docks until word came from the trading house directing which parts would be loaded onto other ships for further trade, which parts would go to the local marketplace, and which parts would be brought up to the house itself.

This last collection of rich merchandise was placed in a secure warehouse attached to the trading house by a walkway. This included the jewels, objects of gold, and other valuable items of exquisite workmanship which made up the city's reserve of wealth. These valuable objects were used, in time, for beautiful civic buildings, for peace-making gifts to kings of other lands, and for future need. With those set aside, and all bills paid, the remainder of the profits from trades were dispersed to the partners of the trading ventures, which is to say, the people of the city.

At first, the trading house would have been where meetings were held and major business decisions were made. But as the number of people in the city grew over the years, getting everyone together for each meeting became impractical. As a result, somewhere around this time the first councils of representatives came into being. An assembly of all the people, possibly held on an annual basis, would have selected the circle of council members and allowed the townspeople to give vent to their pleasure or displeasure over what had transpired since the last assembly. In this manner a broad agenda could be set

Fig. 18   Trading house at Byblos

for the coming year. Thereafter, the council members would meet as necessary and serve much like the board of directors had previously done on individual ventures, making the important decisions. Just as the early trading ventures had selected a managing director to make the day-to-day decisions, the council also granted to one of its members the right and responsibility to make daily decisions, to be the visible leader of the city, and to assemble the council members when major decisions were needed.

Throughout the Phoenicians' long history, this tradition of "leader who consults with a council before making significant decisions" has been frequently noted, but virtually never understood by outsiders. This lack of understanding by others was perfectly acceptable to the Phoenicians, who were becoming more and more secretive with the passage of time.

Their growing penchant for privacy had a very simple reason for being. Each day their wealth grew and they became a larger and more desirable target for people who lusted after easy riches. They had spent hundreds of years gathering what they had now—and were adding to it at an incredible rate. Yet a single man with a sword and enough soldiers could take it all in a single day. So they relied on the shared culture and reverence-for-other-religions mentioned earlier, as well as the large wall that now surrounded the city. Their other essential defense was secrecy.

Avoiding public display of wealth and keeping it in one's home would not work if people talked about everything they had. So to outsiders they said nothing about their private affairs or business affairs. And in a surprising extension of this practice, they said virtually nothing about their public affairs either. The first two "say-nothings" were not too unusual, but the third one definitely was. And the way it was accomplished was quite curious.

During the thousands of years of their existence, the Phoenicians carved no busts of their great leaders. They engraved no commemorative plaques to extol their accomplishments. And they raised no arches to celebrate their triumphs. Try for a moment to imagine the Greeks, Romans and Egyptians without those things.

Yet the Phoenicians could not go through the outside world refusing to talk at all. That would excite too much unwanted attention from people who wondered and guessed at what was being withheld. So they filled the quiet gaps with representations that made them seem like the people around them.

One of the ways they did this was by noting their major customers, the Egyptian people, were led by kings. This was also true for several of the Canaanite cities. So the Phoenicians of Byblos decided to call their leader a king. This was a stretch because kings traditionally first came to power in a land through conquest and bloodshed. During all the years of their existence, that was never the case with the Phoenicians.

In addition, a king's rule in other lands was usually supported by military force. Consider Narmer, Alexander the Great, and William the Conqueror, for example. The difficulty for the Phoenicians in this regard was that they were not a warlike people and were not led by a military ruler. However to be treated as an equal—or at least as a respected group when dealing with other kings and their people—it was felt that they needed to have a "king." So the title was given.

Once done, it was relatively easy to keep up this image, since their leader—chosen by the council with the approval of the city—would normally have come from one of the leading families. When it came time to name a successor to the king, selecting one of the previous king's children was traditionally the easy choice around the world—

and in some societies the succession was mandatory. The Phoenicians usually followed this course of choosing one of their leader's children, thereby supporting the image that they had a traditional king. But it was also possible for the choice to be switched to a member of another family. It was more important that the leader was a good choice to lead the city's trading business than for any rigid rules of descent be followed.

When a king did not measure up, it was fairly easy for the Phoenicians to make a change since it only took a group decision to do so. Over the many centuries that they had kings, there was no record of a violent takeover by a Phoenician to claim the king's position—contrary to what has been found in almost every other country's list of kings. Deficient kings could be deposed, but the Phoenicians seemed to do so only when there was widespread support for the change.

Each time a new king was selected, there was a real risk that the new leader might become enamored with the trappings of power and seek to make himself a real king—and become a dictator over the people. But one of the things that made it easier for the Phoenicians to go forward with this selection was their lack of a military force. For most of their existence, the Phoenicians never had a land army. This seems almost incredible, given the history of virtually all other countries, but it was true. At most they had a few gendarmes within the city to keep order, but no force to march outside the city and do battle.

Since a king among the Phoenicians had no army to enforce his will, the council and people were not at great risk. The second protection retained by the people of the city was the requirement that all major decisions come back to the council. Their king could not create foreign agreements that accrued new powers to the throne because at the first hint of such action the council would install a new king. In later years there was a colorful story of a Phoenician king replaced in this manner.

So Byblos began its tradition of having a king, and continued it thereafter. It is believed that the king lived in the residential part of the trading house, close to all of the daily operations with which he was charged, and amid the wealth of the city. Much like a managing director or chief executive officer of a modern corporation, he had a staff of people who performed the actual work under his supervision. And he reported to a board of directors, just as a CEO would do.

By the beginning of the third millennium BC, Byblos appeared to have become the dominant seaport on the Mediterranean. Larger cities were in existence, but they were located inland. Within this flowering city on the sea, a culture of life evolved around ever-larger boats, freedom of movement from place to place, and an international swirl of fashions, customs, foods and goods. It was becoming a city like no other.

Even so, there were compelling reasons for the Phoenicians not to stay bound inside one city but to spread out to others. And once this expansion began, it became a trend of epic proportions. It all started simply enough.

As the people of Byblos came to enjoy these many benefits from sea trade, they developed a deep concern about losing the source of their comforts. This was quite natural because survival hung by a very thin thread during these early days. The good news was that the Phoenicians had a huge base of customers in the land of the Nile who desperately wanted the cedar and other woods of the Lebanon Mountains. The not-so-good news was that these much-desired trees grew on mountainsides under nature's blue skies, so anyone could come and take them if they wished.

If the Egyptians had decided one day to come get the cedars themselves in these early times instead of relying upon the Lebanese people to bring them, the Phoenicians would have been put out of business—and for all intents and purposes, would have disappeared from history. They would have made such little impact by that point that they could quickly have been lost in the sands of time. There would have been no string of Phoenician cities around the Mediterranean like a necklace of pearls around the neck of a grand lady. There would have been no sea-based empire and all the wonders it placed into the cribs of young civilizations.

But the Egyptians were held back by two aspects of their culture, and that made all the difference. They were consummate river travelers beyond all doubt. As we have seen, however, there was a marked difference between river travel and sea travel. The Egyptians exploited their reed boats to move extensively along the Nile and its many branches in the delta, but found these craft to be at a severe disadvantage upon the sea. When foreigners showed up in boats of wood and were quite willing to bring anything the Egyptians wanted to the foot of the Nile, there was no need to agonize over how to build new boats nor suffer through learning the harsh lessons of the sea. The easy way forward was to accept the service.

The other Egyptian trait at play was their view that the Nile was the center of the world and everywhere else was a great wasteland. Certainly this view had considerable basis in fact within Egypt. But it was not just a physical "wasteland" they had in mind. To them, Egypt was the center of culture, the center of riches, and the center of power. As a result, it was deemed among the worst of all possible fates to be assigned to some location outside of Egypt, and even the border areas such as the mines of Sinai were viewed with displeasure. So imagine trying to drum up interest in going hundreds of miles outside of those borders—and across the sea—to fetch something that others were perfectly willing to bring to you. An insanity verdict for such an Egyptian would have been quickly rendered in any court of local opinion.

These considerations resulted in the Phoenicians' early riches, due to the Egyptians giving them as much business as they could carry. But no reasonable person would count on this arrangement lasting forever. As history has abundantly proved, a show of determination by the pharaoh was all that was required for Egyptians to overcome great difficulties and dislikes by the populace in order to accomplish monumental feats. The word of the pharaoh had already diverted the Nile to build the city of Memphis. So anything could happen.

The Phoenicians had hundreds of years of experience working with the Egyptians at this point and were well aware of these things. So they prudently took steps to protect their lifeline of trade. Recognizing that the Lebanon Mountains stretched for eighty miles along the Mediterranean coast—and that one city at the midpoint of that range could not protect it all—the people of Byblos extended their reach.

About forty-six miles to the south lay a small village on the seacoast which had been in existence from time to time since the Stone Age. One day it would become known as Sidon, but at this juncture it was only a collection of huts. This modest village occupied a desirable promontory of land sticking out into the sea. It was also blessed

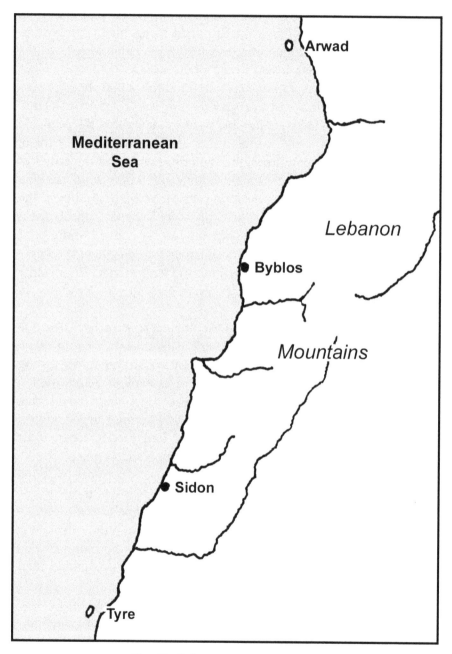

Fig. 19   Lebanon coast in 2750 BC

with a rocky outcropping which emerged from the water and formed a straight line parallel to the shore, just touching the end of the promontory. This created two natural harbors, one facing north and the other to the south. In this it mimicked the two harbors at Byblos, which had proven to be an ideal port arrangement for trading-ships.

Most powerful cities desiring such an occupied location would have simply sent their army southward. They would have owned the smoldering ruins by nightfall. But that was not the Phoenician way. For one thing, the people of Byblos did not possess an army. Even more to the point, they owned something that was almost as strongly compelling: vast economic power. Although these were still the early days of the Phoenicians' existence, they were already far ahead of almost all their neighbors in the amenities and wealth they had accumulated.

It is not known if the land on the promontory was purchased outright or if the members of the village were permitted to join the Phoenician society, but in all probability it was some of each. In this case each family in the village would have had to declare if it was being bought out and leaving, or if it was joining the group and staying. The whole fabric of Phoenician society required a clear understanding of whether a person was in or out—much like the division caused by the wall that now surrounded Byblos. Consider the code of secrecy that had already been established and would continue to get stronger. Who was allowed to learn their private information? There had to be some commitment or pledge on the part of a new member of the society not to divulge the secrets, with that commitment backed up by a stiff penalty if the pledge was broken.

Equally as important, if not more so, was the issue of sharing the profits of the sea trade. The members of the society were all shareholders in the ongoing ventures. They participated in the decision-making process, and worked at some aspect of the trade whether aboard ship or on land. They bore their share of the losses when a ship went down, and they shared in the rich profits when ships came home. Clearly people had to be in or out. And there were powerfully compelling reasons to be in.

No doubt many of the fortunate people who were offered this chance to be part of such a rich society accepted readily and made the necessary commitments. Those who chose not to accept would have been offered a lucrative inducement to move on. In any event, the city of Sidon suddenly appeared early in the third millennium, formed by an influx of people from Byblos.

This gave the Phoenicians two strong cities where they previously had only one. And it gave them a commanding position on the major beachhead south of Byblos that had access to the valuable cedars on

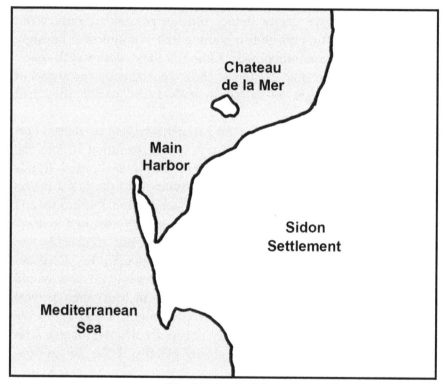

Fig. 20   Early Sidon

the mountainside. This was an essential location because Egypt lay to the south. But the Phoenicians wanted something more.

One of the great benefits accruing to a sea-faring people by having a port city located on a promontory sticking out into the water was that land armies from warlike neighbors could only approach them from the landward side. The seaward side was naturally protected from soldiers marching or cavalry riding against the city. And borrowing boats to attack a Phoenician port was a fairly useless exercise because these intrepid sea-traders had vastly more ships at their disposal than any land power could hope to muster. So locating a city on a promontory was an excellent choice. But there was a better one.

Farther down the coast, about twenty-three miles south of Sidon, lay a pair of rocky islands about a half-mile offshore. These outcroppings were basically useless to anyone except a sea-going people, so

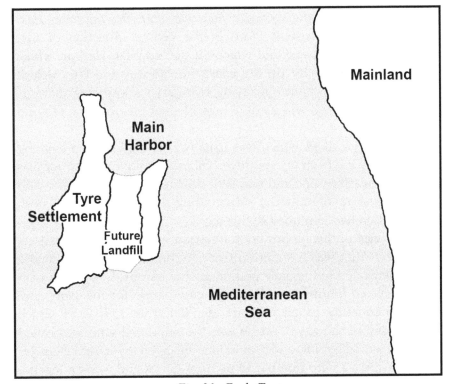

Fig. 21 Early Tyre

they lay virtually undisturbed. But the Phoenicians saw in them a chance to create the ideal port city. It was a base that could not be attacked by land powers from any direction. So they sent an enterprising group of colonists there from Byblos—probably skewed heavily toward the younger seamen and their wives—who would be willing to endure initial privations and hardships in exchange for being the founding families and leaders of the city. This fledgling port and city was given the name *sor*, which meant "rock." But it has come down to us through history as the majestic city of Tyre.

In the beginning this port city was anything but majestic. A small rise at the middle of the larger island afforded a modestly suitable central place to locate a rustic trading house. Nearby a temple was dedicated to Our Lady, surrounded by an enclosure to set it apart from the many dusty activities that quickly filled the available land. The island was an elongated one, stretching north and south parallel to the shoreline. At the southern end was built the Egyptian Harbor—so named because it faced in the general direction of that country. At the northeast end was built the Sidonian Harbor, which looked toward that city up the coast. In this way the Phoenicians preserved their penchant for having two harbors, ensuring that one was always protected and useable regardless of the direction of wind or storm.

In normal weather, which was usually fairly mild, the prevailing sea currents were from the southwest. Since the Sidonian Harbor was on the northeastern side and was well shielded from the currents and waves, it was favored as the shipbuilding center and trading port. That tradition has continued to this day.

To the east of this harbor lay the second, much smaller island. Its main use at first was a significant one to the new settlers: It held a temple dedicated to the male god of sea and storms. In keeping with the Phoenician tradition of allowing many names for the same god, he was frequently called Melqart, derived from *malek qart* which meant "king of the city." Yet he was the same god who was called Baal Shamem in Byblos, and would later be given the names Heracles and Hercules—a hero familiar to us from Greek and Roman legend. This temple would figure greatly in the history of Tyre. It even had a role in passing along to us the founding date of Tyre, which otherwise would have been lost in the swirling fog of antiquity.

This last gift came to us by way of Herodotus, the Greek writer who was quoted earlier. He was the first among the Greeks to travel widely and write extensively about how things came to be the way they were around 450 BC. Others followed quickly, but he was the one who paved the way and preserved a prodigious amount of unique facts and observations which have shed light upon many intriguing and eye-opening corners of history. For this prodigious effort he has been called the father of history, and his major work is simply titled, *The Histories*.

Prominent among these ancient observations were his frequent comments about the Phoenicians. The way he discussed these people showed clearly that they were well known by the peoples of the ancient Mediterranean, for he gave no introduction to them or explanation of who they were. In similar fashion, he did not describe where the city of Athens was located, since it was assumed these facts would be self-evident to all his readers. His perceptive comments also revealed that it was virtually impossible to write a history of those times without mentioning the Phoenicians in most major activities and locations.

Nothing showed this better than the first sentence of his lengthy book, which followed a brief introduction of himself. It read:

> According to the Persians best informed in history, the Phoenicians began the quarrel.
>
> Herodotus 1:1

Strangely enough—though his *Histories* manuscript was replete with mentions of the Phoenicians—each succeeding history written by those who followed him over the centuries have given the Phoenicians fewer and fewer mentions. These people from Lebanon were set aside in favor of individuals more closely involved with the writers' own country or point of view. With rare exception, this unfortunate trend has continued down to the present day.

In Herodotus' time, however, the Phoenicians were highly visible, active, and could not be ignored in any credible telling of events.

His extensive travels included a visit to Tyre. There he saw the old temple to the male god known to him as Hercules.

> In the wish to get the best information that I could on these matters, I made a voyage to Tyre in Phoenicia, hearing there was a temple of Hercules at that place, very highly venerated. I visited the temple, and found it richly adorned with a number of offerings, among which were two pillars, one of pure gold, the other of emerald, shining with great brilliancy at night. In a conversation

which I held with the priests, I inquired how long their
temple had been built, and found by their answer that
they, too, differed from the Greeks. They said that the
temple was built at the same time that the city was
founded, and that the foundation of the city took place
two thousand three hundred years ago.

Herodotus 2:44

When we add 2,300 years to the date of Herodotus' visit (450 BC)
we get 2750 BC as the founding date for Tyre. Normally, one must be
somewhat tongue-in-cheek when considering ancient writings about
events that were said to have occurred many years earlier. Some of
those declarations were simply fanciful, but others proved to be
amazingly accurate.

In this case we are not left to wonder on the matter, since archaeologist Patricia Bikai did an excellent excavation at Tyre which
clarified the picture significantly.[22] In 1974, she dug carefully all the
way down to bedrock, going layer by layer and dating each successive slice of history she uncovered. This was done by identifying
recognizable pieces of pottery whose age had already been established by other archaeologists through previous digs in the Middle
East. After much painstaking work, she identified the founding of the
city to have taken place in the first part of the third millennium BC—
in other words, from 3000 to 2700 BC. With this verification in hand,
the date given by Herodotus of 2750 BC turns out to be one of those
"amazingly accurate" observations, and is widely accepted today.

Once this frontier town became established upon the island, Tyre
immediately took on a key role in the newborn Phoenician trading
empire that now stretched from Byblos to Sidon and Tyre in terms of
permanent cities—but also reached all across the eastern part of the
Mediterranean in terms of small outposts and ships at sea.

Of all the routes plied by these ships, the one running south to
Egypt was the most critical, and now Tyre sat astride it. This fresh
port and its quickly-growing fleet provided the excellent defensive
position the Phoenicians had wanted against incursions from the
south—whether from Egyptians or any other people who were
desirous of what the Phoenicians possessed. But it served another

key role as well: It shortened the critical voyages to Egypt. Goods could now be brought to Tyre from all points north and be gathered onto larger ships, staffed with fresh crews, and be taken on a shorter run to the mouth of the Nile. All of this reduced the risk that was inherent in trade carried by sea, and allowed more of the ships to come home safely with their prized cargoes.

Far to the north the Phoenicians set up a similar outpost on an island called Arwad. Located about sixty miles past Byblos, this delightful isle was more round in shape than Tyre and had the traditional two ports they desired. Both of these faced the shore, which was about two miles away. Today the mainland and this small island are part of Syria, and a significant city known as Tartous has grown up on the coastline. But in those days it was all relatively unpopulated. As Tyre did in the south, Arwad supported Phoenician trade to the north, mainly to Anatolia but also to Cyprus and the Aegean. While this trade was good, it was still secondary to the main route that ran to wealthy and populous Egypt. Like Tyre, it also played a defensive role by protecting Phoenician interests and trade from any incursions by Ugarit and the other ambitious towns north of Arwad. Although this island settlement would one day grow into a bustling city, it never gained the prominence of Byblos, Sidon and Tyre to the south.

Smaller outposts also appeared at other places along the coast between these great cities, including one at a place called Beirut. In time, this would also grow to be a great city, but its day had not yet come. This was still a time for the sowing of seeds, leaving to nature the encouragement of growth that would come over the years.

The spread of the Phoenician people to these other cities underscored what became the sixth principle of their society: equality and sharing the wealth.

This is not to say that every member of the society was exactly equal in every way. Some families may have been especially active in trade ventures and accrued additional wealth for themselves. The Phoenician concept of equality meant that even the poorest among them participated in the proceeds earned by the community to some degree, and this had a remarkable effect. Although the international trade, shipbuilding, and production of goods such as their famous royal-purple cloth made the Phoenicians person-for-person one of the richest societies that ever existed, there was less of a gap between the richest and poorest among them than in most other societies of their day.

Other lands were often ruled by a forceful king and a handful of ultra-rich families who presided over a minimal middle class and a large population of people living a hand-to-mouth existence. Among the Phoenicians it became common for even the least of them to live in multi-room homes, at a time when a single-room hut was the norm in neighboring lands. By choosing—and removing—their councils and kings, the Phoenicians made sure no family acquired too much of the community's wealth. The personal palaces of Egypt, Persia and other lands were not imitated in the Phoenician cities.

In Phoenician society each person had a voice in the affairs of the community and a stake in its success. This principle of equality produced some truly remarkable results. First, the concept of social revolution was unheard of during their long history. The relatively small gap between the highest and lowest strata left no motivation for this to arise. Instead of struggling against each other, they turned their attention to the civic business of international trade. They were confident that their path to success lay in working *with* other members of their community, and the results certainly justified this view.

The incredible wealth generated by their society enabled each of them to live at a level roughly similar to a minor lord or lady in neighboring lands. They were strongly motivated to hold this principle close to their hearts, and they preserved it inviolate throughout their long existence.

Yet even after founding all these cities, they still felt exposed and were driven to do more, because Egypt was still growing stronger. And though no one could have predicted it, the pharaohs would soon begin demanding huge amounts of supplies to build their Great Pyramid.

CHAPTER 6

RAISED UP STONE BY STONE

Although the Phoenicians had now given themselves some protection at home against others coming to take the treasured cedars and lands of the Lebanon Mountains, they were still left with the concern that the people of the Nile might learn to build sea-worthy boats in imitation of the Phoenician craft and thereby acquire the means to make such a foray northward.

Their defense against this was fairly straightforward action. They would work to keep their ships out of Egyptian hands by no longer sailing into Egyptian ports to do trade. Instead they would build their own port where the large Phoenician ships could unload and where smaller local craft could then come to pick up the goods. This practice became a normal part of the Phoenician *modus operandi* when dealing with major customers, and it was quite reasonable that it began with the Egyptians. The choice of such a port was a critical one, since all the riches of trade with Egypt would pass through this vital harbor.

The only problem with trying to locate this early Phoenician port in Egypt today was that no one knew where to find it. As a result, I found it necessary to begin a search for the missing port much as the ancient Phoenicians might have done originally—just substituting ancient maps and other records in place of observations taken by sitting in a wooden boat while carefully scanning the Egyptian coast.

On the coastal route southward from Tyre I passed many small Canaanite villages on the shore of the Mediterranean before reaching Sinai. There the shoreline turned and led westward along the barren shore of Egypt. At Lake Manzana, I reached the easternmost part of the delta where several branches of the Nile once terminated and their water flowed into the sea.

In searching this part of the delta for a suitable island—and the Phoenicians clearly preferred islands as their first choice, settling for a promontory only if no isle was available—it became obvious that the muddy condition of the land was a serious problem. The shifting waterways and the ability of this muddy soil to ooze up or down below the water level was not only a serious difficulty for a port town, but an impossibility in terms of providing hull clearance for the large ships the Phoenicians were using.

The search continued past Tamit on the Damietta branch, beyond a minor branch that led past the major city of Buto, beyond Rashid on the Rosetta branch and past the minor Canopic branch marking the westernmost edge of the delta. After all this way, nothing suitable had yet presented itself.

A little farther west on the coast there was an interesting island, but it seemed a poor location, not being near one of the Nile branches. It also was not near a major Egyptian city, at least not in those days. But with nothing else emerging as an attractive alternative, it had to be considered.

The island was Pharos. About 2,500 years after the arrival of the Phoenicians, Alexander the Great came to this place fresh from his conquest of the main Phoenician cities, and found virtually nothing on the shore. He decided to build the grand city of Alexandria on this spot, and it eventually grew to become Egypt's second-largest city. But in his day, it was mostly sand and a small fishing village called Rhakotis. That was essentially what the Phoenicians found two-and-a-half millennia before him.

But it had possibilities. The modest Egyptian village of Rhakotis lay on a small stretch of land less than one mile wide, which separated freshwater Lake Mareotis from the salty sea. The reason why it was a freshwater lake was that a small channel connected it to the Canopic branch of the Nile, the source of its water.

Now the search was becoming more interesting. One could easily envision Pharos Island meeting the Phoenicians' stringent requirements. As a rocky island not near the silt of the Nile, and surrounded by the open sea, it could comfortably support a deepwater port for large ships. Being separated from Rhakotis by the sea, it was well away from prying Egyptian eyes. The local lake's overflow formed a small river that ran directly beside Rhakotis, providing a clear avenue for goods to be ferried up the short river from the seacoast to the town's lakeside docks. From there, riverboats could take the goods up that branch of the Nile to the heartland of Egypt.

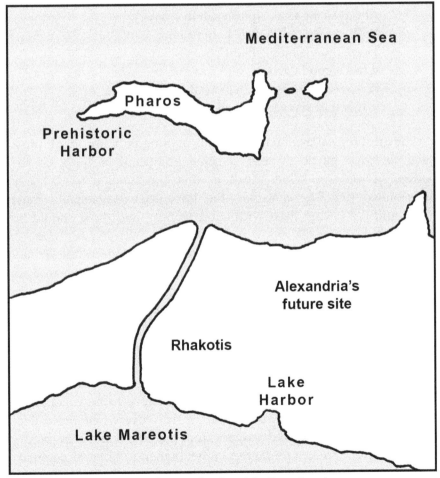

Fig. 22   Pharos Island and the Egyptian shore

It was perfect—but with just one problem. Historical records attested that when Alexander the Great arrived, he found nothing there. This was amended in some written accounts to admit Rhakotis existed, but beyond that, nothing. If the Phoenicians had built a port on Pharos, where had it gone?

If there was less evidence, the search might have been dropped at that point. But the conditions were too perfect. Even Homer told about this place in *The Odyssey*—about five hundred years before Alexander.

> Now off Egypt,
> About as far as a ship can sail in a day
> With a good stiff breeze behind her
> There is an island called Pharos
> It has a good harbor
> From which vessels can get out into open sea
> When they have taken in water.

The most logical explanation for this missing port was that it must have subsided into the water at some point and be lying on the bottom of the sea. While much of that construction might have deteriorated over the centuries, the Phoenicians reasonably must have built the harbor itself with cubic stones—and those should be *somewhere.*

As it turned out, there had been quite a bit of underwater archaeology done in the Great Harbor at Alexandria since 1990 by Jean Yves Empereur and Franck Goddio, both of whom became internationally renowned for their work. Mr. Empereur found an array of stones from the legendary Lighthouse at Pharos, which was one of the Seven Wonders of the World. The blocks lay just outside the harbor on the floor of the sea, indicating that the towering edifice had once stood on the site where Fort Qaitbey now rests. Mr. Goddio located on the bottom of the harbor what many believe to be Cleopatra's palace, and has brought to the surface a truly overwhelming collection of statues, columns and artwork from the time of the pharaohs.

While trying to contact these two gentlemen in hope of persuading them to divert some exploratory effort to the search for the Phoenician harbor, Lady Fortune intervened.

Before my next trip to the Mediterranean—which would include a visit to Alexandria to pursue this possibility—I happened to contact Professor Alaa Ashmawy at the University of South Florida in the United States. Dr. Ashmawy was born in Alexandria and received his bachelor's degree there. He directed my attention to E. M. Forster's book *Alexandria, a History and a Guide*, published in 1922. Lo and behold, there in the book was a map showing the location of a "prehistoric harbor" on the western end of Pharos!

Of course in Forster's time, as at present, sand had filled in to connect Pharos to the mainland, making it a promontory instead of an island. The land area that had been the island was then called the Ras-el-Tin district. But in the time of Alexander, it was still a separate island surrounded by the deep waters of the sea.

And yes, the author was *that* E. M. Forster, the famed writer of *Room with a View, Passage to India* and *Howards End* among other works. During World War I, he was stranded in Alexandria while the war raged on. He made the best of it by researching every possible aspect of Alexandria and writing those discoveries into his aforementioned book. One of his sources was a work written in French titled *Les Ports submergés de l'ancienne Isle de Pharos*, written by M. Jondet, the man who discovered the ancient submerged port while he was the harbormaster of Alexandria. In true Phoenician fashion, there were two harbors. Here is how Forster described what was found. It is perhaps the clearest picture of an ancient Phoenician port anywhere in the Mediterranean.

> It is the oldest work in the district and also the most romantic, for to its antiquity is added the mystery of the sea.
>
> Long and narrow, the Harbour stretched from the rock of Abou Bakr on the west to an eastern barrier that touched the shore beyond the Tour de la Mission d'Egypt. These two points are joined up by a series of breakwaters on the north. Having rounded Abou Bakr, ships turned north under the Ras-el-Tin promontory, where there is deep water. To their left were solid quays, stretching to Abou Bakr, and recently utilised in the foundation of the modern breakwater. To their right was

another quay. Having entered, they were well in the
middle of the main harbour, with a subsidiary harbour
to the north.

The visit to the Harbour is best made by boat, since
most of the remains now lie from 4 to 25 feet under the
sea. They have, like all the coast line, subsided, because
the Nile deposits on which they stand are apt to com-
press, and even to slide towards deeper water. They are
built of limestone blocks from the quarries of Mex and
Dekhela, but the construction, necessarily simple, gives
no hint as to nationality or date. The modern breakwater,
being built across the entrance, makes the scheme rather
difficult to follow.

THE PREHISTORIC HARBOUR

Modern work shown thus ....
Ancient work shown thus _____

Fig. 23 Pharos ancient harbor

The Small Quay (a) is in perfect condition, and not
four feet under water. Length: 70 yards, breadth, 15; the
surface curves slightly towards the south. The blocks,
measuring about a yard each, are cut to fit one another
roughly, small stones filling up the joints. The Ras-el-Tin
jetty crosses the end of this Quay; the point of intersec-

tion is near the red hut on the jetty. At the north end of the Quay is an extension (b) that protected the harbour entrance.

Further north, well inside the harbour, is an islet (c) covered with remains. Some are tombs, and of later date; submerged, are the foundations of a rectangular building (30 yards by 15) reached on the south by steps, and connected by little channels with the sea on the north. This islet may have contained the harbour offices.

From the modern breakwater the Great Quays (d) show here and there as ochreous lines below the waves. They are 700 yards long, and constructed like the Small Quay, but from larger stones. They connect with the rock of Abou Bakr (e), the western bastion of the Prehistoric Harbour; it is a solid mass over 200 yards square; most is on the sea level, but a part juts up; it is marked all over with foundation cuts and the remains of masonry. West of Abou Bakr is a double breakwater (f) further protecting the works from the sea and the prevalent wind; and on it hinges the huge northern breakwater (g) also double in parts, which runs with interruptions till it reaches the eastern barrier (h). The rock is named after the first Caliph of Islam.

The outer harbour (i) has not yet been fully explored.

Upon arriving in Alexandria to see what might still exist of this ancient port, I met with Dr. Ahmed Abdel Fattah, General Director of Museums and Antiquities of Alexandria, and with Dr. Mervat Seif el Din, General Director of the Graeco-Roman Museum in Alexandria. They were quite knowledgeable, and Dr. Fattah gave me a helpful collection of reports on underwater archaeological exploration at Alexandria harbor.[23]

After that it was time to see what could be seen. At that point, modern political necessity unfortunately intervened.

As testimony to the Phoenicians' ability to select ideal locations for their ports, their ancient harbor had now been turned into a Marine base and was home to Egypt's Admiralty. Judging from the number of young men in the area wearing sparkling dress whites, it probably also included their equivalent of a Naval Academy. Needless to say, the entire area was off limits. Though I was unable to go onto the site during that visit, a ray of hope remained.

The military installation surrounds a presidential palace, to which selected visitors are certainly invited. I sincerely hope the country's leader will see the diplomatic value in allowing a small party of Egyptian and international experts to observe the site of the ancient harbor and document it for posterity. This needs to be done before the wear and tear of water and human activities reduce the cubic stones to small, loose rocks adrift in the tide.

To make a long story short, the Phoenicians were successful in their early quest. It was quite likely that they made some economic concessions to Egyptian leaders in exchange for the right to free and untrammeled use of Pharos Island as their personal base for conducting Egyptian trade. Thereafter they were able, much like at Tyre, to consolidate many small shipments of goods from the mainland into warehouses, which were then disgorged into the large, sea-going ships for the voyage north. And all of this was done in the privacy of their own seaport.

In this we see the seventh of the Phoenician principles: the strong preference for privacy and even a degree of secrecy in their personal and professional affairs. We saw suggestions of this earlier in their avoidance of ostentatious display of wealth in public, keeping in their homes whatever treasures they collected. This was also intimated in their desire to blend in with the people around them, adopting clothing and usages appropriate to Egypt when in Egypt and appropriate to Canaan when dealing with their Canaanite cousins.

With respect to professional affairs, privacy was not limited to choosing separate port cities where their boats and shipments would be protected. We will see some of the lengths they went to in order to hold secret the sources of their trade goods, which prevented others from sailing to those undisclosed locations to steal the trade. There was even an illuminating report of a captain who was being followed on his way to one of these private sources and purposefully lured his pursuer into the shallows where rocks destroyed both ships, thus preventing the private source from being revealed. In these and other ways it soon becomes clear that they took their professional secrets seriously.

In a manner similar to the way they established their Egyptian outpost in the south, the Phoenicians also created small outposts in the north and west. These were on the copper-producing island of Cyprus as well as isles in the Aegean Sea and other locations. Although relatively modest at first, some of these outposts would gain considerable importance in the fullness of time, as we shall see.

While those beginnings were quite promising, Egypt was unfortunately going through internal difficulties which undermined some of the gains the Phoenicians had made. The people who lived in the delta area significantly outnumbered the Egyptians who lived south of Memphis along the long and winding Nile. And it seemed that the bitterness over being conquered by people from the south had never gone away.

Sporadic acts of rebellion and instability had already broken out during the rule of the fourth king after Aha Menes. By the time of the seventeenth king, Khasekhemwy, the northern rebels had attacked all the way to Hierakonpolis, the ancient southern capital. During the course of this warfare the Phoenicians' trade with Egypt became progressively more hazardous, and within the country trade in general seemed to have been often disrupted.

The critical moment came during Khasekhemwy's reign when this civil war threatened to split the country in two. He counterattacked, and the resulting bloodshed was staggering. Eventually he was successful on the field of battle. But then he had to fight for peace. To do this he pursued and won the best possible ally in the land: He married Nimaathapu, a proud woman who was of royal northern lineage. In all these things he found himself walking in the footsteps of Narmer, the first king.

The two men shared something else in common. As a result of this watershed moment, a new dynasty was declared in Egypt. Yet it began not with the king who had fought to bring the country together, but with his son. Once again, having a Southern father and Northern mother made the son the symbol of unity, and suitable to be the first king of the new dynasty.

The elder pharaoh made two additional contributions before his long reign ended. Widespread trade was resumed in the re-unified land. This was as much a boon to the long-suffering Egyptians as it was to the Phoenicians, who gladly restored their high volume of shipping.

The other contribution would prove to be significant to Egypt's culture from that day forward. Khasekhemwy built a great wall of cut stone around an area he wanted to use for his tomb and its related funerary buildings. Although the ambitious project was never completed, it was the first known use of cut stones for building in Egypt; and it would inspire some of the Nile's greatest monuments.

The pharaoh's older son may have ruled briefly, but it was his younger son Djoser who became famous as the builder of Egypt's first pyramid. This in turn would profoundly affect the Phoenicians.

In all the years preceding this time, Egyptian kings had been buried in underground vaults. The first of these were simple shafts called *mastabas*, but they developed into imposing underground structures consisting of many rooms lavishly stocked with precious possessions for the king's journey into the next life. Above ground, all that could be seen was a low, flat structure made of mud bricks which covered the rooms below and provided a surrounding for the doorway and stairs leading down into the tomb. There were variations on this design, of course; but broadly speaking, this was the tradition.

The origin of the pyramid is usually laid to the perhaps-fanciful story that Djoser built a stone-block wall around his funerary complex just as his father had started to do, but became disappointed about being unable to see the low structure covering his prospective burial place when standing outside the walls. To solve this problem he ordered a second flat structure of slightly smaller circumference to be built atop the existing structure on his burial place. He then ordered a third level slightly smaller than the first two, and continued for several more levels until he had run out of space and could add no more. This mound of stones could then be seen clearly from outside the walls.

The structure came to be known as the Step Pyramid and still stands today at Saqqara just outside Cairo. It was given this name due to each level having a vertical wall topped by a flat section before the next level's vertical wall began. Curiously enough, the deterioration and crumbling that has happened over time has filled in most of the large "steps," giving it more of the smooth shape commonly associated with pyramids.

The Phoenicians had long ago noticed at Hierakonpolis that the Egyptians spent freely when it came to building temples and religious sites. So they were eager to help with this marked expansion of the Pharaoh's burial place. But these sea traders were not yet noted for their surprisingly precise stonework—that distinction would come later. How, then, could they make themselves valuable to the Egyptians in this regard and earn more of the free-flowing payments?

Fig. 24   Djoser's Step Pyramid

It turned out there was a way they could accomplish everything they wanted. To see this, however, we need to follow their other voyages across the Mediterranean before we return to Egypt.

Trade to the north helped balance the Phoenicians' trade with Egypt, and proved to be an essential key to their survival. Egypt's appetite was huge and demanded much more than Byblos could supply from its own resources. Since it was crucial that they satisfy their customer's appetite, the Phoenicians had to barter for large quantities of goods from their northern neighbors to meet the southern demands. Egypt was putting into Phoenician ships a wealth of precious metals, fine fabrics and other exotic produce. Some of this the sea-traders kept, while the rest was used to obtain more raw materials from the north. It was good trade for all.

Moreover, to be totally dependent upon one customer would have left them in an exceedingly weak bargaining position. If trade fell off with that one client, it could have broken their back. So they always kept trade paths open to Ugarit in Canaan, to Cilicia in Anatolia, to the island of Cyprus and other places. Bits of this trade had been in place before the bonanza on the Nile opened, and was relatively easy to maintain.

Then came the explosion when Narmer unified Egypt and trade demand rose to a fever pitch. The Phoenicians pressed farther and farther west along the coast of Anatolia until they came to the Aegean Sea between the two lands that would become known as Greece and Turkey. Many islands filled the sea between these two mainlands. Local products, wines and oils from all these places quickly filled the ships' holds for the return trip to Byblos and onward to Egypt.

In dire need of an outpost in the Aegean to handle the many small trades with so many towns and islands, the Phoenicians chose a small, centrally located isle that had very few native people on it. The reason for this location's meager population was the simple fact that it had a large, active volcano at its center. And the paucity of water, coupled with cinder-laden soil, made subsistence there a difficult challenge. But for sea-going people who just wanted a harbor of their own and no warlike neighbors with which to contend, the choice was perfect. Since this little island was exactly round in shape, they were said to have called it *Stroggili* or *Strongyle,* meaning "round one." In time it would be known as Thira—and then as Santorini.

South of this outpost by a half-day's voyage—given calm seas and a favorable wind—lay what many called a continent in those days: the vast island of Crete. Here was a land rife with low-level conflict between its towns and cities, but also rich with natural produce such as olive oil and herbs that were in high demand elsewhere. To win this trade without getting drawn into tawdry local conflicts, the Phoenicians established a port on uninhabited Dia Island, which lay offshore in reasonable proximity to one of the provincial centers there which was known as Knossos.

To the west of Crete the small island of Cythera rested just off the coast of mainland Greece. In time this also became a useful port, though ultimately not as important as the other two.

These lands, from the Aegean to Byblos to Egypt—and all the ports in between—comprised the Phoenicians' trade routes of the time, forming a wide arc around the eastern Mediterranean Sea.

The Phoenician willingness to take risks, to explore, and to enthusiastically pursue opportunities for trade—as well as the good fortune to have developed a close relationship with Egypt at an early date—led to a significant trading empire upon the blue waters of the sea. While others pursued empires on the great land masses, the Phoenicians continued to put larger and larger ships upon the sea.

This wide-ranging travel produced another benefit as well. By viewing the stars at night from widely different places, they came to realize that one's location and direction on the water could be known by reading those stars. Their travels forced upon them the need to become navigators, so they learned from every society they touched and added many observations of their own until they became the master navigators of their day.

While most early sea travelers felt compelled to stay within view of land to know where they were, the Phoenicians became skilled at shortening their trips by charting paths across the open water to reach their destinations.

And without question, one of the key ingredients in the growth of their maritime empire was their willingness to explore. Having pushed outward to Crete and the Aegean, they then continued westward across the Adriatic Sea to the southern end of what would become known as the Italian peninsula. Rounding it, they found a beautifully placed island which would bear the name Sicily, and would eventually host many Phoenician settlements. Just south of this island they made two more intriguing discoveries that would open doors for them. One of these was the north coast of Africa, far west of Egypt. At this site they would one day place a colony called Carthage, which became a great city in its own right.

The other discovery was a small island between Sicily and North Africa, which had a much more immediate impact on the Phoenicians. It was Malta.

They found the people of Malta to be fairly isolated in the middle of the Mediterranean Sea, and well-insulated from the periodic violence that wracked the mainlands far to the north and south. These people lived in simple farming communities on the rolling hills of the main island, as well as on its smaller sibling isle of Gozo. They were a peaceful people who revered their ancestors and worshipped

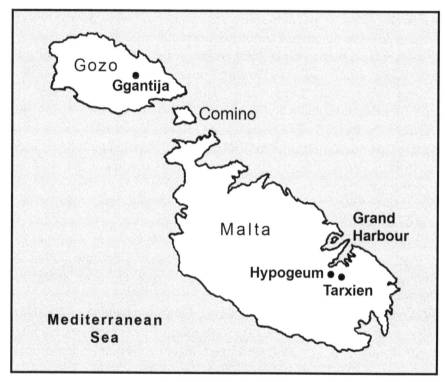

Fig. 25   Malta and Gozo

Mother Nature in the form of a large, expectant woman. They also built absolutely spectacular temples in which to practice these gentle beliefs.

For a long time they had honored their recently departed elders by placing their remains in underground chambers cut into stone. These resembled clusters of rounded rooms, and some of them involved many such clusters. Then in 3600 BC they began to build stone structures above ground where the living could gather and commune with their beloved family members who had gone before them. These above-ground temples were essentially mirror images of the underground burial chambers, being built of huge boulders standing on end and held in place by other stones beside them. In some places there were several courses of large stones, one above the other, reaching over twenty feet high. The net effect was to recall the feeling of being completely surrounded by the stone of the underground chambers. The rooms of the temples were rounded and grouped in clusters, much like the resting places of their ancestors.

Fig. 26 Ġgantija temple on Gozo

One of the earliest and largest of these temples still stands on the island of Gozo and is called Ġgantija. This temple, and the dozens of others scattered across the hillsides of Malta, are now famous as the oldest manmade structures in the world—although women probably had a hand in building them as well.

It is common today to mention men first and women second, if at all, but the opposite was true in Malta. In that land it was the departed matriarch of the family who was highly revered, and it was in her honor that many of the temple rites seem to have been practiced. In silent witness to this role were the ubiquitous statues of large women of childbearing age that were found throughout the temples and underground chambers. The degree to which this extended to women taking the lead in the communities of the living is not yet known; but without question, women held an honored place in the society.

These magnificent temples typically began as smaller, rough-hewn affairs and then grew over time. Reuben Grima, the curator of World Heritage Sites at Malta, took some time from his duties to help me understand the evolution of these ancient and awe-inspiring structures.

Ġgantija, which meant "the giantess," began as a temple of three rounded chambers built with huge stones in the odd shapes they had when found in the ground. Smaller stones were placed in the crevices between them to form the fairly solid walls. Later, five more chambers were built beside the original cluster, with a central hall uniting the five. Finally, two more chambers were added to the original cluster of three, producing two side-by-side clusters of five chambers each. Both groups of chambers had a long hallway that led to impressive entrances on the southeast side.

Since the ancestors of local families were being honored in these temples, it is quite reasonable that new families who appeared in the community also wanted space dedicated to the honor of their ancestors. If they wanted it strongly enough, they might be sufficiently motivated to provide the resources and labor necessary to build those additions, possibly joining together with other families similarly inclined.

It should be noted that as each successive addition was made, the stonework became better. The giant pieces took on more clearly defined rectangular shape, with straight, smooth sides. They also began to be fitted together side-by-side in tight seams that required no intervening stones.

These temples have stood on open hillsides exposed to rain, sun and wind for over five thousand years and have naturally become a bit worn. But we have been given a beautiful rendition of how they looked when they were new, bequeathed to us by the original builders. An underground series of burial chambers known as the Hypogeum was also started in 3600 BC, and seems to have been reserved for the most distinguished among the local people. As such, it was gradually expanded to three full levels, built around a central temple constructed in similar design to those above ground. The difference between the Hypogeum and the above-ground structures is that the underground temple was carved from living rock and sealed tightly until 1899. In the Hypogeum we do not see weathered rocks. Instead we observe smooth lines of finished stone just as they looked when originally built, complete with decorations and painted ochre symbols. The result is truly beautiful.

Fig. 27   The Hypogeum burial chambers.

It was into this peaceful land of Malta that the Phoenician explorers first set foot. Imagine for a moment the impression it must have made on them. After landing on countless warlike shores, ever watchful for those who might—and sometimes did—steal their cargoes and covet their ships, they landed here. The peaceful people of these farming villages had not a single weapon among them: no sword, shield or helmet. They had only their magnificent temples and their Large Lady statues.

The Phoenicians must have thought that they had died and gone to heaven. After so many years of having to work hard developing relationships with people who had strange beliefs and customs, here were people whose life revolved around peacefulness and family. The Phoenician voyagers explained their feelings about this place better than anyone else could do for them. They called the land *Malet*, which meant "refuge."

If trade was their only interest, there would have been little reason for them to come here again. There was no rich royal family to buy their goods, and no great surplus of olive oil or other commodity for locals to give in return. Yet the Phoenicians came back many times.

Fig. 28   A chamber in Tarxien temple on Malta

And when they later established permanent colonies in this part of the world, Malta would be one of them. The attraction was not trade.

This quiet island seemed to have become their refuge, their place of rest on the long voyages around the Mediterranean—a place to revive not just the body but the spirit in these awe-inspiring temples. In exchange they brought many desirable things not naturally found on the island, particularly the sharp obsidian needed to make cutting tools. It was quite likely they also brought gifts for the temples and for the people who maintained them.

Certainly in 3000 BC, after the bounty of the Egyptians had been showered upon the Phoenicians, a significant change came about among the temple-builders of Malta. They began to modify the earlier temples to add additional chambers, the artistic decorations were improved, and protective walls of large, regular-cut stones were added. It was as if a rich sponsor had taken an interest in their well-being.

In time there came a day when the Maltese seemed to have been asked to return the favor—and unwittingly, the price was a high one.

Far to the east of this little island, Egypt's pharaoh Khasekhemwy built that land's first stone structure around 2650 BC. By that time the Maltese had been building stone temples for almost a thousand years. The Egyptians had vastly more resources at their disposal, but the Maltese had knowledge drawn from long experience and had developed a high level of craftsmanship. In their many stone temples they had already cut, moved and erected massive stones up to fifty tons in weight. And the Phoenicians were frequent visitors to both lands.

When the new pharaoh, Djoser, wanted to go beyond his father's simple wall and construct a towering edifice upon his prospective tomb, it would not have taken the Phoenicians long to realize how to curry his favor. Ever careful to protect their sources, they probably did not divulge the location of Malta but only the existence of expert stonemasons they could bring to help ease the path for the pharaoh's monumental project.

The cooperation between Phoenicians and Egyptians seems to have worked well. The Step Pyramid was successfully built, and in similar manner the burial pyramids of Djoser's successors were also raised as needed. Throughout these years the Phoenicians were able to successfully maintain their coveted position as the suppliers of sea trade to the people of the Nile.

Then came the first king of the fourth dynasty, whose name was Snefru, and things began to change. This king was a forceful man who led a brutal military campaign against Nubia to the south of Egypt and brought back seven thousand captives from this small country, largely depopulating the land. Then he attacked Libya to the west and brought back eleven thousand captives. Returning home he began a massive building campaign and sharply turned up the heat on his suppliers of wood and stone: the Phoenicians and the quarry miners. Of particular concern to the Phoenicians was that he not only wanted to build pyramids and buildings, he also wanted to build boats.

While they had brought enough cedar to Egypt in the past to satisfy that land's basic requirements, the Phoenicians had never saturated the market by bringing too much wood. This practice was reflected in the fact that cedar stayed in high demand throughout these times and never became a common commodity. It also mirrored their fear that the Egyptians might one day become major builders of seagoing ships and drive them out of the business of trade. Snefru's desires were therefore quite ominous.

Brief descriptions of these times are found on the famous Palermo Stone, which was discovered along the banks of the Nile and moved to a museum in Palermo, Sicily, where it received its name. On it were recorded the deeds of many Egyptian kings, including Snefru. One of the statements it made about him was that he "brought forty shiploads of wood." This was understood to be cedar from Lebanon because he subsequently used cedar to build great riverboats for use on the Nile.

Some people have assumed that—since Snefru caused this wood to be brought—he must have sent Egyptian ships to get them. But of course, no such ships existed yet due to the Phoenicians' actions and lack of Egyptian interest. Yet that was starting to change. Forced to bring the forty shiploads of precious cedar by this military-minded king, the Phoenicians could only watch nervously as the new Nile riverboats he had his people build became much larger. Some even reached 170 feet in length.

Snefru's pyramid-building was likewise of a scale never before seen. He created not one but *three* major pyramids. The first was a step pyramid like that of Djoser. Apparently not satisfied with it, he ordered the Bent Pyramid to be built—which was even larger and had relatively smooth sides like a traditional pyramid. Unfortunately the slope of this second pyramid did not taper enough, and it had to be changed to a much steeper slope when half done. This led to its "bent" appearance. Being the forceful man that he was, he could—and did—command a third pyramid be built. This one, called the Red

Pyramid due to the color of its stones, was a true pyramid in shape and was the largest ever built up to that time.

Upon Snefru's passing, his son Khufu—also known as Cheops—followed in his father's footsteps. Inheriting his father's forceful nature but none of his diplomatic skills, Khufu became hated by his own people and by others upon whom he imposed his will. But he pressed forward nevertheless and created in his own time the Great Pyramid, the first and largest of the three major pyramids at Giza beside the Nile. Throughout ancient and modern times these three

Fig. 29   The Great Pyramids of Egypt

pyramids—built by himself, his son and his grandson—would be viewed as awe-inspiring marvels.

But at such a cost. The resentment of his people was part of the price. The Phoenicians likewise—under what was no doubt enormous pressure—provided two complete cedar boats to be placed beside the Great Pyramid for use by the king during his eventual trip across the river of the dead. Though they tried to make the design as much like a riverboat as possible, that was not their skill. As a result, the vessel gave away some of the design secrets they had labored so hard to retain. Worse yet, the boats had to be shipped from Byblos in pieces and assembled in Egypt, giving away even their methods of construction.

We know these things because the two boats were discovered in 1954 buried in two protective vaults beside the Great Pyramid.[24] The boats were found disassembled, but each piece of wood was marked to show how it was to be assembled again. Wood shavings on the vault floor indicate that at least one of them was put together and taken apart again to test the design. It may even have been used one time to ferry Khufu's body across the Nile amid lavish ceremonies. This boat has now been completely reassembled and stands on display in a protective structure beside the Great Pyramid.

Fig. 30   Cedar boat at Khufu's pyramid

Existing documentation also shows that the process of Egyptians buying pre-cut cedar boats from the Phoenicians for religious purposes—to be assembled in Egypt—was repeated many years later when it was no longer necessary to hide this information. But at the time of Khufu, the release of these design elements was a major breakthrough for the Egyptians and a huge blow to the Phoenicians.

Yet this may not have been the greatest loss to be suffered. In a possible echo of Snefru's virtual depopulation of the Nubian lands, the entire population of Malta suddenly disappeared from their island at this time. Searches across the main island and Gozo have found no signs of natural disaster or violent attack. There were no signs of epidemic, no signs of a society wasting away over time. They were there, and then they were not.

There has been no way to know with certainty what happened on Malta. Were the Egyptian demands too great? Was some amount of force applied to the Phoenicians or some beguiling inducement offered to the Maltese to accomplish this wholesale moving of several thousand people from the islands? Perhaps it was promised as a temporary activity, while the greatest religious structure in the world was being built. "Temporary" may have dragged on as a second, then a third, great pyramid was built.

All we know for certain is that the people of Malta, the world's most experienced builders of stone structures, suddenly disappeared at this time. Dust, sand and wind-blown debris piled up on their dozens of magnificent open-air temples. This detritus covered the walkways, the tables for offerings, and the statues of the Large Ladies. For hundreds of years the land knew no visitors other than the seabirds that paused as they crossed the waters. For whatever reason, the passing Phoenician ships could not bear to land. It was a loss felt by many. A beautiful, peaceful culture was gone.

CHAPTER 7

TO FOLLOW A CHANGING WIND

Phoenician fears about the Egyptians building sea-going boats came to be realized eighty years after the death of Khufu and his burial in the Great Pyramid. When King Sahure took the throne in 2487 BC, he set his eye on taking a more dominant position in wealth-making through foreign trade, and quickly ordered such boats to be built. In response to his wishes the first known sea-going boats produced by the Egyptians were launched. This historic moment was recorded with great pride in beautiful scenes carved into the stone of his pyramid complex at Abusir. The Phoenicians followed each step in this process with growing dread.

A distinctive design characterized these sea-going Egyptian boats. This was true not only at the time of Sahure but also at the several later times in their history when they would again attempt to create a navy. The design was easily recognizable in paintings and carvings, and grew directly from their extensive Nile riverboat experience.

Egyptian riverboats had gradually evolved from the original simple bundles of papyrus reeds, primarily by adding short planks of wood to them to serve as decking. When this skill was mastered, wood planks were then used instead of reeds for the hull itself. Eventually this resulted in riverboats being fashioned completely from wood.

However the only home-grown wood Egyptians had to work with was from the small acacia tree, which yielded planks only about three feet in length. This resulted in a very unique style for their boatbuilding, which remained virtually unchanged down to the time of Herodotus. This is how he described it on a visit to Egypt.

> The vessels used in Egypt for the transport of merchandise are made of the Acantha (Thorn), a tree which in its growth is very like the Cyrenaïc lotus, and from which there exudes a gum. They cut a quantity of planks about two cubits in length from this tree, and then proceed to their ship-building, arranging the planks, like bricks, and attaching them by ties to a number of long stakes or poles till the hull is complete, when they lay the cross-planks on the top from side to side. They give the boats no ribs, but caulk the seams with papyrus on the inside. Each has a single rudder, which is driven straight through the keel. The mast is a piece of acantha-wood, and the sails are made of papyrus. These boats cannot make way against the current unless there is a brisk breeze; they are, therefore, towed up-stream from the shore.
>
> Herodotus 2:96

In imitation of the reed boats that had gone before them, these riverboats made of planks had flat bottoms and two-footed masts. Such a mast was used to support the sail because these boats had no solid keel running down the middle to which it could be attached, and the small planks could not support it. As a result, the mast was made in an upside down "V" shape with one foot resting on each side of the boat, distributing the load.

When Sahure ordered the construction of sea-going boats, this same design was used, and vessels were produced using many small planks and having a two-footed mast. They immediately discovered, however, that the sea was not the same as the river. While the surface of the river was basically flat, the sea had waves of various heights. These combinations of crests and troughs in the sea caused the boats to go up and down in the water. Since these boats were made of many small planks and had no solid keel, they were flexed by each passing wave and quickly split apart.

The Egyptians' solution to this problem was to tie thick ropes around the part of the hull farthest forward and also the part farthest aft. These two were then connected by equally thick ropes held above the deck by "Y-shaped" sticks. These ropes, which ran the length of the boat, were then tightened until the front and back ends of the vessel were lifted enough to stop them from flexing with the passing waves.[25]

Fig. 31   Engraving of trussed Egyptian boats

This solution, though inelegant, at least worked well enough for these craft to go to sea. It also made the Egyptian sea-going boats instantly recognizable. The stone engravings at Sahure's pyramid clearly showed the rope trusses around the front and aft of the boats, connected by the thick cables running above the deck. It also showed the two-footed mast that would support the furled sail. The cargo being unloaded from those boats seemed to include logs of cedar from Lebanon, which was still one of their most highly prized imports. Intriguingly, the crew of the boat includes both Phoenicians and Egyptians. This is understandable since these were maiden voyages for the Egyptians, and they would have wanted people on board who were familiar with sailing these routes.

The other use to which these boats of planks and trusses were put was to sail on the Red Sea to Punt—which is believed to be the

Egyptian name for the area around Ethiopia—to bring back myrrh, malachite and other exotic goods.

Fortunately for the Phoenicians, the trussed boats were not very effective on the Mediterranean, and Egyptian interest in pursuing such voyages soon waned. The calmer waters of the Red Sea were more hospitable, however, so use of these boats to Punt continued for some time. Two hundred years after Sahure's venture we are told that trade relations with Byblos were flourishing again, indicating the Phoenicians were still in the middle of that trade. After that, the power of the pharaoh and the central government deteriorated and Egyptian sea travel appears to have been abandoned.

So the Phoenicians had dodged the frontal attack on their sea trade. But they were not as fortunate in an attack by others closer to home. This was a time of troubles which would unwittingly push them to the heights of their first empire.

Into the crossroads known as Canaan came the Amorites, a fierce tribe of itinerant shepherds whose clans forced their way into whatever lands they needed to graze their herds.[26] In 2150 BC, they decided the land near Byblos would suit their needs. Descending upon the city's walls and gates with a vengeance, the Amorites forced their way in and partially burned the homes and temples within.

With help from their sister cities on the coast of Lebanon, the people of Byblos were able to rebuild the damaged structures and reinforce the broken city walls. But what they could not repair was the serious damage to the community's feeling of security. Like a person who has suffered a violent rape in her own home, they had lost faith in the protection of the walls around them. To make matters worse, the clan of Amorites did not move away but instead took up residence well within striking distance. Even if the thicker walls of the city should hold, the population of Byblos had grown so much that many of their people lived outside the walls to the north and east. Each time the intruders practiced their frightening habit of making incursions into the area, the outlying people had to flee and hide within the walls. That left their property and animals to be plundered, and unlucky stragglers to be killed.

Although they had long realized that islands were the best place to put new settlements—and had put that knowledge to good use at Tyre, Arwad and other locations—the Phoenicians now began to consider something much more extreme. They began to contemplate the relocation of their land-based cities to a large island, where land armies and raiders could not reach them.

They had already taken over the two largest islands on the eastern shore of the Mediterranean—Tyre and Arwad—but those were too small to hold the Phoenicians' existing population, let alone provide room to grow. So they looked farther away.

It did not require a great deal of imagination on their part to see the large island of Cyprus sitting 120 miles northwest of Byblos. Without question, it had enough room for them to grow. Byblos rested on perhaps twenty-five acres of land, including the homes outside the city walls, and the other Phoenician cities were smaller. Cyprus had over two million acres of land, though admittedly much of it was on steep mountainsides. More to the point, it had over three hundred miles of excellent coastline.

Nor was it unknown territory. Being practically in their back yard, the people of Byblos had been going there and trading for copper for about a thousand years by this time.

Unfortunately, their timing was terrible. Only a couple of hundred years before, colonists from Anatolia had arrived and brought the Bronze Age to the simple farmers and miners who lived there. Originally, these new people settled in the north of the island—the point nearest to the land from which they came—but then the colonists spread over the entire island. They had even reached the southeastern shore, which faced toward the Phoenician cities.

An appeal to the new masters of Cyprus for some type of accommodation apparently fell on deaf ears, for no relief was given. Still, the Phoenicians persisted.

At home, they followed their time-honored practice of trying to blend in with their new neighbors. They began to adopt some of the Amorite personal names, fashions and customs. Perhaps they felt they were making progress and that a major change in their lives would not be necessary.

Then, close to 2000 BC, the Amorites fell upon the city again in a show of destruction even more devastating than before. The walls fell, and much of the city was put to the torch. If Byblos had been a single city standing on its own, this might have been a devastation too severe for them to survive. However once again—in a pattern that would be repeated many times throughout the Phoenicians' long existence and become one of their trademarks—the pain of one city was felt by all. The healing resources flowed from Tyre, Sidon and the other Phoenician communities. Byblos was immediately rebuilt with thicker walls, its temples were refurbished, and its houses were restored.

But it was a brutal beating they could not forget. Any further delay in seeking an island haven was now unacceptable. Any inconvenience caused by moving far away was brushed aside as inconsequential. That this was going to happen was clear. The question was: where?

Having found the door not open at Cyprus, and having neither the military power nor inclination to attempt fighting their way in, the Phoenicians looked westward along the coast of Anatolia. But there were no islands large enough until they came to the Aegean Sea between Anatolia and the future land of Greece. Suddenly, they went from having no choices at all to having too many. Islands were everywhere, in every possible shape and size.

Their outpost at Santorini[27] reasonably received first consideration because it was already theirs. The few local people were friendly and the location was perfect. It stood midway between the two mainlands, which put as much water as possible between the island and any land-based warriors similar to those who had stormed Byblos. Being near the center of all the other islands also made it attractive in terms of local trade. All of these things were good.

Unfortunately it had several characteristics that could not be ignored. In the middle of the island stood a smoking, active volcano. During the roughly seven hundred years they had been using this outpost, the simmering volcano had come to life once or twice each century and added a little more lava to the towering black mound that was its home. The earthquakes which accompanied each minor eruption caused some inconsequential damage that was easily repaired, since the settlement was so small. The long-term residents had become accustomed to it over time. But for newcomers—

especially those whose nerves had recently been scraped and were still raw—this was not appealing.

The more decisive consideration was water. The small island had virtually none. The few trickles which existed largely determined where a few settlements could be, and local people were already occupying most of those places. The small rivulet that crept down the hillside to their port at Akrotiri could only nourish a small town.[28] How they would support their growing population was a critical concern.

So they turned their eyes to the neighboring islands—and the unexpected happened.

To the south of Santorini, across a significant expanse of open water, lay the immense island of Crete, their major customer in this part of the world. And just offshore from it was the small Phoenician outpost on Dia Island. A quick inspection of Dia showed it was even less suitable than Santorini in terms of meeting their needs.

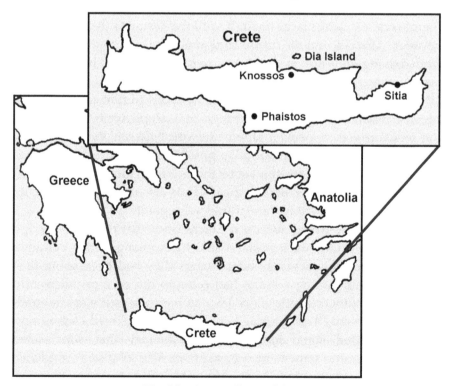

Fig. 32   Aegean Sea and Crete

But the people of this outpost had something intriguing to report: The longstanding Phoenician custom of blending in had worked perfectly here. There were many reasons why this large island might be the sanctuary for which the Phoenicians were searching.

When they first stumbled across the island of Crete around 3000 BC, after early Egyptian trades sent them down this path of exploration and sea trade, the Phoenicians had found the local people living a very simple existence. Many still lived as hunter-gatherers, while others had made the step to shepherd or subsistence farmer, raising what was needed for their own families and little more. Their homes were basically one-room huts, though many still lived in the open or in caves as their ancestors had done for thousands of years.

The people on Crete, as well as on the mainland and other islands at this time, would later be called Pelasgians by the ancient Greeks. This term came to mean all the people who inhabited these lands before the first Greeks "came down from the north" around 2000 BC, and settled in the land known today as Greece. The Pelasgian people spoke their own language, little of which has survived, and had their own customs. It was these Pelasgian people that the Phoenicians first encountered on Crete in 3000 BC.

The local Cretan people were able to live in such a rustic manner because their island had a temperate climate dominated by warm, gentle winds and soft rain. The land was rich and fertile, blessed with mountains, valleys, bright sunlight, flowing rivers, green forests and wide fields. All of these things supported an abundance of grains, fruits and wildlife. It took little effort to eat well, and the need for shelter was not as great as in other less temperate lands.

So despite their lack of apparent achievement, the people of Crete multiplied and thrived. And they did so on an abundance of land. Stretching 150 miles from east to west and averaging about 25 miles from north to south, their home was roughly the same size as Cyprus but with much more of it suitable for cultivating. The three mountains higher than 7000 feet and the many deep valleys gave these people a great range of choices for where to live and earn their sustenance. Occasionally a few huts would be aggregated into a small village, and three larger settlements that might actually be called towns had formed. One was at Knossos in the north-central hills of the island near the seacoast, one was at Phaistos in the south-central valley, and the other was at Sitia in the eastern part of the island.

In conditions such as these, the initial trades between the people of Crete and the Phoenicians were fairly basic. The local people discovered, however, that with a little more effort they could produce an excess of food and natural products such as oil pressed from olives. In return for these things, they could obtain attractive cloths, bright jewelry and tools to make farming and home-building much easier. The Phoenicians, in turn, took the food obtained here and traded it to those who dwelled on the rocky islands and mainlands of the region. The highly useful and desirable olive oil was earmarked

Fig. 33 Mountain ranges and valleys of Crete seen from Phaistos

for the long haul back to Egypt and the correspondingly richer exchange which made this effort worthwhile.

As the Phoenicians became comfortable with navigating across the open sea and learned the prevailing winds and currents which flowed across the central expanse of the Mediterranean, they eventually devised a southern route across the open expanse of water. It took them southward from Crete to the coast of North Africa and then eastward to the Nile Delta.

This simple discovery proved to be a remarkable breakthrough in Mediterranean trade. It completely eliminated the need to turn around in the Aegean and go back the way they had come with all of their goods—back to Anatolia, Byblos, Sidon, Tyre, southern Canaan and the Sinai—just to get to Egypt again. Now they could take their trade in a large circle, from Byblos to the Aegean to Egypt to Byblos. And instead of spending half their time fighting winds and currents, they could move with these forces of nature at their back over virtually the entire trip.

This also proved to be the confirming reason for the Phoenicians' choice of Pharos Island as their permanent Egyptian outpost, since it lay at the western end of the Delta and was the point of arrival at the Nile when following the circular route.

Fig. 34   Dia Island

The people of Crete knew nothing of these matters, of course, being concerned only with their fields, their expanding herds, and the doings of their neighbors up and down the valley in which they lived. What they did know was that these visitors came by boat from their port on Dia Island[29] to places along the northern shore and seemed to be non-threatening. They carried no weapons and had no soldiers—unlike the aggressive visitors from the mainlands and some of the other islands who occasionally had to be chased away.

And they brought a moveable marketplace on their boats which was like no other. Unlike the coarse but serviceable material of local weaving, they brought fabrics soft to the touch, colorful and interwoven with designs made of bright threads. They brought tools of a new metal called bronze, which was incredibly superior to the soft copper that had never really replaced their ancient stone tools. It became true that a man was not a man unless he had a sharp, shiny knife of bronze in his belt. But he could not buy the knife until he had first bought the cloth for his wife's special dress—unless he wanted to sleep outdoors at night and find no food on his table. So he labored a little longer in his field and produced something extra against the next trading day.

In the early years it is likely that much suspicion existed on both sides and many precautions were taken. But gradually a measure of trust built up, and the locals came to accept these genial visitors who did their best to blend in. As they always did, the seaborne traders would begin to sport the same clothing and manner as the people of the land, albeit with the benefit of fine fabrics and personal jewelry equal to what the richest locals might possess. There would be an effort made to learn the local dialects and courtesies, giving their customers the feeling they were dealing with a rich uncle who had come to visit. But an uncle who, unfortunately, could not make the trade for that low an offering and could something more be proffered to secure this beautiful item for themselves rather than have it fall to their neighbor?

Beyond that, the revered Mother Nature was also worshipped by these seafaring people. What better proof of their good character could be offered? The visitors even brought exquisite figures of the mother goddess holding her full breasts, all carved from flawless marble.

Unfortunately, offering prayers to Mother Nature did not keep the local people from violence. Fighting seemed to break out without too much provocation between neighboring groups, sometimes simply as proof of manhood or other times to establish a new local "pecking order." Weapons were built and proudly owned for such purposes. At times in between, those sharp instruments seemed to be displayed as a show of strength. The only good news from all of this was that it was amateur fighting. By all indications, when tempers got hot or someone wanted to assert himself over a wider area, he got his neighbors together, they went down the road and fought, somebody won, and they all went home to sleep it off.

No sign of permanent military institution occurred. There was no standing army, and any manner of fortification was a rare occurrence. On the distant mainland, different cultures pushed each other into raising battlements for defensive needs or offensive desires, but they did not appear in this rural land. These people were far removed from the various armies and roving, warlike tribes of those faraway lands.

The newcomers, who identified their homes as being in Byblos, Sidon, Tyre and Arwad, even seemed more loyal to the peaceful precepts associated with Mother Nature than were the Cretan people themselves. This earned them the locals' grudging admiration. Of course, the strangers did not *have* to fight here. Whenever a local disturbance broke out, they could simply load their boats and retire to Dia Island until it blew over.

More to the point, however, the visitors refused to take sides. As a result the traders were not feared. And because these traders stayed above the fray, they eventually became trusted. This was a pattern the Phoenicians repeated again and again across the Mediterranean as they established their many trading outposts.

These relationships continued to grow over hundreds of years as the villages became towns, and some of the towns grew to become larger and more important than the others, dominating large regions. The leader who ruled each region was a lord who held real power; but that power was never secure, given the long history of personal feuds and shifting local leadership. So each lord kept his weaponry on display as a symbol of his right to rule. And among all the lords, the one at Knossos—the closest town to the source of trade goods at Dia Island—became recognized as the supreme lord: the king. This king took as symbol of his power the Cretans' most impressive weapon: the double axe. This weapon had a single handle with one axe blade facing forward and another facing rearward.

This was the land of Crete that the Phoenicians began to consider in 2000 BC. They came with the lashes of the Amorites still fresh on their backs, and seeking a place of peace in which to live.

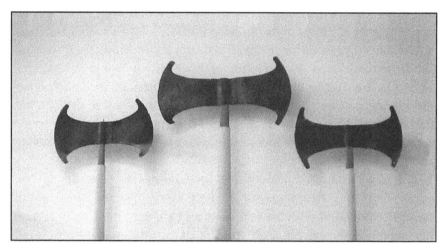

Fig. 35   Double axes from Knossos

Up to this time Phoenician trade had brought some measure of prosperity and growth to Crete, but the local people were still far away from realizing the powerful palace society they would become. So what happened during these days?

For a long time there was active debate over whether the local people pieced together that golden society all by themselves—a process given the grand name of "indigenous development"—or whether they were aided by "Eastern influence." This latter term referred to involvement by either the Anatolians (people from modern Turkey), Phoenicians, Egyptians or others. During the course of resolving that issue, a rich and intricate picture of the rise of this golden society emerged.

As we have seen with legends such as those of the Trojan War, fanciful ancient stories often had elements of actual history in them. They cannot be taken at face value, with gods causing events to happen. But comparing those tales to archaeological evidence has sometimes showed us clearly which parts are true.

The ancient Greeks recorded their understanding of how the Minoans came into existence. They did this in the legend of Europa which was passed along from generation to generation. In this colorful account, Zeus first saw the Phoenician princess Europa at her home in Tyre, Lebanon. She was walking beside the sea gathering wildflowers, and he fell in love with her. The classical poet Ovid described their encounter this way, with Zeus....

....headed for the shore, where the great king's daughter, Europa, used to play together with the Tyrian virgins. Royalty and love do not sit well together, nor stay long in the same house. So the father and ruler of the gods, who is armed with the three-forked lightning in his right hand, whose nod shakes the world, setting aside his royal sceptre, took on the shape of a bull. [He] lowed among the other cattle, and, beautiful to look at, wandered in the tender grass.

In colour he was white as the snow that rough feet have not trampled and the rain-filled south wind has not melted. The muscles rounded out his neck, the dewlaps hung down in front, the horns were twisted, but one might argue they were made by hand, purer and brighter than pearl. His forehead was not fearful, his eyes were not formidable, and his expression was peaceful. Agenor's daughter marvelled at how beautiful he was and how unthreatening.

But though he seemed so gentle she was afraid at first to touch him. Soon she drew close and held flowers out to his glistening mouth. The lover was joyful and while he waited for his hoped-for pleasure he kissed her hands. He could scarcely separate then from now. At one moment he frolics and runs riot in the grass, at another he lies down, white as snow on the yellow sands. When her fear has gradually lessened he offers his chest now for virgin hands to pat and now his horns to twine with fresh wreaths of flowers.

The royal virgin even dares to sit on the bull's back, not realising whom she presses on, while the god, first from dry land and then from the shoreline, gradually slips his deceitful hooves into the waves. Then he goes further out and carries his prize over the mid-surface of the sea. She is terrified and looks back at the abandoned shore she has been stolen from and her right hand grips

Fig. 36 Europa coming to Crete

a horn, the other his back, her clothes fluttering, winding, behind her in the breeze.

Ovid, *Metamorphoses* Book II: 844-875

Once they arrived on Crete, Zeus and Europa became lovers. The king of the gods made her pregnant, and the Phoenician princess gave birth to sons Minos, Rhadamanthys and Sarpedon. Minos was then crowned as the first king of the Minoans.

If the Greeks had honored one of their own people as king of the Minoans, that might not have carried as much weight. Because legends and historical writings often reflect some bias in favor of the author's own people. The fact that the Greeks accorded this honor to an outsider—in this case the son of a Phoenician—makes it more likely that they were simply reporting events as they happened.

The Greek historian Thucydides told us more about King Minos himself.

> The first person known to us by tradition as having established a navy is Minos. He made himself master of what is now called the Hellenic [Aegean] sea, and ruled over the Cyclades, into most of which he sent the first colonies, expelling the Carians and appointing his own sons governors; and thus did his best to put down piracy

in those waters, a necessary step to secure the revenues for his own use.

Thucydides 1:4

This description of the Minoans' power upon the seas reveals an essential point which is often overlooked in the rise of the Minoan palace society. We have already seen the history of the Cretan people up to 2000 BC. They were rustic people who lived by simple farming, herding livestock and fishing from small ports. There was no sign of massive shipbuilding at great harbors, nor great skill at sea trading with foreign powers.

The Phoenicians, on the other hand, had all these things in 2000 BC. Their cities at Byblos, Sidon and Tyre had been conducting sea-trade for over 700 years by that time, while bolstering their harbors and boatbuilding facilities.

Yet when the golden Minoan society was launched, the people of Crete suddenly had all this sea-faring and sea-trading experience. And they had so many ships that they could command the seas around them.

In keeping with the arrival of Europa and some number of Phoenicians, this fairly abrupt change in Cretan culture would only make sense if it was accompanied by a significant number of arriving sea-traders and boatbuilders from Lebanon. Archaeological evidence in Lebanon does in fact show a decrease in the population there, as we will soon see.

As for the plight of Phoenicians being driven overseas by hostile neighbors, what reasonable course of action could they have pursued with the leaders of Crete at this time?

Most other neighboring societies would have pulled together a large army and proceeded to invade the island. With soldiers every-where, they could have taken part or all of the vast land for themselves. But as we have seen, that was not how the Phoenicians did things. Countless times in their long history the Phoenicians found themselves facing larger and physically stronger foreigners while needing to find a solution to the problem confronting them. And they virtually always handled it the same way. They came bearing breathtaking gifts and began to negotiate.

Let us consider how that would have looked if they brought their traditional—and so often successful—approach to the leaders of Crete. The Europa legend suggests that their rich gifts could have been offered as a massive dowry, in return for which the Cretan king would marry a Phoenician princess and name their son as his heir.

Their son, Minos, would then be raised with full knowledge of the Phoenician principles and secrets. When he came of age and was crowned king of Crete, the Phoenicians could safely bring much or all of their sea-trading empire under his control. And they could bring as many Phoenicians to Crete as necessary to manage that extensive trade network across the Mediterranean.

This would allow exactly what archaeologists have discovered: the sudden proliferation of ships and sea trade controlled by King Minos on Crete, followed by great wealth and the rise of a palace-building society.[30]

True to the Phoenician desire to blend in, King Minos and his successors clearly left in place as many outward trappings of the Cretans' culture as possible. Even though Knossos was several miles inland, it was kept as the capital and the king's main residence.

As the Phoenician principle of peaceful resolution of differences became an accepted rule on the island, the occasional squabbles among Cretans faded away, and the few fortifications which had previously been built fell into disuse.

Even so, the double-axe was kept as a symbol of the king's power, despite the shifting of real power to the tremendous profits earned by trade. This was apparently done for a simple reason: If people were used to giving their allegiance to a king at Knossos backed by a double-axe, then *be* the king at Knossos backed by a double-axe and receive their allegiance.

Other subtle changes were made to reflect the growing importance of sea trade. The sleepy port of Poros—which lay on the coast just north of Knossos and faced Dia Island across seven miles of open sea—took on new importance. A much larger harbor was built and virtually all the operations from Dia were moved to this place. It became in a very real sense the new heart of Crete and played a central role in all that would come.

Nota Dimopoulou, the Director of Iraklion Archaeological Museum on Crete, was the one who impressed on me the importance of

Poros harbor. At her office in the museum she described her personal research into this valuable early port, and it was eye-opening. I urged her to publish those intriguing findings, and she did in fact produce that work three years later.[31]

So many ships began to call at Poros that another harbor had to be built at Amnissos four miles to the east to share the burden. Other ports were enlarged or built all along the coast of Crete, with most of them being on the northern shore. This took advantage of the many natural bays which existed there, and the fact that they were sheltered by the island's large mass from the deeper waters and tempestuous storms of the Mediterranean to the south. Each of these ports was tied back to Poros, and from there a direct road was built straight to Knossos, linking the island's visible and working centers. This stone-topped highway came to be known as the royal road.

This growing importance of trade and the king's control over it soon became established in a very visible way at major towns across the island. This was achieved by constructing a large trading house in each of these region-leading towns. Much larger and more elaborate

Fig. 37   The royal road arrives at Knossos

than any existing building on the island, their presence in the major population centers became solid testimony to the new way of life.

These trading houses were not just for show, however. They were essential if the people of Crete were going to accept the son of a foreigner as their leader. And along with that, accept the possibly uncomfortable changes being made to their society. Prosperity had to come to these people or violent uprisings might well ensue.

So the trading houses encouraged and rewarded surpluses by the local farmers, shepherds, olive pressers and artisans. The merchant houses did this by buying whatever the local people produced. In short order, the obtaining of luxurious foreign goods was no longer a matter of long trips to occasional markets but instead became an easy and local affair. The quality of life for people in the towns and surrounding fields quickly began to grow.

Local leaders seemed to profit even more. Their small homes now grew into villas. Compared to what they lived in before, each of these homes was a grand edifice and a source of pride. Quite purposefully, however, these structures do not seem to have been allowed to approach the size and grandeur of the trading houses.

The skilled stonemasons, woodworkers, plasterers and roofers who built these imposing residences also became available to the general populace. As prosperous locals satisfied their need for everyday items, they began to consider the luxury of adding a second room to their tiny single-room homes—and later, to add a third. It was a prosperous time.

But the local people were not the only ones who had to adjust their life under this new arrangement. While most Phoenicians continued to sail the sea and hold traditional positions in their many scattered ports and outposts, a significant number of them began to immigrate and make the adjustment to life in this new land. Many of them swelled the size of new or existing port towns such as Poros, Amnissos, Malia, Sitia, Kato Zakros and Kommos. But some had to relocate inland—certainly to larger towns such as Knossos and Phaistos where trading houses were established and their presence was needed.

So they settled on the land and built villas for themselves similar to the ones being raised for local leaders. They planted vineyards and olive groves to make the wine and olive oil that were among the most prized exports of this land and for which there was a growing demand.

Whatever trepidations the first generation of Phoenicians might have had in making this transition to living on acres of countryside, their children and grandchildren seemed to take to it quite readily. This presaged a soft division among the Phoenician people, which eventually would lead to a social eruption and major change of direction. But that was still many years in the future.

And so the Minoan empire was born. The local people of Crete, and the Phoenicians who arrived by ship, merged into a new society that had not existed before. Many elements of this new life were drawn from the old Cretan society, but its business skills and rules came from the Phoenicians. It grew into a unique and beautiful culture.

This was something completely unanticipated for the Phoenicians. They had expanded many times in the past—to new settlements at Sidon, Tyre, Arwad and countless outposts. But this was the first time they had ever committed so many of their people. And it was the first time so many outsiders had been involved.

It put everything they had built over the years at risk as they ventured into untested waters. Adjustments had to be made in Lebanon when so many people departed for Crete, and the effect was substantial. In addition, their trade secrets and the private matters of their society risked exposure. The peacefulness they had worked hard to preserve amid warlike surroundings might be trampled if people on Crete could not make the change. The Phoenicians were, after all, vastly outnumbered in this merger. They had only their economic strength and tight-knit organization to help them hold their own. It was a terrible risk. But they knew it was only a matter of time before Byblos and their other cities would be overcome by the land-powers around them, so this drastic change had to be made.

Yet they were always practical in the steps they took, and now remained true to that ingrained practice. They did not insist on establishing a completely Phoenician way of life as they had done in creating Sidon, Tyre and other cities up to this time. This was a blend of two societies, and was not fully Phoenician or Cretan. It was something new which we have come to know as Minoan. In a very real sense the Minoans were the children of the Phoenicians and

Cretans. As such, they were related to the Phoenician family, but with their own special attributes.

Shortly after the arrival of the Phoenicians, the building of magnificent palaces began in earnest around 1950 BC.[32] And the golden society of the Minoans began to thrive.

CHAPTER 8

THE LABYRINTH

The large and impressive trading houses erected in major regional centers across Crete soon began to serve several purposes. In addition to conducting trades, one of their main functions was to be a storehouse for the wealth of the kingdom. Part of this abundance was the locally-purchased goods about to be shipped out, alongside the recently-arrived goods flowing into Crete. The rest were the earnings from past trades which were earmarked for public projects as well as for distribution to the king and local leaders.

The trading houses also provided working-space for the king's administrative staff, which is to say for the fledgling government of the island. In the emerging cities of Crete, as in all Phoenician cities, the distinction between business and government was a difficult one to make, if indeed there was any such distinction. The many clay tablets found in these administrative offices showed that most of their concern was with trade and other business matters over which the king presided.

Some of the Minoan trading houses also provided residential chambers for the king or local governor. These individuals served not only governmental roles but also as managing directors of this trading business. Large rooms were provided so public and private meetings related to business and government could be conducted.

The public meetings were carried out with great pomp and circum-stance, as attested by the magnificent chambers and grand central court where they were performed. These displays gave assurance to the local citizenry that they were part of a great and thriving enter-prise. Less is known about their private meetings, which reasonably dealt with the actual affairs of state and trade.

Eventually, religious leadership also came within this overall so-cial fabric, and even into some of these buildings. There was never any doubt that local worship had been and would continue to be centered on Mother Nature. She was revered by locals and newcom-ers alike. But the Phoenicians had learned a valuable lesson from the Egyptians, and they put it to good use in Crete and all their other trade locations.

The high priests of Egypt exerted a great deal of influence over their people, and when the pharaoh kept these religious leaders within his sphere of influence, the government was strong. But when the high priests chose a contradictory course to that being followed by the pharaoh, civil unrest, revolts and the fall of dynasties were the order of the day.

To avoid those problems the Phoenicians, as was their wont and normal practice, went with the simple solution. The king became anointed as the chief priest and presided over the highest religious ceremonies. And so the religious leadership and senior level of public ceremonies on Crete were brought into the king's building. This included giving the high priestess lavish space and honors at Knos-sos.

Within a hundred years the coalescing of all these activities into what had started out as simply a trading house in major towns created a serious need for larger buildings to house all these func-tions. Another pressure for expansion was the level of trade in Crete, which multiplied as the local people gained immediate rewards from this activity and rushed to produce additional quantities of goods. Still more pressure was provided by the growth of local villas in size and substance due to leading families competing to show their affluence. In time, these homes began to compete with the once-dominant trading houses as symbols of power. Local earthquakes were also a factor in upgrading these buildings, including a major one around 1700 BC which led to the redesign of some palaces.

Fig. 38   At Knossos outside the king's chambers

So the Minoans reached into the rich vaults of these trading houses and created new buildings vastly more majestic than anything else in the land. As a result, these structures once again became awe-inspiring, and reestablished visible proof of the king's ascendancy.

Since these vast edifices were ultimately controlled by the king, they were called palaces. Yet clearly they were not palaces in the usual sense of the word. Traditional palaces were the opulent homes of kings and queens. That the highest affairs of state were conducted in a traditional palace was also true. However its primary purpose was not normally to be the main business house of the realm, nor was it usually the house of parliament or the national cathedral.

In Crete, the largest of these incredibly lavish and extensive new buildings were all of these things. And given their close relationship to the king as well as their luxurious décor, these massive buildings continue to be called palaces down to the present day.

All these things became abundantly clear when the ancient palaces of Crete were finally unearthed by archaeologists and preserved for us by able conservators. Yet before they were excavated, the concept that these palaces existed at all was held up to ridicule for many years. This was due to the main evidence for their existence being a handful of tales from mythology. These stories harked back to a then-poorly-known time before the emergence of the classical Greeks in Athens, Sparta and their related cities.

However a few individuals were willing to go against the tide of established opinion. They searched for some historical basis behind these legends, to see if that existed. As mentioned earlier, one of those individuals was Heinrich Schliemann, who had previously pursued the possibility of there being some truth in Homer's epic poem *The Iliad.*

Schliemann did in fact unearth Troy, though exactly which level of the city witnessed the Trojan War has been debated. It also was the case that this explorer probably enjoyed publicity too much. Yet his contributions proved to be tremendously significant. His work at Mycenae and Tiryns revealed much about Mycenaean Greece.

He also believed there might be something of value at Knossos relating to these times, and sought to perform excavations at that location in Crete. Unfortunately the site was on private property and he failed to secure the rights to dig there. Sir Arthur Evans, curator of the Ashmolean Museum at Oxford, was inspired by Schliemann's discoveries at Troy and Mycenae and took up the challenge. He successfully gained the rights to dig on that property in Crete.

What Evans found there in the year 1900 AD was the palace of Knossos—and the Minoan civilization.

Excavations at Knossos and other ancient sites across Crete provided a wealth of information about the Minoans and piqued people's curiosity about how this magnificent civilization had come into being. This led to the competing theories of "indigenous development" versus "Eastern influence" alluded to earlier.

Researchers noted the Eastern Mediterranean influences on the architecture and other aspects of this society, and Phoenician origin of the Minoans was strongly considered.[33] But at the time substantive proof of such a connection had not been produced, so that view faded into the background.

In its place Colin Renfrew and others raised the possibility that Crete evolved solely on its own, with no outside help, and called this indigenous development.[34] However that theory was unable to successfully explain the suddenness and impetus for these changes on Crete.[35] In more recent times, Eastern Mediterranean influences have received more attention again. This was due in part to the highly controversial work by Martin Bernal. But more importantly due to the more traditional approach used by L. Vance Watrous and others. As a result, the pendulum began to swing back the other way.

After all those searches, I believe the necessary evidence has now been found to resolve the matter, and it came from an unexpected source.

The archaeological excavation performed at the ancient city of Tyre in Lebanon by Patricia Bikai was mentioned previously as the work that established a reliable founding date for the city of Tyre. This date of 2750 BC is now widely accepted and commonly used. Yet she found something else in her excavations which also turned out to be quite important: around the year 2000 BC, the city of Tyre was abandoned.[36] The archaeological findings show no indication of widespread destruction in the city at that time. The people seemed to have simply picked up their possessions and left.

It should be noted that this was the same time the Phoenicians began arriving on Crete in large numbers, and the Minoans took a great leap in sea-trading along with beginning to build palaces.

It is also worthy of mention that this was not the migration of a few people from Tyre but rather the entire population of the city. This made it a highly visible event. Even so, these matching dates on Tyre and Crete might have been a coincidence. But there was more.

A growing layer of fine sand accumulated on top of the deserted city of Tyre for hundreds of years. Occasionally a burial was performed in the sand, but otherwise the place was left undisturbed. And this sand layer was not minor. It grew to more than three feet in depth before new construction showed the return of people to resettle Tyre. All of these things are clearly documented in Bikai's excavation report, including the sand in layer 18 (stratum XVIII):

> That there was an abandonment and that it was complete seems clear from the archaeological evidence. Immediately above the rocks of Stratum XIX there was a layer of sterile sand.... This sand, in the areas where it had not

been disturbed by later pits, varied in depth from 90 to 140 cm (35 to 55 inches).

Stratum XVII—This stratum, consisting of dirty brown sand and pottery is the first evidence of human habitation after the Stratum XVIII sand. The picture which emerges of this stratum then is one of a long period of sporadic visits to the area by people coming either from the mainland, or from a part of the island where there was a permanent village.

Stratum XVI—In this period there seems to have been a more or less permanent occupation at this location.

There was no human habitation during the period ca. 2000 to ca. 1600 B.C.[37]

Patricia Bikai, *Pottery of Tyre*

The distinctive pottery found among those buildings indicated the new arrival of people began in 1600 BC and the permanent re-occupation reached this part of the island in 1425 BC.

Minoan society on Crete was also going through changes at these times. The highly destructive volcano eruption on Santorini around 1600 BC heavily damaged the Minoans. But they managed to rebuild and hold on until violent earthquakes later led to their destruction. Invaders from the mainland forced the leaders of the Minoans to flee, and their civilization ended. The date this happened was right around 1450 BC. It is clear that these damaging changes on Crete took place at the same time as the gradual re-occupation of Tyre.

So we saw the Phoenicians left Tyre at the same time people arrived on Crete and Minoan society arose. The arriving people brought Eastern Mediterranean influences to that island, as noted by Sir Arthur Evans and others. And when invaders later stormed Crete and many Minoans fled, the island of Tyre became permanently repopulated. Those simple facts would seem to be enough to settle the long-standing question of where the people came from who created Minoan Crete.

But there was even more evidence.

At the city of Sidon, just up the Lebanese coast from Tyre, permission for archaeological excavations has been difficult to obtain due to the modern city of Sidon having grown over the ancient one. Even so, recent excavations by foreign archaeologists in cooperation with local organizations have produced intriguing finds. Just as at Tyre, a surprisingly similar layer of sand was found. Work is still under way and opinions vary, but the roughly three-foot thick sand layer suggests Sidon was likewise abandoned for the several hundred years during which Minoan civilization existed.

Nor were the people who came to resettle Tyre and Sidon strangers to the land. Prior to being abandoned, these cities had been an integral part of Phoenician society, and bore the recognizable characteristics of that society. The returning people still had those recognizable characteristics and usages of Phoenician society. They resumed their fraternal relationship with the people of Byblos who had remained in Lebanon during the whole time the Minoans rose and fell. They continued to be Phoenicians—albeit ones who had experienced unique events which would color Phoenician actions and history from that point onward.

There was one last thing. For a long time, historical records have shown a puzzling anomaly. Some sources stated that the Minoans dominated sea-trade at this time,[38] while others said it was the Phoenicians who dominated the seas.[39] This has always seemed quite strange. Which account was correct? And if both societies sought to dominate sea-trade at the same time, surely there would have been highly visible fighting between them for that valued position.

Yet in all the records carved by the Egyptians into stone, and in the verbal history and writings which have come down to us from Homer, Herodotus and others, there has not been a single mention of confrontation between Minoans and Phoenicians. No assertion has been made of competition between them in any port, nor any alliances formed with land powers against the other.

Contrast this with what happened a thousand years later when the classical Greeks set out to establish themselves upon the same seas that had long been sailed by the Phoenicians. The annals of history have furnished us with a plethora of clashes between them: competition in ports, competition on islands such as Sicily, and outright confrontation on the seas in the Persian War. This demonstrated clearly what happened when two powers sought to dominate the same seas. It was a lesson also demonstrated by Venetian, Turkish, Spanish, French and English navies, among others, over the centuries that followed.

Yet there was not a hint of conflict between the Minoans and Phoenicians.

Now that archaeological evidence has demonstrated the Phoenician contributions to Minoan civilization, those historical records finally make sense. The two civilizations did not fight each other, because they were both members of the same family.

And the Greeks finally have the last word. Recall for a moment how Homer's stories of the Trojan War, once thought to be only mythological, turned out to be largely true. Now we see the Greek story of Europa—the Phoenician princess who came to Crete and gave birth to the Minoans—has turned out to be largely true as well.

When the Phoenicians mixed with the people of Crete, a truly marvelous world came into existence. And thanks to the work of many archaeologists, we now get to see glimpses of their world as well.

Over the years, the impressive site at Knossos has been beautifully restored. Since this was a unique find at the time, the manner in which some of the artifacts were reassembled may not have been completely correct—as revealed by later excavations and research. But in the main it has been excellent work. Seeing Knossos has filled a huge gap in our knowledge of what happened in this time before the Greeks began to meticulously commit to writing the events of history.

The many uses and attributes that made these palaces unique become immediately apparent when one sees them in person. I found it an inspiring experience to walk the stone courtyards and floors trod by those people almost four thousand years ago. It was possible to touch the massive walls and see the beautiful paintings which were an important part of people's lives in those days. Consider some of the images and insights that occurred on a recent visit.

Most people still arrive on Crete today the same way the Phoenicians did so many years ago. They take a boat across the expanse of blue water which stretches between the Aegean islands. These ferries from other Greek isles pass Dia Island on the inward journey and land at the place now called "New Harbor." From this vantage point

Fig. 39 Light-well to royal chambers, Knossos

the city of Heraklion—also called Iraklio—can be seen a half-mile westward along the shore, surrounded by thick stone walls built in the Middle Ages. Close to those walls, one can make out the smaller "Old Harbor."

It is another tribute to the Phoenicians' ability to select the best locations for their ports that the current ferry terminal actually stands on the original Phoenician harbor. This is where the ancient port of Poros once thrived, and served as the palace of Knossos' gateway to the sea.[40]

As you walk from the ferry terminal property with knapsack over one shoulder and the northern sea behind the other, the choice is to stroll a half-mile west to the modern city or to go straight ahead—due south—for a three mile walk to Knossos. It is no coincidence at all that the road leaving the ferry terminal is the shortest route to the ancient palace. This trek to Knossos can be accomplished in just over an hour, but those preferring greater comfort can make the journey by car in less than ten minutes.

Crossing the first hill puts the sea out of view, and one is immersed in a wonderfully green countryside of trees, fields and farms while drawing closer to the site of the legendary palace. After donating a few Euro toward the upkeep of the grounds, there is a temptation to rush forward to the nearest side of the imposing stone-block palace. But to experience this vast building the way the Phoenicians and Minoans did, it is better to turn left and go down to an excavated route called the royal road. This roadway of closely packed, smooth stones ran directly from the port of Poros to the palace and was designed to provide quick and reliable transport of goods between the two centers regardless of rain or mud.

In a manner totally confusing to people who are expecting a traditional palace and do not understand why this imposing structure at Knossos was created, the royal road forked as it approached the building and went to two places (see Fig. 37). On the left was the outdoor reception area where the king formally received honored guests. Originally this area was called a theater by those who discovered it. It is now recognized to have consisted of a high platform for the king, and adjacent rows of steps descending toward the royal road where lesser officials would stand in their finery to make an impressive show for the visiting dignitary. Just behind the king loomed the towering palace of Knossos.

The other branch of the royal road went directly to the nearby northern side of the massive building, where all goods brought from the ships in the harbor were inspected and recorded into the trade ledgers. Significantly, this was also one of the two main public entrances into the palace. The other entrance was on the south side of the palace, where a frescoed passageway greeted visitors from the fertile plains and many villages of central Crete.

After the honored guests' arrival on the royal road and short walk up the steps to the king's platform, they would be escorted along that second branch of the road to the massive square pillars of the north entrance into the palace. Since this part of Knossos also served as its trading house, the large rooms would have been filled with exquisite goods of all kinds amid bustling activity in this busiest of all the trading houses on the island. The coursing flow of riches must have

Fig. 40 North entrance, through the trading house, Knossos

been an eye-opening experience for local leaders and foreign dignitaries alike.

A walkway from these trading offices led deep into the heart of
the palace. It rose up an incline and passed the impressive wall
decoration which showed a massive bull, a potent and oft-repeated
image in the palace. The end of this walkway emerged onto the
spacious central courtyard of the palace, around which all the rest of
the vast, sprawling structure was oriented. It has been estimated that
there were a thousand rooms in this palace scattered across the five
different stories of the structure. These were all interconnected by a
warren of large and small hallways repeatedly turning left and right.
From this came the legend of the Labyrinth, an intricate maze
prowled by the Minotaur. According to legend, visitors were hopelessly lost in the Labyrinth until they were found by the Minotaur
and eaten. Labrys, by the way, was the name given to the double-axe,
the symbol by which the king was recognized. The legendary Labyrinth was his palace.

From the expansive central courtyard, some of the other functions
of the palace quickly became apparent. There was a Throne Room
with the throne still there—a fairly modest chair with a high back and
an intricate wavy design. There was some controversy over whether
the king or the high priestess sat in this chair. Given the Phoenician
practice of having the king be the high priest,[41] it could be argued
that both sides were right. The other rooms adorning the western
side of the palace included many deemed to have been designated for
religious purposes. But here was also found the West Magazine—the
extensive warehouse area filled with row upon row of giant storage
jars called *pithoi*. These vessels once contained olive oil, wine and
other valuable goods. Clearly there was a mix of functions being
served by the people who lived and worked here.

At the far southwestern corner of the palace was the beautiful
Procession fresco. This long and detailed wall painting lined the
Corridor of the Procession near the south entrance, and created
vibrant imagery reminiscent of the wall paintings at Santorini. Seven
female and male musicians played flutes and harps, as they followed
five men bearing ornate gifts. In front of them several men raised
their hands in adoration as they approached the goddess who was
the center of attention. In the same fresco but standing on the other

Fig. 41   Throne room, Knossos

side of the goddess and facing her were several more men with their hands raised in adoration, and behind them were two more gift-bearers. The musicians wore long robes flowing from their shoulders to their ankles, while the male gift-bearers and adorants were bare-chested and wore only colorful kilts that hung from their narrow waists to mid-thigh. The goddess wore a flowing dress that left her breasts uncovered, and stood with each hand raised in acknowl-edgement—one to the adorants on her left and the other to those on her right. All of the people in this elaborate wall painting had dark hair falling in loose ringlets at least to their shoulders and in several cases below the waist.

Fig. 42   The Procession fresco

Returning to the central courtyard, this was where the major cer-emonies would have been performed. Some of these affairs took place on holidays and were religious in nature, reaffirming the king's role as high priest of the land. Others would have been governmental in nature, coinciding with visits by high dignitaries or special decla-rations by the king which needed a bit of pomp to reinforce the fact that they carried the force of law. The third cause for lavish gatherings in the courtyard was purely social in nature, including the ever-popular athletic events. In a place of honor among these athletics was the dangerous and exciting bull-leaping, which was immortalized in another of the magnificent wall paintings.[42]

This brightly colored fresco pulsed with the excitement of the moment as a large and powerful bull lowered its long horns and charged forward. A woman stood directly in the bull's path and grabbed its horns, beginning to lift herself onto them. A man who went before her had already been flipped over the bull's head and was doing a handstand on the animal's back. Another woman, who had apparently been the first of the three to approach the bull, had already completed her back flip and was about to land on her feet on the ground behind the charging bull.

Fig. 43 Bull Leaping fresco

This magnificent wall painting not only vividly portrayed these people's love of athletics and the details of this particular sport, but attested to the high level of equality between men and women seen throughout Phoenician society, which clearly took root in Crete as well. That women could participate in athletics alongside men was a highly liberating experience—and one that was unfortunately not echoed in the male-oriented cultures of the mainlands.

This great courtyard had originally been a hilltop. As a result the surrounding buildings not only rose two and three stories above this open yard, but as one moved away from that central place it was also possible to descend to other levels as well. This was most visible on the eastern side of the palace, which was extensively given over to grand rooms for the king and queen and impressive meeting rooms of varying size and decoration.

The grand staircase located here was believed to have originally run five stories from top to bottom. The upper floors might have been where government minions labored away, but the lower levels of this wide staircase led into the lavish rooms of the king and queen.

The king's royal chambers were masterfully arranged so that only a series of columns stood where dividing walls would normally have been expected. The result was a much more open and airy feeling than thick walls of stone normally conjure. The large Hall of the Double-Axes contained a throne quite similar to the one in the room beside the central courtyard, and apparently was used by the king for royal audiences. Being on the far eastern edge of the palace, the windows of this room looked out across a small ravine toward verdant wooded countryside.

Looking the other way toward the interior of the palace, the series of rooms was brightly lit by a large light-well which was purposely

Fig. 44 King's chambers

Fig. 45   Queen's chambers and Dolphin fresco

left open beside the grand staircase. This concept of creating a large open shaft in the middle of a huge building to allow light and air to reach inside apartments would later be used to great advantage in densely populated urban areas such as New York City.

Adjacent to the king's chambers, the queen had a similar suite of ornate rooms. Here was found the colorful Dolphin fresco that showed several of these large fish admired by the Phoenicians. The dolphins were portrayed in bright blue and were swimming among their smaller brethren.

Elsewhere the captivating Ladies in Blue fresco showed how the queen and the ladies of her court dressed and styled themselves in those days. Their dark hair was gathered into waves by strings of jewels, bright beads and other ornamentation, while stray locks were sometimes left to fall in loose ringlets. Colorful clothing with fields of smooth fabric was edged by an accentuating color and laid beside tasteful but eye-catching swaths of contrasting stripes to create a

Fig. 46   Ladies in Blue fresco

detailed and pleasing appearance. Necklaces and bracelets of gold and other precious materials completed the ensemble.

The queen's chambers included one other essential: a regally appointed bathroom. This lavish area was complete with dressing area, hand painted hip-bath, and a fully functional toilet. This miracle of indoor plumbing, as it turned out, was not just a staple of the palaces of the land but was also used to a certain degree in the neighboring towns, where pipes inside the houses led to outside drainage systems. To put this accomplishment in perspective, the kings and queens of Europe would suffer through their days without indoor plumbing until more than three thousand years later.

Ascending from the royal chambers to the central courtyard again and walking northward through the bustling trading house's receiving rooms, one came back to the royal road. Walking on the smooth stones of the road, one would have passed a number of the large villas belonging to local leaders, before plunging past the thousands of buildings that made up the actual town of Knossos. A few of these structures have been revealed through painstaking work, but most still slumber under the mounded green hills of soil and vegetation which have accumulated on top of them over the years. The well-worn stone road then continued onward through the countryside to Poros and the sea.

As we saw earlier, before the arrival of the Phoenicians, the indigenous people of Crete were oriented toward the land. Their modest homes were in the valleys and foothills where they lived as farmers and shepherds. The villages they formed were more likely to be inland than on the seacoast. To these people and their leaders, their dealings were with others up and down the rural roads, not across the sea to vaguely comprehended lands. The Phoenicians not only brought the wealth of sea trade, but a new level of civic life as well.

Perhaps the most visible aspect of this was the way Crete went from being an absolute unknown on the world stage to suddenly being a major dealer in commerce and dominating the seas of that time. Their empire gradually spread across many islands in the Aegean Sea, from Cythera near the Greek mainland to Rhodes near the coastline of Anatolia. Their influence reached much farther. Given their Phoenician heritage, this was not too surprising.

The change from rustic homes to palaces over such a short time was likewise astounding. They had progressed as far as multiroom structures on their own. But virtually overnight they possessed the craftsmanship to build palaces with perfectly-cut ashlar stone, light-wells for ventilation and indoor plumbing. The Phoenicians were able to help in this regard. The seafarers from Lebanon had supported the Egyptians in building temples and palaces for hundreds of years by this time, and could draw upon the best craftsmen from hundreds of ports in many lands.[43]

Yet the local people of Crete also brought critical contributions to the table. The Phoenicians—with all their accumulated skills and resources—were still a sea-oriented people and stingy with their use of land. The temple of Our Lady at Byblos had become a beautiful display of stonework and craftsmanship, but it still stood on only a small footprint of soil. Alone, the Phoenicians would be unlikely to have contemplated, let alone built, the gargantuan palaces at Knossos, Phaistos, Malia and Kato Zakros. But to the people of Crete there was more land available than anyone could use. So in the merging of cultures, the palaces became not only possibilities but realities in all their beauty.

For better or for worse, the weaponry of the indigenous people became part of the Minoan heritage, including the double-axe that was their recognized symbol. During the years of this thriving Minoan civilization, there were stirrings among the more militarily-skilled people of the mainland. Despite the mainlanders' evident desire regarding the riches of the Minoans—which were reflected in their mythology as well as the historical record—they were held at bay perhaps as much by the imagery of weapons possessed by this largest of all the Aegean islands as by the miles of water that separated the two lands. So perhaps having these weapons as part of Minoan heritage played a constructive role.

The exquisite Minoan artwork, including delicately carved marble figures and the lifelike wall paintings in the palaces, must likewise be credited to the talent pool of Crete and its neighboring islands. There was virtually no sign in the years before this time that the Phoenicians possessed this masterful artistic ability with respect to sculpture and painting. But the sea-traders were generous patrons of these arts, and with their support the arts flourished.

The merging of the Phoenician people with the people of Crete on a fertile and well-placed land caused this magical moment to happen. The marriage of these two cultures created a peaceful and rich society that literally worshipped nature, art and beauty. They lived surrounded by luxuriously warm sunlight, sprinkles of rain, overgrown green countryside, and vast expanses of the clear, blue waters of the surrounding sea. This idyllic time and place had become a paradise on earth.

Yet the Phoenicians were also confronted with daunting new challenges. These came to light as they stretched themselves between Lebanon and Crete, trying to maintain their commitments in both of these camps.

CHAPTER 9

A WELL IN BEIRUT

When the Minoan empire came into being, the city of Byblos—like its sister cities—allowed many of its people to go to Crete. However, in several other respects the leaders of this ancient Phoenician municipality took a completely different course. It became impossible for them to face abandoning the Temple of Our Lady, so the priestly staff was left in place. Along with them there were enough supporting people to provide food, shelter and basic services. Having done that, they decided to maintain the other temple as well, in addition to several minor shrines.

The story which then was broadcast to all their neighbors—and was largely true—was that Byblos had been converted into a religious city. Their sincere hope was that the Amorites would not attack a religious center, especially when such a place no longer held the glittering wealth gleaned from widespread sea trade.

Time proved their gamble to be a good one. The Amorites, who seemed to find joy and great rewards in raiding the merchants' till and taking the proceeds, seemed to find no motivation in robbing a church's collection plate. The city of Byblos was left in peace.

It should be noted that the Amorites' behavior in this regard was not completely altruistic. They found themselves intensely busy pursuing a much larger prize. Mesopotamia's early Sumerian empire, formally known as the Empire of Akkad and Sumer, had become weak and listless. The old empire's problems were exacerbated by the abrasive Amorites who raided deep into their lands, just as those raiders had done with Byblos and the land of Canaan. These raids undercut the once-great, but now tottering, Sumerians and their empire fell into ruin. The Amorites surged into this void and established themselves in the previously unremarkable city called Babylon.

A hundred years later an Amorite king in Babylon known as Hammurabi wrote his name large on the pages of history by conquering all the cities around him and establishing the first Babylonian Empire.

All of those activities in Mesopotamia did not harm the people of Byblos in any way, and in fact served to take off some of the pressure. A number of the Amorite clans still lived nearby, however, so the people remaining in Byblos had to proceed cautiously with their lives.

Being Phoenician, of course, the people of Byblos did not give up sea trade completely. It would have been easier to ask them to give up breathing. A major reason why they continued to trade had to do with Egypt.

From their earliest days—even, as we have seen, before Narmer and the first dynasty—the people of the Nile had highly regarded Byblos as the source of their much-desired cedar. When other Phoenician cities came into existence and many of the wood-bearing ships then sailed from Tyre, the Egyptians still called the vessels Byblos-boats[44] and referred to that wood as coming from Byblos. This proved to be a blessing after Tyre was evacuated. The Egyptian orders for cedar were still delivered to Byblos, and Phoenicians were there to receive them.

This required some sleight-of-hand, as a magician might describe it, because Byblos had nominally become a religious city. How could it continue to receive and fulfill shipping orders while keeping up those appearances? The people of that city did not have to look far for an answer, because their principles and practices were almost tailor-made to handle such a situation.

The main principle they used in this was their devotion to privacy. The shipping orders were accepted and no outsiders were allowed to hear about them. The curtain of privacy covered every inch of their society down to the lowest cook or clerk—so no one would tell. In other cultures, leaks and disclosures were almost certain to occur. In this society one could count on silence. To do otherwise would have been unfathomable—especially when accompanied by the very real threat of expulsion from this rich society.

Another major attribute which came into play was their penchant for mixing the roles of government, business and religion, which was clearly seen in the palaces of Crete. Since the king of Byblos was also the high priest, he continued to rule this religious city in his sectarian role. Yet he was also the managing director of all trade that passed through the city.

As managing director, he had previously played up his role as king and confined public priestly appearances to the annual spring fertility rites and little else. Now there was a reversal. He played down the role of king, and priestly vestments became more commonly seen. Throughout this process he continued his role as head of the city's enterprise, but it was not easy.

The difficulties he faced were twofold: population and distance. Much of his city's population had migrated to Crete, leaving him short-handed. Yet to recall significant numbers of these people to Byblos, or to recruit more in their place, would destroy the newly established "religious city" image which was essential to their survival.

The solution, using the Phoenician principle of creating strong partnerships, was quite simple: The king's trading house continued to operate, but now served only as a clearinghouse and center of control. The actual log-cutting, shipping and handling of trade goods appear to have been moved to an outpost farther down the coast. And the name of that outpost was Beirut.

Among the outstanding advantages which recommended Beirut was its location to the south, in the direction of Egypt. The people of the Nile were still the major customers the Phoenicians had to satisfy. Being only twenty-four miles away, Beirut was much closer to Byblos than the deserted Tyre or Sidon. This made it much easier to maintain the surreptitious communication of shipping orders and trade decisions to this outpost. Also, the stretch of shoreline that there was uninhabited and had no neighboring villages—a significant plus in terms of maintaining privacy and security.

This location had previously been passed over in favor of Sidon and Tyre because it lacked the wonderful natural harbors that graced those other two sites. Still, its proximity to Byblos and isolation from others made Beirut the best choice at this time.

The relatively virgin countryside that the Phoenicians found here was part of a large triangle of land—about six miles on each side— which protruded from the foothills of the Lebanon Mountains into the Mediterranean Sea. The point of the triangle was a highland that became known as Ras Beirut, and its edges fell in sheer cliffs to the water below. This did not make an appealing location for a port.

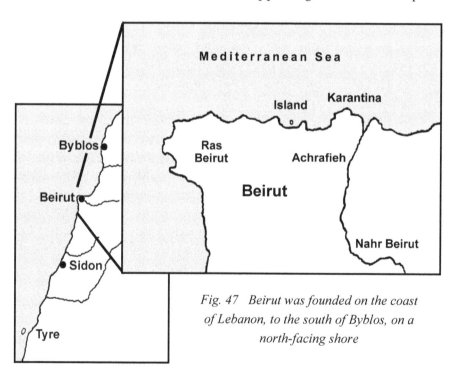

Fig. 47 Beirut was founded on the coast of Lebanon, to the south of Byblos, on a north-facing shore

Other difficulties beset the western edge of the triangle, where the cliffs became sandy shore and merged with the coastline flowing south beside the foothills. This shore was exposed to the prevailing winds and currents that came from the southwest, which made it unsuitable for a major harbor.

That left the upper edge of the triangle, which followed a roughly west-to-east line before meeting the normal northward-bound coastline. Protected from the wind and currents, this was where the port and outpost would have to be placed. Not finding a magnificent natural harbor, the Phoenicians had to search for a suitable place.

At the eastern end of this piece of coast—just before it turned north—was the mouth of a river which in time would be called Nahr Beirut. Wandering groups of people had made temporary settlements here as long ago as the Stone Age because the river offered a source of water. Unfortunately it also created a wide, marshy delta, which was a haven for mosquitoes and proved to be an unhealthy location. As a result, no permanent village or town had taken root. This silt-filled area was also a poor choice for ships that needed deep waters, so it clearly could not be the port.

Immediately to the west of the river was a significant hill in the neighborhood of Achrafieh and Karantina, with the latter area being on the coast and making a cliff-like descent to the sea. Between the cliffs of Karantina on the east and Ras Beirut on the west was found a long and normal, but rock-strewn, coastline. Somewhere along this coast was where the port city of Beirut would have to be placed.

It was here that the Phoenicians found something so appealing they could not pass it up: a small island. To the east and west of the island were promontories that extended from the mainland into the water, forming something of a bay between them, with the island near the middle. This did not offer the two-harbor arrangement they would have preferred, but under the circumstances it was the best they could find—so they took it.

The only problem with this location seemed to be drinking water. There was none visible at the proposed site. Off to the west there was only a small creek at Ain al-Mreisseh. To the east, one had to go to the foot of the Karantina highland to find another small creek.

The one saving grace of this area was an underground stream flowing down from the Lebanon Mountains. It passed between the hill at Achrafieh and the one at Ras Beirut. It came down to the shore, miraculously enough, just inland from the small island. That it would be necessary to dig wells for water here was no impediment to the Phoenicians. Their original home at Byblos was built around a freshwater well which made that city possible. And they could see

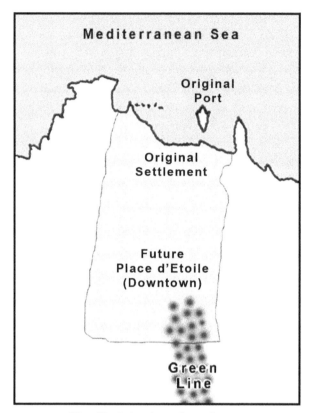

Fig. 48 Beirut's early settlement

exactly where to dig their wells in the Beirut area. Because the underground stream made a green line of trees and bushes across the land roughly following what is known today as Rue de Damas.

Thousands of years later, when troubles in Beirut would tear the city apart for fifteen years, the dividing line of the city would follow this same route, and it would be called the Green Line. Yet in the beginning this path of trees and bushes was not a sign of division, but rather of what brought people together in this place and made life possible: it was the source of precious water.

The Phoenician name for the town that they planted here was *brt*, which meant "water well." The wells were dug along this naturally green line.

In true Phoenician fashion, the earliest outpost here was apparently on the small island. It afforded one of the best accesses to deep water. And it was somewhat protected from passing tribes of people on the mainland because of the small passage of water between it and the shore. But the huge amount of trade being diverted from Byblos at this time would have made a larger port town on the shore almost immediately necessary. Today this location is where the streets beside the Place des Martyrs approach the water's edge, and where ancient walls can still be seen protruding from the ground.

Fig. 49   Ancient and modern Beirut

While Beirut was growing into a major port, life at Byblos went on as before. The guise of being a religious city continued, though the trading house was as busy as ever. Instead of walking to the harbor at Byblos to see the trade goods arriving and departing, however, the king and council had to receive reports from Beirut. But the trade flowed.

The image of Byblos as a religious center was aided by a local legend whose fame had become widespread. It was the story of Adonis. Born a beautiful baby boy named Tammuz, he was left without parents to care for him. Our Lady fell in love with him and placed him in the care of the goddess of the underworld for safekeeping. Unfortunately when Our Lady went back to claim him, the other woman had also fallen in love with the child and would not give him up. As a compromise it was agreed that the boy would live half of the year with each of them. Nurtured by the love of these two women, he grew into a handsome and influential young man in the hills above Byblos and became known as 'adon, which meant "lord."

In a twist of fate, one of the male gods became jealous of Adonis. The rival changed himself into a wild boar and fatally gored the handsome young man. As Adonis lay dying in the arms of Our Lady, drops of his blood spilled out and stained the anemone flower crimson red. When he was gone, Our Lady went to the goddess of the underworld again to see if their bargain could be restored. Her outpouring of grief and love was so strong that it was agreed Adonis would live again. He would stay in the hills of Byblos for six months each year during spring and summer, and then return below for fall and winter.

In observance of these things, the river which coursed down from these hills to a place near Byblos was called the Adonis River (today, Nahr Ibrahim). Each year when runoff from the Lebanon Mountains turned the river red, it was said to be the blood of Adonis. The crimson-red anemone continued to bloom there each year. And the grotto at Afqa on the side of the mountain from which the Adonis River flowed became a place of pilgrimage.

In his honor "Adonis gardens" were grown each year by sprouting seeds in a dish which sprang up bright and green but then perished. This was done every year in memory of his life and death. At the same time, a period of mourning was declared during which women would wail and expose their breasts in an expression of grief. After seven days of mourning, Adonis was reborn amid effusive celebration and festivities that could be quite arousing in nature.

The Greek people later became so caught up in these emotional observances that the legend of Adonis was brought completely into their mythology. And through them the imagery of Adonis came to the West.

In Lebanon the month of July is still called Tammuz in his honor, and aspects of his annual festival are still seen in the growing of Adonis gardens and other traditions. Each year the joy of life is reborn in the mountains of Lebanon and flows down to the people. And Adonis lives.

Across the sea, the flourishing Minoan empire reduced the burden on old Byblos and young Beirut by taking on the arduous task of record-keeping. On the island of Crete legions of scribes tracked the yields from trading voyages and assured all participants in this widespread Phoenician network of receiving their fair share. In silent witness of this, deep piles of clay tablets have been found in these Minoan palaces, marked with record-keeping that has yet to be adequately deciphered.[45] When finally mastered, those records may produce some intriguing insights into these times.

Unlike the people of Byblos, the Minoans were able to do these things freely, untrammeled by jealous and warlike neighbors. At least none who could march onto the island. The waters of the Aegean Sea and the ships of the Phoenicians created a barrier around Crete which none could cross.

When the Phoenicians had first arrived on that island, the Pelasgian people they found were similar to the ones who occupied the mainland and the other islands of the Aegean. They all spoke a similar language and had similar customs. Though they might fight among themselves from time to time, their basic preoccupation was with farming, fishing, tending flocks and enjoying a fairly simple life. Remnants of their language still exist throughout the area, recognizable from their many words ending in "ossos" and "assa," which are still seen in names for some cities such as Knossos.

But while the Phoenicians and Cretans were busily building their first Minoan palaces, a new people swept down from the north and established their mastery over the mainland. They spoke Greek, and settled in places such as Mycenae and Argos. These people would come to be known as the Mycenaeans.

These new masters of the land tended to build their small settlements on hilltops and surround them with thick walls, positioning themselves to command the surrounding valleys and to resist counterattacks. When not conquering new lands, they honed their skills in local fights and by going on raids to distant islands. It was this raw energy that converted the whole mainland peninsula into a Greek-speaking land, and would eventually spread across the many islands of the Aegean.

All of this was viewed with some alarm on Crete. Phoenician influence had led the merged culture which we call Minoan toward a more peaceful course than before. But it also placed a greater reliance on sea trade. Now that trade was putting the Minoans into direct contact with these people on the shore, incurring a significant risk to their safety and their way of life.

Trading in any foreign seaport had always involved some degree of risk. The desire by physically strong individuals to take from others had led to many small raiding parties and large armies marching across the lands and harbors of every country. The only reason why the seas were not plagued by constant campaigns of the same kind was that seamanship was not a skill to which most were born. Those who drew their first breath on land often learned to fight on land as part of their everyday experience as they grew up. Relatively few knew the sea with that same degree of familiarity.

In those early years, the Phoenicians were more likely than most land-dwellers to spend teenage years hoisting sail, learning to row on choppy seas, and moving the rudder to hold a course through changing wind and currents.

Others who ventured to sea with dreams of piracy and easy wealth which could be obtained at swordpoint on the bounding main usually found themselves chasing a quarry they could not catch. In equal boats, the Phoenicians could move much more skillfully.

The advantage shifted further in the Phoenicians' favor because the boats were not equal. While land-oriented people spent time concerned with homes, farms and weapons, the Phoenicians spent time on their boats. With unlimited wood at their disposal, they could try every conceivable improvement and keep the ones that worked. Their boats became faster. With their safety and their lifeline of sea trade dependent upon this, they managed to stay well ahead of any predators for many centuries in terms of ships and skill.

But their success pushed them into a difficult position. As they took on larger and larger quantities of trade, they had to build heavier ships to carry the loads. These large vessels in time grew to be huge merchantmen with rounded hulls and a vast capacity. While excellent for trade, these giant craft no longer had the advantage of speed.

This posed a huge problem for the Phoenicians, since their characteristic first response to every problem was to avoid conflict and try to negotiate a solution. When dealing with well-established societies such as Egypt, Cilicia and others, they could use economic pressure to prod the local king into cleaning up nests of pirates on their shores. This did not eliminate piracy, but made it much more manageable.

With the Mycenaeans, they had no such leverage. Raiding was not only endorsed, the local kings joined the sorties. Homer's *Iliad* documented what was perhaps the greatest of these campaigns they ever mounted: the one that destroyed the city of Troy and created an epic story of legendary proportions. But that event was still many years in the future. At first the Mycenaeans simply honed their military skills at the local level. And they could find no more worthy targets than the huge Minoan trading ships serving ports in the Aegean.

One of the adjustments which seemed to be made in response to raiding along the coast was to restore Santorini's role as a hub of Phoenician trade routes in the Aegean. Prior to establishing their agreement with Crete, the Phoenicians had used centrally-located Santorini as a focal point for trade in the area. Their expanded role at Crete had shifted part of that load to the larger island. Now it became prudent to return to the earlier arrangement. Although a bit cumbersome, it was tremendously safer to have the huge merchantman ships put into port only at Santorini and the middle of Crete, keeping them far away from the mainlands.

From Santorini a fleet of small and medium-sized trading vessels could fan out all over the Aegean carrying trade from Crete and other islands, as well as from distant Phoenician ports. With their smaller cargo holds, these craft put fewer trade goods at risk should a pirate vessel take up pursuit. And since they were not as huge or as ungainly in the water, they stood a better chance of escape.

Even so, the raiders had smaller boats, no cargo and only a crew of fighters and rowers. So they still had a clear advantage, and ships were lost.

The second adjustment was a drastic one for the Phoenicians, and one that was only made possible by their partnership with the people of Crete. They began to build fighting ships to confront the sharp increase of piracy on the seas. Taking a leaf out of the raiders' book, these craft were sleek and fast. No room was left for cargo and the maximum number of oars were built into them. Passenger space was standing-room-only and was designed to accommodate a contingent of Cretan fighters who were skilled in the use of their ancestors' weapons. The sides of the vessels were built high to protect the rowers from arrows and spears, and the whole construction was made more solid to withstand impact with the pirate boat when it was time to board and fight. Sometimes the impact alone was enough to shatter the mainlanders' boats, which were not built to the rigorous specifications of people who made their life upon the sea. In later years a battering ram would be added to the front of the boats for this purpose, but that time had not yet come.

Thucydides described these confrontations between Minoans and the mainlanders this way.

> The first person known to us by tradition as having established a navy is Minos. He…did his best to put down piracy in those waters, a necessary step to secure the revenues for his own use.
>
> For in early times the Hellenes [Greeks] and the barbarians of the coast and islands, as communication by sea became more common, were tempted to turn pirates, under the conduct of their most powerful men; the motives being to serve their own cupidity and to support the needy. They would fall upon a town unprotected by walls, and consisting of a mere collection of villages, and would plunder it; indeed, this came to be the main source of their livelihood, no disgrace being yet attached to such an achievement, but even some glory. An illustration of this is furnished by the honour with which some of the inhabitants of the continent still regard a successful marauder, and by the question we find the old poets everywhere representing the people as asking of voyagers whether they are pirates, as if those who are asked the question would have no idea of disclaiming the imputation, or their interrogators of reproaching them for it. The same rapine prevailed also by land.
>
> And even at the present day many parts of Hellas [Greece] still follow the old fashion, the Ozolian Locrians for instance, the Aetolians, the Acarnanians, and that region of the continent; and the custom of carrying arms is

still kept up among these continentals, from the old pi-
ratical habits. The whole of Hellas used once to carry
arms, their habitations being unprotected, and their
communication with each other unsafe; indeed, to wear
arms was as much a part of everyday life with them as
with the barbarians. And the fact that the people in these
parts of Hellas are still living in the old way points to a
time when the same mode of life was once equally common to all.

Thucydides 1:4-6

Eventually the outbreaks of piracy were beaten back and the Aegean Sea was swept clean. The Mycenaeans then had no recourse but
to focus their military campaigns on targets within the Peloponnesian
peninsula and the mainlands around the Aegean. Even so, the image
of a raiding leader who could take his men on daring forays proved
irresistible to young Mycenaeans. This was especially true for princes
who wanted to command the respect of fighting men when it became
their turn to be king. So with their fathers' blessings the princes
would set out on daring raids to other islands or in search of a
merchant ship. And sometimes they succeeded. But other times they
failed. The patrolling ships caught them at sea and they were never
seen again.

These occurrences seem to have made their way into the legends
of King Minos. The Mycenaeans quite reasonably would have
wanted to present themselves in a good light, and it was *their* story of
King Minos that was passed down to the classical Greeks. This
legend told about the son of Minos dying while among the early
Greeks in Athens. As a result the angry Minos was said to have
defeated the mainlanders in battle and demanded annual tribute of
fourteen young people who were then devoured by a monster known
as the Minotaur.

Try to imagine the peaceful Minoans conquering the militarily
superior Mycenaeans on their own land. That would have to be
considered doubtful at best. Try to imagine the trade-oriented
Minoans demanding payment in people instead of valuable trade
goods. Also highly unlikely. Then try to imagine a half-man, half-bull
Minotaur devouring people. That fairly well speaks for itself.

On the other hand, the idea of mainlanders losing young men and princes at sea due to the Minoan navy had a great likelihood of being true, given their confrontations over piracy. Note that the legend served as a wonderful way for mainland leaders to save face by explaining the disappearance of these highly visible young people in their society. The Minoan monster did it! This story had the added advantage of drumming up public disgust against a perceived opponent—and planting a justification for any future attack upon the Minoans.

When all was said and done, however, the raiders were held in check and the Minoan people prospered for several hundred years. Their ships patrolled the Aegean and peace reigned. But the day when the Mycenaeans would be able to turn the tables on the Minoans was drawing closer.

During all these peaceful and busy times, Santorini flourished. Blessed with the coastline of an island many times its size, Santorini was able to handle the many demands placed upon it relatively easily. As noted earlier, the island was completely round and unbroken except at the southwestern edge. Boats sailed into that gap and reached the vast inner lagoon. There they found not only a smoking volcano but also narrow beaches around the harbor where landings could occur and cargoes were transferred.

More anchorages existed on the outside of the island facing the surrounding Mediterranean Sea. As one moved inland from the gentle seaside beaches, flat plains gave way to rising hills. Continuing upward soon brought visitors to high viewing points above the inner harbor. From that place the land descended steeply or precipitously to the clear water surrounding the black cone of the volcano.

On the outside shore of Santorini, facing south toward Crete far across the sea, was the major port city that we know as Akrotiri. Here the huge merchant ships tied up at the quays as stevedores unloaded their enormous stores of goods. The workmen then brought aboard the outgoing loads of materials and valuables bound for Crete or some foreign port outside the Aegean. Small craft ferried light loads from this port to other anchorages around the island where medium-sized ships awaited to receive cargoes destined for local islands or the Mycenaean mainland.

Fig. 50   Flotilla fresco, people in Santorini greeting arriving ships

In the midst of all this bustling activity, Santorini seemed to retain aspects of its old pre-Minoan ways, learned when it was solely a Phoenician colony.

In that regard it differed from Knossos and the rest of Crete, which reveled in a wonderful culture of mixed Phoenician and Cretan provenance. The mixing was necessary to win over and keep the support of local people on Crete. But at Santorini there were no "outsiders" who needed to be won over or to be presented with a modified view of the Phoenician people. On this small island they had no neighbors at all save the few indigenous people with whom they enjoyed a live-and-let-live relationship. Even ancient Byblos had been forced to hide its light of Phoenician culture and enterprise under a religious cloak in order to survive its destructive neighbors. On Santorini the Phoenician people could do, feel and act exactly as they pleased, able to enjoy their heritage purely and without constraint. And that appears to be exactly what they did.

For example, there was no Minoan palace at Akrotiri. The trading house at this major port retained its pure and original form and function as the center of enterprise and of government. There were no hundreds of rooms in its structure, nor a huge courtyard for grand public displays. Religious rituals were performed in a separate building down the street. These reflected fundamental differences in the nature and function of the societies they served. In all its essential details this city was highly Phoenician.

In fact, Akrotiri seems to have been one of the most frank and honest expressions of Phoenician life that existed in its day. And—as is well known—this view of life was sealed and preserved for us under hardened lava after a massive eruption of its volcano. Now that it has been unsealed again after all these years, the town is gradually being reconstructed. This work goes slowly because funding is unfortunately quite limited. As a result, only a portion of Akrotiri has been excavated. Many more pieces of beautiful frescoes and other discoveries remain to be found. Surely this is one place where an increase in support would bring a treasure trove of art and understanding.

Beautiful re-creations of the frescoes of Akrotiri can now be seen on Santorini. And it is possible to walk once more through the streets and buildings of that once-thriving city. Putting all these pieces together now enables us to bring this ancient port and its people to life once more.

CHAPTER 10

FLYING TOO CLOSE TO THE SUN

The treasure of Santorini rests on its southern shore, where undulating hills partly cover and partly reveal the city of Akrotiri. At one time this ancient port bustled with life when Phoenician and Minoan ships plied the surrounding sea. Today, the city is approached by walking up a dusty road where the busy docks and harbor once stood. Volcanic ash long ago covered those maritime features, then sand, earth and vegetation took root on top of it in the millennia that followed. The shore of the Mediterranean now stands some distance away on a beach covered with small mounds. But once the blue waters had surged forward to the carefully placed stone blocks of the quays and breakwater that made up its harbor.

A ship's captain disembarking from one of those cedar ships onto a crowded quay would have had to make his way past workmen loading and unloading the exotic cargo from many ports. Reaching the main square of Akrotiri, his duties would have taken him first to the three-story building on the right-hand side of this plaza: the massive and impressive trading house. Testimony to the building's importance and wealth was immediately conveyed by the fact that all four exterior walls were built with superbly cut ashlar stones,[46] each one hewed so perfectly that no mortar was needed to hold the building together. A significant part of these magnificent walls are still in place today, and are one of the first things seen in the excavated town.

The captain would have gone inside the trading house and crossed to the grand staircase which spiraled upward to the other floors. These stairs also attested to the purpose of this building through the impressive fresco lining both sides of the stairway. Portrayed in it were many men making their way up the steps bearing items of trade.

Christos Doumas, who has for many years directed the excavation at Akrotiri and the reassembling of its beautiful frescoes, showed me the many pieces of this magnificent new mural. His staff labored all around us in the excavation workshop as they carefully positioned those fragile pieces. When completed, this vast artwork should be a stunning addition to the frescoes already released to the public.

Upstairs, the captain would have presented his cargo manifest and his report on the voyage. With that done, he was free of his duties and able to enjoy the port from which he had so long been absent. Stepping out of the trading house into the boisterous public square, he would reasonably have made his way directly across the crowded plaza to the imposing temple of Our Lady, as many sailors did upon returning safely from the sea.

Almost as striking as the trading house, this temple was adorned with two exterior walls of costly ashlar-cut stones. Entering through the main door, he would have found himself in the grandest space of the old temple, where three rooms stood open to each other and soared two stories high.

Magnificent wall paintings surrounded him, depicting salient moments in people's lives as they grew up in this remarkable society, and especially the rites of passage from child to adulthood. Although the building has not been officially named, other than having an excavation number, I have always described it as the Place of Passage due to this collection of beautiful frescoes.

In one of these murals, several young female Adorants reverently approached the seated Mother Nature. Among them was a woman in her twenties with curly brown hair plaited into an elaborate hairdo. She wore large, round earrings of similar hue. Her eyes were lined with a dark cosmetic and her eyebrows were shaped and darkened, very much in a modern style. But the most striking aspect of her face

Fig. 51   Woman in the Adorant fresco

was her expression, formed by bright, intelligent eyes and slightly open-mouthed lips shaped into the beginning of a smile. She clearly had great confidence in herself and enjoyed her life. The impression given was that she would be a joy to be around, whether as a friend or lover.

Her skirt was intricately woven in tasteful yet colorful designs. The exquisite detail of the work suggested fine embroidery and expensive threads. She was a woman who was used to being well dressed, and wore rich fabrics as if to the manner born. Yet it was her blouse that was the triumph of both couturier and artist. The actual garment was of the thinnest gossamer, intentionally made to see through and to show in its best light the young woman's natural beauty. With just a hint of light blue throughout and highlighted by darker cuffs and a seam of the same color, the diaphanous fabric and design revealed arms and breasts of a most appealing shape and youthful firmness.

Yet one more characteristic was worthy of note. While this woman was eminently pleasing in appearance, with hips not overly broad and a torso that suggested an active life, she was not thin. Beneath her chin was the slight curve of a well-fed person, her breasts were generous, and her arms seemed full yet smooth and well proportioned. She appeared to be a woman unfamiliar with dieting, but very familiar with an active life—especially walking, and possibly dance or sport.

Her overall bearing added to the confident and happy expression of her face. She carried in her hand a beautiful necklace as a gift, and seemed completely at ease and pleased to be among the Adorants in her society who were partaking in this lavish ceremony.

The extremely talented artists who created this work and the others around it gave this young woman and her people immortality, for they walk and talk, work and play, express love and revel in life with us today, just as they did then.

It should be noted that the Phoenicians of those days were not renowned for their artistic talent. So they would have retained Aegean artists to paint the frescoes in these buildings. That would explain the similarity of styling and colors with frescoes found at Crete and other parts of the Aegean. But the scenes portrayed here showed life and rituals as the Phoenicians experienced them.

For example, rites of passage are not noticeably visible in the Minoan palaces on Crete. But among the Phoenicians this was a critical part of their society. The shroud of secrecy which they so famously pulled around themselves required that they know who was—and was not—eligible to receive those secrets. The rite of passage would not only have welcomed a young man or woman into adulthood, but also given them the right to know those secrets. At the same time it would have impressed on them the seriousness of keeping those secrets until the day they died.

The ritual of passage for young men was depicted on the farthest wall to the left. It showed naked youths with their hair partially shorn, ready to make their ritual commitments. When presented with

Fig. 52   Naked Boys fresco

the *zoma* kilt to cover their loins, they walked out not as naked youths but as men ready to take their place in the community.

In other frescoes young women appear with almost all of their hair shorn off, just like the young man who was going through the rite of passage. They might possibly have been going through a similar ritual.

Near those initiation rituals on the high soaring walls was the magnificent expanse dedicated to Our Lady. This set of frescoes presented a vast field of delicately colored crocus flowers, with women moving among them collecting the fragrant blooms with their yellow-orange pistils from which the much-prized saffron was made. One of the women emptied the collected blooms from her basket so that they came to rest at the feet of the Mother Nature goddess herself. The Grand Lady sat on a high throne attended by birds and animals, even snakes and insects, all in sumptuous colora-

Fig. 53 Mistress of Animals fresco, showing Mother Nature

tions. The ornaments of one necklace she wore were made to look like small ducks. Clusters of grain adorned the blue trim of her dress. Her lips were slightly open as she acknowledged the gift of saffron being presented to her.

Crossing to the offering table in the center of the room, a visitor would give some silent words of thanks for his or her safe return, and possibly leave a small gift. Embraced by memories of their own passage to adulthood, they then walked back out into the sunlight.

In the raucous square with its many voices from different lands and warm Mediterranean sun, the ship's captain might quickly move along to pay respects to his eldest relatives in the town, and be welcomed back into the bosom of his family. Making his way to the northern side of the square to Telchines Street he would pass between the residential buildings of the city and up the gently sloping hillside. Walking in that direction meant passing a multi-story building on the right where the fresco of Boxing Boys decorated one of the walls. A little further was another beautiful painting, this one showing a gathering of antelopes frolicking in the wild.

Fig. 54 Antelope fresco

Soon the narrow road opened into Triangle Square, a public plaza with only three sides. If his eldest relatives lived in the large house there, that would have been fortuitous, for the West House was definitely worth visiting. Unlike most buildings in this port which were built in townhouse style—with the walls of one edifice touching the walls of the next in a manner creating one continuous block of housing—this house stood alone.

At the front door a younger relative might greet him and escort him up the stairs to meet his elders. The large room at that level was marked by an impressive window roughly ten feet wide that looked out over Triangle Square. However, since this would normally be a family room filled with implements for weaving or other productive pastimes, the visit with his elders naturally moved to the adjacent room which was richly decorated and suitable for small meetings or receiving guests.

While sitting, talking and enjoying refreshments, there was ample opportunity to admire the magnificent frescoes adorning the walls. These paintings on pure white plaster commemorated several pivotal chapters in the history of his people. Their simple beginning as fishermen was reflected in pictures of two young boys in their carefree, unclothed state holding large catches of fish. The other stages appeared in the extraordinarily long fresco covering the upper portion of all four walls.

It portrayed a difficult decision being made by council members, followed by the destroying of ships from a fortified city on the mainland which housed many soldiers. It showed trips to the land of a great river which he understood to be the Nile, shown as a place of exotic animals and well-tended palm trees. It also revealed a lush land with high mountains, many trees and abundant wild game. From an island in front of this land, a flotilla of many boats sailed across the sea on a joyous voyage—accompanied by leaping dolphins—to the port of Akrotiri. The entire city turned out for this occasion, with many residents peering from the city's multistory buildings while others walked down to the harbor to meet the arriving boats in person.

In due course the visiting captain would have excused himself to go home to his wife and family. Once on Telchines Street again he could continue north and pass the home of one of the great families

Fig. 55 Fisherman fresco, boy with fish

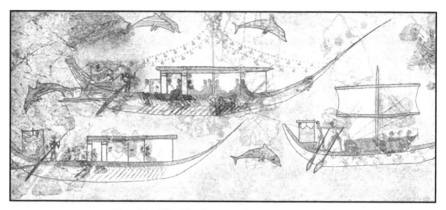

Fig. 56   Flotilla fresco, ships crossing the sea

of the city. This residence has now popularly become known as the House of the Ladies due to the frescoes of women portrayed there. But a more important place lay before him—where his family, food and friends awaited—a place called home.

About 3600 years later the director of the excavation team at Akrotiri, Dr. Doumas, explained to me how a pre-eruption earthquake probably saved the lives of thousands of people in this city. That earlier damage was severe enough so that the town stood virtually empty while workmen made necessary repairs. A limited number of merchants may have been conducting business there when the massive volcanic eruption took place. Those people apparently made good their escape by boat, for no bodies were found in the city.

The fiery eruption blew the top off the volcanic cone at Santorini and threw a huge torrent of lava and ash skyward. This proved to be one of the most devastating eruptions ever to occur in recorded history. It surpassed even Vesuvius, which buried Pompeii; and Karakatoa, which shattered Indonesia. Dark clouds of volcanic ash were spewed upward and filled the sky for many days, blotting out the moon at night and the sun by day. Plumes of lava and molten rocks streaked the ash-choked skies with streamers of red.

The ground pounded so violently that a huge tidal wave was sent outward.[47] On neighboring islands, seaports were instantly demolished by a tsunami roughly fifty feet high. The devastation on Crete was especially great because the island's major seaports lined its northern coast and faced toward Santorini. Ships at sea and in port were hurled to their destruction, along with the loss of their crews and rich cargoes. Port facilities and warehouses were smashed to pieces by the wall of water which towered many stories above them. It crashed far inland against buildings of mud brick and timbers, then retreated back to the sea and took everything with it.

The full flower of maritime life in the Aegean Sea was destroyed in one frightening heartbeat. Lesser destruction was caused all across the eastern Mediterranean. But the losses were not all suffered through fire and water. Massive earthquakes accompanying these upheavals shook buildings throughout the region. The hardest hit were the multistory structures on Santorini and Crete. The magnificent palaces of Crete—most of them well inland and protected from the tidal wave—once again had sections toppled by the force of these quakes.

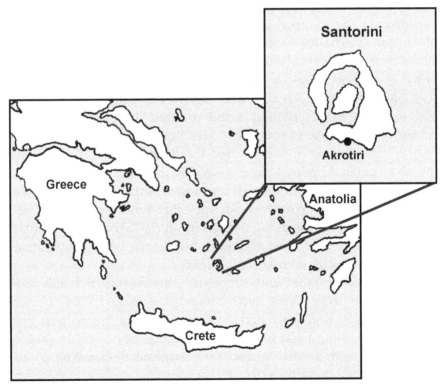

Fig. 57   The Aegean Sea and Santorini before 1628 BC

On Santorini, lava oozed into the steaming sea, and volcanic ash fell like heavy snow across Akrotiri and the rest of the island. The ash piled up day by day and week by week until it formed a blanket roughly twenty feet thick on top of the broken buildings and all else that remained. This material solidified into a hard mass which was compressed by its own weight and formed an airtight seal over the entire city.

The only silver lining around the dark cloud of what had happened was that this incredible center of Phoenician life and all its beautiful frescoes were sealed in a time capsule and held safely for us over the intervening millennia. It was not until 1967 when Spyridon Marinatos opened this sealed capsule with his excavations at Akrotiri that these marvelous finds came into our hands to be admired and appreciated.

Yet the spectacular display of nature's incredible power on Santorini was not over with the passing of the eruptions. During this fiery performance the volcano had spewed a staggering seven cubic miles of molten magma into the sky. The then-empty cavern under the island, from which this lava had come, could not support the weight of the volcanic cone above it. So in a paradoxical display of nature, that which had gone up now went down. The entire volcanic cone and part of the surrounding island plunged downward into that cavern and disappeared from view. The blue water of the Mediterranean quickly flowed in and covered the steaming hole. As a result, the island of Santorini no longer looked like an almost-complete letter "O" with a dot in the middle, but was now shortened to a "C." In the thousands of years which passed since that time, the volcano has crept upward again, breaking the surface of the lagoon at the center of Santorini and once more forming a black cone with an attendant wisp of smoke which shows it is still alive.

The violent eruption and subsequent destruction not only destroyed many lives, ships and harbors, it damaged Crete's vital lifelines of trade which spanned the Aegean. With many harbors lost and Crete faltering, what had been the beating heart of this golden society went into cardiac arrest. Like surgeons responding to an urgent call, the surviving ships of this maritime empire came from great distances to this devastated land. Though this meant yielding some amount of trade to competitors in other parts of the Mediterra-

Fig. 58   Santorini volcano surrounded by the lagoon today

nean, they had no choice. The Phoenicians had committed everything to Crete; and until this natural disaster, it had paid off handsomely. Crete had to be kept alive.

And revive it they did. The harbors of all the northward-facing cities were rebuilt better than before. The palaces likewise were painstakingly rebuilt to a larger scale and grander manner than what had stood earlier. Santorini could not be repaired due to the countless tons of smoking pumice and ash that now covered it, so all resources which had once been used there now came to Crete as well.

In time, Crete thrived again and life seemed much as it once was on the shores and hills of this extensive island. But elsewhere in the Phoenician domain, a more somber picture was seen. It would probably take centuries to restore the coffers which had been emptied to make the miracle on Crete possible.

As years rolled by, the prosperity of Crete helped to soothe the pain and all seemed well on the way to recovery. Even the wonderful frescoes in Minoan palaces had been carefully repaired or completely redone, making them fresh and clear. The damage at Phaistos palace, however, was so severe that restoration was unreasonable. So a completely new design was implemented, with some functions being performed at nearby Agia Triada.

Unfortunately, the hand of fate intervened once again, just over a century after the eruption at Santorini. Another massive earthquake whipped the region back and forth, sending the palaces and ports tumbling again. Just as before, commerce in the Aegean came to a complete standstill. But this time the Minoan and Phoenician pockets were empty.

In what had become almost a ritual, the harbors of Crete were cobbled back together well enough to accept shipping, and repairs were begun on the palace at Knossos. But the slow pace at which this work was able to proceed opened a window that had not existed before—and the Mycenaeans took advantage. With Minoan harbors and boats depleted, the waterway between the mainland and Crete stood open. The Mycenaeans, who had long been held back by Minoan patrol ships, seized their opportunity.

Raids were launched across the open water against the less-populated western coast of Crete. And once the Mycenaeans established their foothold on the shores of the island, the end was near. The Greeks were highly experienced with fighting on land, and proved to be virtually invincible.

This desperate situation presented the Phoenicians with a difficult decision. Was it time to finally abandon their peaceful way of life and fight? That seemed to be the only way to preserve the miracle created on Crete.

This was a critical moment from which there could be no turning back. If they built an army and abandoned their principle of peacefully resolving conflicts, the Phoenicians would become like the land powers around them. Up to this point, the trait of peaceful existence had been a major force in much of what they did in life. The negotiating, blending in, and being fluent in many languages all grew from walking a path other than the "manly" one of picking up a sword to settle differences. They had already come half-way toward making that change by merging with the people of Crete and agreeing to put local fighting men on board patrol boats. This was a "necessary evil" which protected their way of life. Now they faced the final step that would make the "necessary evil" a core part of their society, as others had already done.

But they could not. Or would not. There has been no way to know how the arguments and discussions went, but the results were clear. The Phoenicians summoned their ships and left Crete.

The rebuilt harbors and restored palace at Knossos were left as they stood. The local leaders were once more on their own. Quite likely, groups of villagers took up arms to defend their land, for they had nowhere else to go. But it did not matter. The Mycenaeans went through Crete like a hot knife through butter. In the years before 1450 BC the Minoans ruled Crete. After that it was the Mycenaeans who ruled. It was that quickly done.

The Mycenaeans moved into the existing palace at Knossos—the only one that was fully restored—and installed their own king. With that, they found themselves immediately operating a lucrative empire in the Aegean.

And the change in Mycenaean society was equally profound.

During the hundreds of years the Mycenaeans had lived on the mainland before 1450 BC, their society had not yet achieved palaces, polished culture, wealth or great tombs. They had conquered, ruled and led daring raids.

Suddenly all of that changed. By taking over the palace at Knossos they not only came into great wealth from trade, but also inherited the bureaucracy which made that wealth possible. The many local people who held middle-level positions in the palace were apparently still there when the Mycenaeans arrived, and were found to be valuable. They knew how to tend the goose that laid the golden egg. As such, their higher-ranking members were no doubt accorded honors and wealth by the new masters of the island—provided they kept the trade machine running. And run it they did.

It was not long before palace life became an acquired taste for the Mycenaean kings. They carried it back to the mainland where their newfound wealth soon begat grand palaces of their own. These were Mycenaean edifices, of course, which meant they were built on high, strategic hills and were surrounded by thick defensive walls. But other than that they were impressive replicas of the Cretan palaces, and they came to life at locations such as Pylos, Mycenae and Tiryns.

The changes even extended to burial customs for the king. Reflecting their new wealth, the simple tombs used prior to this time now were replaced by grand chambers called *"tholos"* built into the sides of mountains. They were then filled with lavish valuables reflecting the king's great status.

The Mycenaeans also inherited writing. Clerks in the Minoan palaces had recorded trades and accounts on clay tablets by using a writing system called Linear A. Its symbols seem to have expressed those accounts in a Semitic language that may have been a blend of Phoenician and Pelasgian. These have not yet been deciphered, but when that happens they should give us a more definite picture of those times.

After the arrival of the Mycenaeans these symbols were used to express trade accounts in the language of the new rulers, an early form of Greek. This written style is called Linear B. Given its Greek linkage, this version of the writing style has been successfully deciphered and has provided much useful information about the Mycenaeans.

However it cannot be said that the Mycenaeans took all these things and gave nothing back. The Greek language that they spoke now became dominant on Crete and throughout the Aegean Islands. Under the Mycenaeans, the Aegean actually became the Greek Sea.

This lifestyle continued uninterrupted for about two hundred years until, almost like clockwork, another great earthquake destroyed the palace at Knossos again. By this time the Mycenaeans had already transferred most of the wealth and control of trade to their homesteads on the mainland. Their towns like Mycenae had become important cities in their own right. With control of trade—and of the surrounding seas—firmly in their hands, there was no need to continue supporting this expensive palace on Crete. So Knossos was never rebuilt.

In time this once-magnificent Minoan creation became covered by drifting soil and overgrown with successive layers of vegetation. It remained in that dormant state until 1900, when the spade of archaeologist Sir Arthur Evans removed the cover and returned Knossos to the light of day.

After leaving the palaces of Crete to lie fallow, the Mycenaeans continued to enjoy the benefits of the life they had acquired, even while retaining much of the life they had always known. It was from palaces on the mainland that they now launched their raids. And far from being confined to the mainland, they covered the Aegean with their boats. They went as far east as the large island of Cyprus, which was an important source of copper. Since copper was a necessary ingredient to make their bronze weapons, this was a trip they made quite often.

They also struck the coast of Anatolia with their campaigns. The great victory by the Mycenaeans at Troy in Anatolia around 1200 BC would prove to be one of the last golden moments of their civilization. Shortly afterward, they fell into oblivion.

Across the Mediterranean Sea in Lebanon, the Phoenicians likewise stood at the cusp of extinction or survival, with a long gauntlet of challenges to be faced.

CHAPTER 11

THE PLUMMET TO EARTH

The loss of Crete spelled the end of an era for the Phoenicians. Their bold experiment with settling on a large island of their own had almost worked. They had been able to live openly in a peaceful, prosperous society, safely protected from warlike neighbors. If it were not for the intervention of volcanic eruption and earthquakes, they could have remained much longer. Who knows how the history of western civilization might have developed if the early influence on the classic Greeks had come directly from the peaceful Minoans rather than arriving indirectly through the Mycenaeans? But all of that was grist for old men to grind at the end of the day, sitting over small glasses of liquor and wondering what might have been. The real world had moved on, and the Phoenicians had to swim quickly or sink beneath the waves.

Their first concern was where to land their people. Ships filled to the brim with families, possessions, and what meager wealth they could bring with them had set sail for the Phoenician homeland. Decisions had to be made. Byblos was still threatened by its Amorite neighbors, but apparently made arrangements to take in some of the incoming flood of people. Beirut had open land, but water was a problem until more wells could be dug. Still, that city probably accommodated as many families as it could. That still left the vast majority of refugees needing a place to stay. The nearly empty Sidon and desolate island of Tyre were available, but would require much work to rebuild them. Of all these choices, Sidon had the most drinking water and one of the best harbors. It seemed to fill quickly with the largest number of Phoenician families evacuated from Crete, with a lesser number going to Tyre. These settlements were not the luxurious surroundings to which the Phoenicians had become accustomed. But the new residents were alive, had roofs over their heads and food to eat. The rest would have to come later.

The problem they faced in trying to move beyond simple survival was that the rich flow of trade and wealth which had always buoyed them before was no longer there. The Mycenaeans took a huge bite by stealing away the Aegean Sea with all its islands and the mainlands that touched it. When the Phoenicians had moved to Crete, they reasonably put more emphasis on that area, and it came at the expense of their trade in the eastern Mediterranean where they had gotten their start so many years earlier. Now the prized Aegean was gone and they had to fall back to the eastern shores where their customers had grown weaker and the competitors had grown stronger.

Egypt in particular had gone through difficult straits. The power of the pharaohs had deteriorated, and at times competing dynasties attempted to rule the land. When the Minoan civilization was at its zenith, the strict practice of keeping Egypt for Egyptians had broken down. Amorites and Canaanites came into the Nile Delta seeking water during dry years, and stayed to live on the land. The outsiders eventually became so great in number that they took over the government in 1674 BC and installed their own king as pharaoh of the land. These Hyksos kings, sometimes referred to as shepherd kings, ruled from the city of Tanis in the Nile Delta. This was a bitter pill to swallow for most Egyptians.

Still, the Hyksos introduced some advances to Egypt such as the horse and chariot, which revolutionized their method of fighting battles. The chariot became an essential part of the Egyptian army from that day forward. Yet the reign of the Hyksos was not long lived. By 1550 BC, the ruling family of Thebes was able to assemble a large force and drive them out of Egypt, pursuing them all the way to the vicinity of Gaza.

Thirty years later, presumably in response to Amorite raids, pharaoh Tuthmosis I assembled a massive force and marched into the Canaanite lands north of Gaza. He was said to have chased these "retreating Hyksos" all the way to the Euphrates River. This put Egyptian soldiers just across that stream of water from the Amorites and the Mitanni, who ruled lands spread across the northern part of Mesopotamia. The Mitanni had previously made deep incursions into the land that would be called Syria, and had absorbed the Amorites into their empire. Now the retreating Amorites confidently fled into the heart of these Mitanni lands and the safety of their protectors.

Byblos had maintained good relations and at least some trade with Egypt throughout the turbulent times that southern country experienced. Even so, the Phoenicians were somewhat shocked by this new development. Their powerful trading partner form the Nile had never campaigned so far north before, and now had brought a huge army virtually to their doorstep. This ability of Egyptian kings to make a personal decision to send their army wherever they wished made the Phoenicians deeply uneasy. That large force might be sent in *their* direction as well.

In keeping with their principle of peacefully resolving imminent conflicts—and using one of their traditional methods for dealing with such danger—the Phoenicians hastily scraped together some of their much-reduced resources and sent expensive gifts to Tuthmosis I. In this way they hoped to keep fresh the memory of their ongoing cooperation, and keep their cities off the "targets for conquest" list. As a result, the Egyptians held on to the captured Canaanite lands south of the Phoenicians but left the sea-traders alone—for now.

Yet when the reign of the pharaoh's successor was cut short and Queen Hatshepsut took the throne, another ominous note sounded. The new queen decided to improve Egypt's fortunes by increasing trade with the land of Punt, near modern-day Ethiopia. She did this by commissioning the building of sea-going ships on the Red Sea, much as Sahure had done a thousand years earlier. The idea of Egypt with its own boats on the sea was extremely troubling to the Phoenicians. Having lost the Aegean, their trade with Egypt was the only lifeline they had left. They probably could not survive if it was severed.

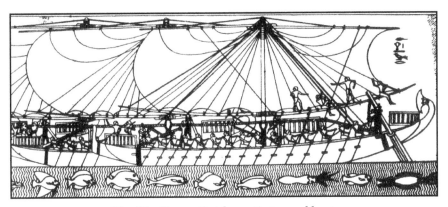

Fig. 59 Queen Hatshepsut's trussed boats

Two strands of hope remained for the tempest-tossed sea-farers and they clung to them. The first was that Hatshepsut had only launched these boats upon the Red Sea, and not yet upon the Mediterranean. The other was that the long period during which Egypt had gone without sea-going boats had apparently produced no improvements in their construction skills. The new boats on the Red Sea were essentially carbon copies of the earlier Egyptian vessels. Commemorative stone carvings from this time showed the queen's boats clearly. Heavy cables were seen tied around the front and rear sections of the hull, and more cables connected these two, passing above the deck from front to rear. Again, the cables were tightened on these trussed-up boats to keep them from falling apart on the sea.

The Phoenician art of shipbuilding meanwhile had sailed far ahead of where it was a thousand years earlier. Larger, sturdier and safer craft built with solid cedar slipped from their dry docks into the water at Lebanon. Any Egyptian who chose to put his life and goods upon the Mediterranean in a trussed Egyptian boat instead of a Phoenician one could reasonably count on being declared incompetent and be removed by his heirs. In the end, good sense prevailed and Hatshepsut's boats did not intrude on Mediterranean trade.

However a new danger arose in 1458 BC when the queen died and Tuthmosis III came to power, dedicating himself to extending the Egyptian empire. In particular he set his eye upon Canaan where his grandfather had previously won great victories. Since that day, the

Amorites had marched south again and were raiding into the outlying Egyptian territories.

The land of the Amorites—from which the raiders came—
extended from just north of Byblos to slightly south of Ugarit along
the coast. It then spread inland as far as the middle of Syria. The
Amorite king's headquarters was at the city of Kadesh on the Orontes
River, just southwest of modern-day Homs. On their raids into
Egyptian territories these warlike people found many allies among

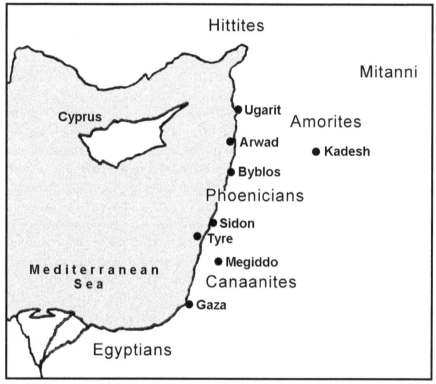

Fig. 60   People and cities in the Levant ca. 1400 BC

the Canaanites who lived in the land south of Tyre and all the way to
Gaza where the former border with Egypt existed. The Canaanite city
of Megiddo in what is now northern Israel served as the joint command post for these raiding parties.

Tuthmosis revealed himself to be a brilliant military leader. In his
first campaign he went from battle to battle the whole way from Gaza

to Megiddo. After a siege of seven months, that latter city fell and he celebrated a great victory. Proclaiming himself the master of Canaan, he returned home. But his problems were not over. The Amorite lands remained untouched, and no sooner had he left than the Amorites began to raid southward into Egypt's Canaanite territory again.

Tuthmosis was outraged and ordered plans for a new campaign to the north. The Phoenicians, who had supplied Egypt's needs for wood and other goods throughout this time, received word of these plans with a mixture of optimism and dread. On the positive side, the potential crushing of the Amorites who lived immediately north of them and who had been a pain in their side for hundreds of years had to be high on the list of things they sincerely wanted to see. On the other hand, there was a tremendous risk that their own cities would be trampled under the feet of the Egyptian army in the rush northward by that force to attack the Amorites. So a simple proposal was made to their powerful trading partner from the south.

In view of the longstanding friendship between Byblos and the people of the Nile, the Phoenicians would transport the large Egyptian army past all the troubled Canaanite lands, bringing those troops directly to Byblos. The Egyptians could then march north from that port directly into Amorite lands. There was no need for the Egyptians to endure the long march through Canaan and take casualties all along the way. The price reasonably asked for this service was that no Phoenician cities be attacked, and that after the campaign, these cities retain their special status as partners and suppliers to their Egyptian friends.

That the proposal was found pleasing is attested by the launching of Tuthmosis' next campaign to the north. Many shiploads of his troops were transported from the Nile Delta to Byblos. From there the Egyptians attacked the Amorite city of Ullasa on the coast, then followed the Eleutheros River inland to sack the Amorite capital at Kadesh. Tuthmosis once again celebrated a great victory—this time declaring himself lord of the Amorites—and returned home. Yet, as before, his problems were not over.

Many Amorites had fled to Mitanni lands to escape the advancing Egyptian force and now returned in raiding parties to their former homeland. There they found many willing accomplices. As a result

Tuthmosis came back immediately, with his troops once more brought by sea to Byblos, and marched on the Mitanni. He crossed the Euphrates River at Carchemish and defeated the Mitanni army. But he did not continue onward to attack their capital city at Wassukkani and, feeling he had made his point, returned home. As it turned out, the point had not been made at all. Ten more years of similar campaigns ensued.

In the end, the Egyptians more or less established themselves in this part of the world and set up three governorships. One viceroy was put over the Amorite lands north of Byblos. Another was placed over the Canaanites to the south of Tyre. Byblos retained the governorship of the Phoenician cities.

But there was a problem. The pharaoh demanded that he be acknowledged as overlord of the Phoenician cities.[48] This exceedingly aggravated the Phoenicians because they had worked hard in support of the pharaoh and expected full independence. Yet they were not ones to react emotionally in critical situations. Upon talking it over in council, they apparently decided there was no real harm in letting the pharaoh claim that title. They were used to giving major customers the feeling that they were all-important, and Egypt was their largest customer. As long as they only had to pretend to the rule and retained freedom of action, they agreed to go along and see if the pharaoh kept his word. Time would show that he did keep that promise.

As governor, the king of Byblos managed the affairs of his own city and those of its sister cities. He had previously done this privately through the Phoenician council system, but now did it more openly. He also let the administrators in Egypt know some of the local actions in order to keep up appearances. The more difficult matter was the cost of sending an annual shipment of free cedar which the pharaoh now expected. Yet in the past they had lavished many gifts upon the pharaoh and his predecessors to keep up good relations, so this was only payment in a different form. Outside of that, the Phoenicians were able to conduct their trade where and when they wanted and to go about rebuilding their personal lives after Crete—and that was what they wanted. So if the arrangement with Egypt was an irritant, it was at least workable.

It was during these difficult days that the Phoenician withdrawal from Crete took place. Those battered shiploads of people returned to Lebanon only to discover that the Egyptians and Amorites had just finished fighting battles on the land behind the Lebanese mountains. The foreign armies were believed to have passed through the Bekaa Valley, stripping the land to meet their needs.

If things were not bad enough, just to the north of the Phoenicians a completely different problem began to grow worse. And it would prove to be the straw that broke the camel's back.

During the same time the Hyksos had moved into the Nile Delta, a people known as the Hittites had established a kingdom for themselves in the middle of Anatolia. They took for their royal city the town of Hattusas, east of modern-day Ankara, then spread south into the land where ancient Çatal Hüyük once stood. They acquired the use of horses and chariots, which enabled them to press their claims even farther afield. After many battles they took Cilicia and gained a broad expanse of coastline on the Mediterranean.

When the army of Tuthmosis had arrived by boat at Byblos to attack the Amorites, the new Hittite nation was presented with a unique opportunity. Their king signed an agreement with Tuthmosis to jointly attack the Amorites. While the Egyptians attacked Kadesh in the southern part of that land, the Hittites were allowed to sack— and keep—the major city of Aleppo in the north. After the dust settled, Egypt held Ugarit and all the Amorite lands south of that city, while the Hittites held the lands to the north.

The part of these proceedings that had the most impact on the Phoenicians was the Egyptians' control over the port of Ugarit. In a single stroke the Phoenicians' virtual monopoly on Egyptian trade had disappeared. Through all the years up to this point the Egyptians had known only one reliable sea-trade supplier in the eastern Mediterranean, and that was Byblos. This was by no means an accident. The people of Byblos had worked assiduously from the first moment Egyptian trade was opened to them to keep it all in their own hands. Having cedar to trade was a huge advantage in their favor, but the rest was all earned by sweat and effort.

Anything the Egyptians wanted that the Phoenicians did not already own, the sea-traders purchased from others and shipped it to the Nile. These others—be they from Ugarit, Cilicia, Anatolia or the

Aegean—were never told that the ultimate buyers were in Egypt and were exceedingly rich. These others knew only that the Phoenicians wanted the materials and paid well in trade. Since some Egyptian goods arrived through those trades, however, people were certainly aware that the country existed, causing local merchants to salivate.

Yet if a local trader from any of these places happened to arrive at the Nile and tried to establish their city as a supplier, they ran into huge obstacles. The Phoenicians seem to have used their considerable influence in Egypt—which arose from control of the much-desired cedar and their many rich gifts over the years to the right people—to freeze out the intruders. Similar pressure was almost certainly brought against the trader's home city with the very real threat that all purchasing of goods done by the Phoenicians from that city would be diverted to other suppliers—a fate worse than death to those who had grown rich from that steady trade.

As a result, goods from all those places ultimately arrived in Egypt with Byblos as the middleman, and goods from Egypt to those places traveled by the same vessels. The Egyptians were so accustomed to doing their sea-trade through this Phoenician city that they called trading ships on the Mediterranean "Byblos boats," because those were the ones they primarily saw.

Ugarit was one of the cities that made a run at the Egyptians, hoping to steal away a piece of this lucrative trade. They exchanged lavish gifts with Pharaoh Senusret I around 1950 BC, and with several of his successors. However nothing appears to have come of it, and Byblos retained its preferred position.

When the Phoenicians merged with the people of Crete and the Minoans came into existence, the Egyptians clearly became aware of the culture and goods of that land. The Great Circle trade route made Crete the last stop for trading ships before coming to Egypt—but it is not clear whether the Egyptians were led to believe the arriving merchants were Minoan or Phoenician. The ships' crews apparently still used Byblos as their identification since it has been seen that the Egyptians continued to call these vessels Byblos boats.

When the Mycenaeans overran Crete, all of this changed. The new owners took over the Minoan ports, the palace at Knossos, and the Aegean trade routes. They seem to have begun servicing the Crete-to-Egypt trade route also, as suggested by evidence from a Greek aristocrat named Solon who traveled to Egypt many years later. He heard stories there that could only have come from the Mycenaeans. This meant the Egyptians were suddenly aware that someone other than the Phoenicians could supply them with valuable trade goods from the Aegean.

This was followed by the much-later acquisition of the port at Ugarit, bringing it into the Egyptian sphere of influence. That immediately gave Anatolia and other northern lands a direct path to Egypt that did not involve the Phoenicians.

These events at Crete and Ugarit shattered the Phoenician monopoly on Egyptian trade like a crystal bowl striking a tile floor. Breaking the sea-traders' control seemed to be what gave Tuthmosis the brash confidence to force his "protection" upon the Phoenician cities. It also gave the Phoenicians no choice but to endure it. The tables had been turned on them completely. Egypt had taken the monopoly into its own hands and could deal solely with the Mycenaeans and Ugarit if it chose—leaving the Phoenicians with nothing but an obligatory annual cedar shipment to fulfill.

Ever practical despite their feelings about how they were being treated, the once-dominant sea traders had to salvage what trade they could. They recognized immediately that competing with Ugarit would produce the horrible result of driving down the value of Egyptian trade to commodity prices, instead of the luxury prices they had always obtained before. So swallowing their pride, they took the boat trip north to Ugarit and created a relationship with those formerly minor competitors. By moving quickly, they were able to retain a fair portion of this commerce, and keep the value of Egyptian trade high.

Of course, the other way to look at it was that after losing all of the Aegean trade, they had now lost about half of everything else to what had once been the runt of the litter: the small port up the coast at Ugarit. The old saying that every dog has its day was apparently true. Ugarit flourished like never before.

The Phoenicians were in a miserable position. They had taken beating after beating and it must have felt as if they had sunk as far as they could go. Unfortunately, it was possible to sink farther.

The Amorite raids continued across the land around Byblos. Protests to Egypt and requests for the protection that had been promised

went unanswered. Dissatisfaction with the new arrangement grew to
a slow boil.

Far down the coast, Sidon also struggled. It had become the Phoenicians' largest city as refugees from Crete flowed in and built
temporary homes, but this brought with it the backbreaking task of

Fig. 61   Sidon Sea Castle, site of a Phoenician temple

housing and feeding all these people. Fortunately the passage of time
slowly healed some of those privations. The people of Sidon were
gradually building proper houses, roads, markets and local trade,
which began to create a semblance of normal life.

Tyre, on its small island, also had endured its days as a homeless
camp and was inching forward to a more permanent settlement.
Already it had attained a population approaching that of Beirut and
Byblos up the coast.

Yet Byblos retained leadership of the Phoenician cities even
though the ongoing raids put it in a precarious position. It was a
problem that needed to be addressed.

Among the Phoenician practices established more than a thousand
years earlier at Byblos and carried to Tyre and Sidon were several
relating to leadership. Each city chose its own council and its own
leader, now styled as "king." This king served as head of the city's
government, trade and religious traditions—in regular consultation
with the council. The king of Byblos, also by tradition, had primacy
of place above the other kings. When major decisions had to be made

concerning them all, the accepted practice seemed to have been for him to convene a high council from all the cities. He then led that council in making the decision, which was issued in his name.

Such a council from all the cities appeared to have been called to address the ongoing raids that were weakening Byblos, because a

Fig. 62   The old harbor in Tyre

change of leadership was made at this time. The position of seniority was passed to the king of Sidon. With this, the authority and responsibility for decisions affecting all of the Phoenician people came to reside with him.

Byblos, the venerable original home of the Phoenician people, continued to be honored, but its day had passed. It retained its disproportionate image of importance to the Egyptians simply because the culture of the Nile had so deeply embedded the name and image of Byblos into its traditions, religious mythology and language. But the reality had changed.

The Phoenicians were able to make adjustments such as this because, in a mixed blessing, Egypt's claim to be overlord of the Phoenicians, Amorites and Canaanites proved to be more claim than truth. That distant land had little to do with daily life in any of these places. The Amorites raided when they wanted, the Phoenicians traded where they could, and the Canaanites struggled with their own problems. The Egyptians seemed content to enjoy their position of superiority and collect the annual assessments. Their only investment in these unruly regions was an occasional military campaign to keep some rudimentary measure of control. Then came the reign of pharaoh Akhenaten, and conditions deteriorated even further.

Akhenaten was the Egyptian king who famously married Queen Nefertiti. He also abandoned the country's long-held belief in Amun and the other gods of the land, raised a single god named Aten in their place, and moved the royal capital from Thebes to Amarna. In the course of doing this, he dispossessed the high priests of their rich income and influence. This caused a huge outcry from these powerful people who immediately set about fomenting rebellion against the pharaoh.

It should come as no surprise that Akhenaten spent all his time dealing with these affairs and paid no attention to matters involving the lands to the north. He received numerous entreaties from those lands to fulfill his obligations, but paid them no heed. Those stacks of clay tablets would be unearthed by archaeologists in the modern age and, popularly known as the Amarna Letters, would yield interesting insights into the events of these times. But in terms of igniting action, they were fairly useless.

While Egypt was preoccupied with Akhenaten's issues, the Hittites in Anatolia took full advantage. Not content with their previously agreed-upon boundaries, they continued to press southward. They swept across the Amorite lands and seized their capital at Kadesh. They also took the port at Ugarit, and the Phoenician city of Arwad along with many other towns.

The Phoenicians were rightfully concerned with this outbreak of military activity just north of them and were outraged over the loss of Arwad. Surely the Egyptians had to wake up and do something in response. But what would the Egyptians do and when?

For a long time, the answer was: nothing. Then, forty years and several short-reigned Egyptian kings later, Ramses II came to the throne. He proved to be a man of action. He fought a major battle with the Hittites at Kadesh, followed by several other engagements. Though he claimed success each time, nothing seemed to be decided one way or the other. Finally he resolved the matter by signing a peace treaty with the Hittites during the twenty-first year of his reign.[49]

To the Phoenicians, the terms of this treaty were shocking. Ramses yielded everything to the intruders from the north. All the Amorite lands were ceded to the Hittites, including Kadesh, Ugarit and even Arwad. All this was given in return for a promise of peace.

Those Phoenicians who had been evacuated from the island-city of Arwad during the previous attacks would now not be going home.

The Hittite warriors had marched south to the border with Byblos. With Egyptian permission, they now rested there with time to regroup and grow stronger. It was painfully obvious that the next time the peace was broken, those warriors would continue their march southward and level the Phoenician cities.

That would put out the flame of their gentle society which had endured 1,900 years from the spark that was lit by supplying cedars to the temple at Hierakonpolis. It had lasted through the beautiful culture of arts and peace on Crete, and had come to this point of standing on the shore looking up the coast at enemy camps—without knowing how to protect what little was left.

Once again, the possibility of fighting had to be considered. They had refused before in Crete, only to end up in a worse situation on the Lebanese coast. Perhaps the time had come to give in, strap on swords, and hope to become good enough with them to withstand the Hittites when they came marching down the road with army after well-trained army.

But if the heavily armed and experienced Egyptian soldiers could not prevail against these intruders, what expectation could a small number of inexperienced people have? And if they shed their principles and their society to do this thing, what would they have left even if they miraculously won?

Despite all that had happened, they still could not bring themselves to fight with sharp weapons on bloody fields. To survive they needed a miracle, but it would have to be of a different kind.

CHAPTER 12

PEOPLE OF THE SEA

In the midst of all these dispiriting problems, there was at least one development that went the Phoenicians' way: The Hittites honored the peace while Ramses II lived, and he lived for a long time.

Finding a solution to the impending apocalypse would have been a consuming passion in anxious council meetings. And somewhere in those sessions someone apparently asked the right question: who were the enemies of the Hittites? To that was added another: might some rich gifts given to such people arouse interest in cooperating against a mutual enemy?

One answer to "who?" was the Assyrians in northern Mesopotamia. The Hittites had already conquered the Mitanni in that direction, leaving them in a tense standoff with the Assyrians who held the immediately adjacent lands. Unfortunately, the Phoenicians had no well-established contacts with these Assyrians who lived far inland. In addition, it was necessary to cross a considerable amount of Hittite country to reach them. If an outreach was made to these people, it met with no success.

But then trading ships came back with a much more intriguing possibility. It had to do with Anatolia, the homeland of the Hittites. As most people familiar with that part of the world are aware, this large land mass was actually a peninsula which protruded from Asia and pointed westward toward Greece. It was surrounded by water on three sides: the Mediterranean Sea on the south, the Aegean on the west, and the Black Sea on the north. The Black Sea was a large body of water, yet has often been overlooked in the annals of history. Perhaps that was because its people for many years tended to be

Fig. 63   Black Sea, Aegean and the Eastern Mediterranean

rustic, tribal and without written records, much like the Celtic and German tribes in northern Europe until the arrival of the Romans.

From time to time ancient narratives have told of people who "came down from the north" into Mesopotamia, Anatolia, Greece and Italy. In the east these people came down from the Black Sea. In the west they came down from central Europe. They may have originated from somewhere else prior to that, but those two staging grounds were used before stepping into the bright light of recorded history. The Hittites, for example, originally "came down from the north," from the lands around the Black Sea.

The interesting fact discovered by the Phoenicians was that the Hittites—renowned as the fierce masters of central and southern Anatolia—were blocked from access to the Black Sea to their north by an even more fierce group of people known as the Kaska.[50]

As additional Phoenician trading ships went through the Aegean and into the Black Sea on missions of trade, the Lebanese seamen brought back word of people in turmoil all across western Anatolia and the fringes of the Black Sea.

As sometimes happened, the population of those lands had increased when food was plentiful and times were good. Then as subtle shifts in climate hampered crops, and warfare cut off supplies that had come from farther away, there was not enough food to support the large population. Conditions began to deteriorate. The growing food shortage seemed to generate anxiety and agitation to find more suitable lands on which to raise and feed their families.

With their rustic background, the people who lived in the hills around the Black Sea tended to subsist in a fairly simple manner, forming themselves into tribes rather than cities. In fact they exhibited some distaste for walled cities and the restrictions on life that came with them. Their rudimentary but sturdy ships took them around the Black Sea, but not many of them ventured through the Bosporus waterway to the Aegean Sea where the Mycenaeans lived and raided. Yet they understood fighting very well, as the Hittites had already discovered.

The people of western Anatolia were a little more familiar with city life than their northern neighbors, living as they did between the Hittites in central Anatolia and the Mycenaeans in the Aegean. But in most of their countryside, life was simple and basic, just as it was in the north. And unfortunately they were frequently at war with the large powers on each side of them, so they often found their access to trade and supplies cut off. Like the northerners, they were gradually becoming more desperate as conditions deteriorated.

Although the Phoenicians did not have much in common with these people in western Anatolia and around the Black Sea, any enemy of the Hittites was a friend of theirs. So the wooing began. Gifts were pressed into the hands of local leaders, and food was brought from lands to the south.

This trading in foodstuffs benefited the Phoenicians as much as it did the starving people who received it. The Mycenaeans were meeting their own shipping needs for grain and other food,[51] while the Hittites' port at Ugarit handled their shipments of grain from Egypt. The Phoenicians were frozen out of those lucrative trade arrangements. So supplying food shipments to the beleaguered people of western Anatolia and the Black Sea was their only way to participate in this trade. And the arrival of Phoenician ships laden with food in those famished ports seemed to have made a lasting impression on the local people.

As they had done with the people of Egypt and Crete, as well as the other places they went, the Phoenicians worked hard to be accepted as friends and compatriots of these people. With the passing of years and the steady bringing of food in their ships, they became appreciated in this hard-hit region.

When the old and feeble Ramses II finally was put into his burial sarcophagus in 1213 BC,[52] the Phoenicians braced themselves for the worst. Throughout the ancient world it was common practice—upon a change of reign—for conquered lands and unfriendly neighboring rulers to test the mettle of the new king by immediately hitting him with a revolt or attack. The object was to see if he would stand and fight or run from the field. Many kings ran, leaving rich plunder and large estates to be taken and doled out by the victorious.

No doubt the Hittites were ready and willing to take advantage of this opportunity to sweep southward, but they were temporarily stymied by problems at home. Crops in the region had failed drastically once again, and they faced a serious need to pacify their people at home before anything else.[53] So they appealed to the new Egyptian king Merneptah for grain to ease their famine. Merneptah, realizing his choice was between fields of wheat and fields of battle, sent the requested grain. As a result, the Hittites forbore and did not attack the lands "protected" by the Egyptians—yet. But their sword still hung by a thread over the heads of the Phoenicians. Eventually, it had to fall.

Meanwhile, the Phoenicians found themselves dealing with ever more restive cohorts in Anatolia and the shores of the Black Sea. Inadequate crop yields and growing desperation sharply increased the pressure for decisive action. Yet the Hittites blocked those people's access south to lands that were imagined to overflow with flocks, fruit and grain. And the Mycenaeans blocked their way south through the Aegean Sea. When word arrived about the Egyptian surplus of grain, the vague desire to go south now had a clear destination.

For their part, the Phoenicians had no problem with any of these desires on the part of the Anatolians and Black Sea tribe members who were working themselves into a lather to attack. The sea-traders had suffered at the hands of these same Hittites, Mycenaeans and Egyptians. If the tables were turned, it would be an excellent outcome.

In 1208 BC a war party plunged southward across the sea to attack the Nile Delta and obtain a piece of that fertile breadbasket.[54] But the raid failed and King Merneptah erected a stele with an inscription carved into its stone surface commemorating his victory over these "peoples of the sea."[55] The name stuck, and that is how they are still known today.

When that first attempt failed, the desperate groups across western Anatolia and the Black Sea struck closer to home, turning loose their countless shiploads of warriors to pour into the Aegean. The Mycenaeans who had been attacking the people of western Anatolia for years were early victims. The raiders fell without warning on the Mycenaean cities and ports, much as the warriors from those cities had fallen upon others. Many cities of Anatolia and some of the Aegean islands joined their more rustic cousins. This swelled the ranks of those who coursed southward. In the places where they swarmed ashore, no one could stand in their way.

The sea-based raids then began to move eastward and struck all along the Hittites' extensive southern coast. The overall element of surprise was now long gone. However it was impossible for the Hittites and their allies to place armies along their whole coastline. They left many pockets exposed, which were successfully hit by quick raids. In addition, the Sea Peoples owned the whole northern coast along the Black Sea and were starting to move southward in massive numbers. The members of the Sea Peoples who lived along the west coast of Anatolia now joined them by marching east into Hittite lands.

The great military abilities that had made the Hittites an invincible opponent to the Phoenicians, Egyptians, Amorites, Mitanni and Assyrians were now put to the ultimate test. The staggering number of people attacking them from all sides made it seem as though the issue would be resolved in a short time. Instead, the Hittites fought valiantly and forcefully for almost twenty-eight years, steadily losing ground but not admitting defeat.

Toward the end, the king of Cyprus sent a letter to Ugarit's king warning him that the invading ships had come all the way across Anatolia and were likely to attack that port-city next.[56] The king of Ugarit died a short time later in 1182 BC, and his city was completely leveled, never to be rebuilt again. Shortly thereafter, the Hittites suffered their final defeat and likewise disappeared.[57]

The hundreds of thousands of Sea Peoples then swept eastward across Syria. Having done that, they turned toward the south.

At this point something remarkable happened. This unstoppable force which was destroying virtually every city in its path turned inland and bypassed the Phoenician cities, leaving them untouched.

It is possible that this was done in exchange for Phoenician support of the Sea Peoples in the raids and migrations that had brought them this far. Yet it is also possible that the memory of malnourished people coming down to their harbors to see Phoenician ships arriving with stores of food had left an indelible mark, and a debt that could never be repaid. Whichever it was, those thousands of Sea Peoples marched past the Phoenician cities as if passing revered ground, and nothing there was disturbed.

The lands of Canaan, on the other hand, had earned no such favor. As the Sea Peoples poured south, they continued to relentlessly destroy major cities in sudden attacks before moving on.[58] Immediately behind them came the long columns of ox-drawn carts bearing their wives, children and household possessions. No sooner was the old culture plowed under than a fresh way of life was planted.

Whether the new way was any better than the old would be a matter of opinion, but it was accepted.

Even though many tribes took part in this flood of humanity pouring over the northern Mediterranean, there was a unique manner to the attacks that marked their many battles. The attacks avoided unnecessary damage or harm to the people of the land. Only ports and civic centers were struck, leaving the countryside leaderless and open to the new people who were arriving. As they moved east and south, these actions were not solely military operations. Behind the warriors came those caravans with their hungry families. If the land was promising, some of them settled there. Since the Sea Peoples had avoided harming the local residents who were already working the land, they were grudgingly accepted.

All of this stood in stark contrast to the usual method of raid and conquest practiced by most marauders. Traditional raids did not destroy the chosen city's ability to produce wealth. It merely reaped everything of value found there. In time, the city would fill with valuables again, making it ripe for another reaping. This repeated raiding is what Byblos had experienced at the hands of the Amorites.

The traditional form of permanent conquest likewise did not seek to destroy the city's ability to produce wealth. It simply transferred ownership of that wealth-making ability to new hands. Those conquering warriors generally established themselves as an elite class on the land, with the prior residents as a serving class. All of the wealth produced thereafter went to the ruling class.

The raids and conquests by the Sea Peoples were considerably different. Against the Hittites and Mycenaeans, they simply wanted to neutralize the people who blocked their access to much-needed food. When they finally reached rich croplands, they fought only as a means of finding good land upon which to live and raise their families. These people showed a pronounced disdain for cities and their wealth-producing possibilities. When they decided to stay and homestead a land, the nearby cities were often razed to the ground. The manufacturing, weaving, jewelry-making and other industries frequently disappeared. They settled the land in the same rustic manner and culture they had experienced before. It was, in the truest sense, not so much a conquest as it was a migration. They lived side-by-side with the "conquered" upon the land.

The one major exception was the Egyptians. The people of the Nile were no more willing now than they had been before to be overrun by ramshackle invaders from the north. And the steady drumbeat of the newcomers' march southward took away any possible element of surprise. During the many years this migration required to cross Hittite lands, Syria and Canaan, the pharaoh Merneptah passed away and was followed by a series of other kings. Each of them ruled for only a few years, reflecting the internal turbulence in Egypt during these times. Then Ramses III took the throne, and he proved to be a worthy adversary.

As the vast horde of invaders ground their way south from the Black Sea, they had steadily planted many of their people on the lands they crossed. This had significantly reduced their numbers by the time they approached Egypt. Even so, they were a considerable force. Ramses III committed every soldier he could wrest from his

Fig. 64   Egyptian battle with the Sea Peoples

cities along the Nile, including captives from previous campaigns, and sent them all to the Egyptian outpost called Djahi near the border with Canaan.[59]

Like the crashing of two opposing waves, the people and weapons of these forces met in the desert and fought for the lands of Egypt. In the end, Ramses III claimed victory, but it had come at a huge cost. And the Sea Peoples were not yet ready to concede defeat. Stopped by land, they made one more thrust by sea. Either their losses had been too great or there was divided opinion on whether to attack Egypt again, for the sea force that approached the delta was not significant. It was easily defeated by the Egyptian commanders who placed archers in boats along the shore and barraged the invaders unmercifully with arrows until the warriors' boats could be boarded and the issue settled in hand-to-hand combat.

To celebrate his victories, Ramses III inscribed on the walls of his temple at Medinet Habu glorious praise for his accomplishments. Included in this were detailed illustrations of those battles. Of his fierce opponents he said:

The (Northerners) in their isles were disturbed, taken away in the (fray) at one time. Not one stood before their hands, from Kheta [Hittites], Kode [Cilicia], Carchemish, Arvad, Alasa [Cyprus], they were wasted. (They set up) a camp in one place in Amor [near Ugarit]. They desolated his people and his land like that which is not. They came with fire prepared before them, forward to Egypt. Their main support was Peleset, Thekel [Tjeker], Shekelesh, Denyen, and Weshesh. [These] lands were united, and they laid their hands upon the land as far as the Circle of the Earth. Their hearts were confident, full of their plans.

Now, it happened through this god, the lord of gods, that I was prepared and armed to (trap) them like wild fowl. He furnished my strength and caused my plans to prosper. I went forth, directing these marvelous things. I equipped my frontier in Zahi, prepared before them. The chiefs, the captains of infantry, the nobles, I caused to equip the harbor-mouths, like a strong wall, with warships, galleys, and barges. They were manned (completely) from bow to stern with valiant warriors bearing their arms, soldiers of all the choicest of Egypt, being like lions roaring upon the mountain-tops. The charioteers were warriors, and all good officers, ready of hand. Their horses were quivering in their every limb, ready to crush the countries under their feet. I was the valiant Montu, stationed before them, that they might behold the hand-to-hand fighting of my arms. I, king Ramses III, was made a far-striding hero, conscious of his might, valiant to lead his army in the day of battle.

Those who reached my boundary, their seed is not; their heart and their soul are finished forever and ever. As for those who had assembled before them on the sea, the full flame was in their front, before the harbor-mouths, and a wall of metal upon the shore surrounded them. They were dragged, overturned, and laid low up-on the beach; slain and made heaps from stern to bow of their galleys, while all their things were cast upon the water.

J. H. Breasted
Ancient Records of Egypt

The greatness of Ramses III was that he preserved Egypt from outsiders. But he could not save Egypt from itself. Amid raging internal dissention, his building projects continued to spend money that his country did not have. He left a penniless land behind him.

Along the coast north of Gaza, the Sea Peoples accepted that they had gone as far as they could go and looked for homesteads where they could begin new lives. The tribe known as Peleset settled here, and from them the land became known as Palestine.[60] North of them the Tjeker tribe settled in the land near Akko. Others settled across Syria and Anatolia. The Kaska took much of the old Hittite home-lands. A few tribes returned once more to the sea and apparently made their homes on islands that received the tribe's name, such as the Shekelesh on Sicily.[61]

This was also the time when one of the epic events in Greek history seems to have taken place—one that we are only now starting to fully understand: the Trojan War. The Mycenaeans left their own homes unprotected and launched a massive attack on Troy at the mouth of the Dardanelles—the passageway between the Aegean and the Black Sea. This spectacular clash of intentions and armor was chronicled in rich detail by the poet Homer and came down to us in his great work titled *The Iliad*. In it, Homer made immortal the heroic deeds of many great warriors and kings such as Achilles and Hector, Priam and Agamemnon, Paris and Menelaus whose names live on because of this honor.

After many heroics and a long war, the Mycenaeans finally won. But at a staggering cost in men and resources. They returned home to mainland Greece only to find ports devastated by the Sea Peoples, which left them poor and unable to recover. Over the next few decades they disappeared as a civilization.

During the forty years that the Sea Peoples' hurricane of destruction swept over virtually every part of the Eastern Mediterranean, the Phoenicians sat in the peaceful eye of the storm. At one time it was assumed that, with all the devastation wrought across this part of the world, the Phoenician cities and all their occupants must have been destroyed as well. That led to misguided statements that the Phoenician people were somehow created in 1200 BC.

As the facts of history show, however, the Phoenician people enjoyed—though sometimes struggled through—a long, rich heritage of sea trade and unique culture from 3200 BC onwards. One might well ask, then: what happened to the Phoenicians at 1200 BC during the onslaught of the Sea Peoples? In terms of destruction and upheaval, the answer is: nothing at all.

Archaeological studies in the Phoenician cities have carefully sifted through the physical records of these times and found no evidence of damage. To the contrary, detailed excavations such as the one by Patricia Bikai at Tyre showed smooth continuity through this period.[62] The city continued to grow and produce items for trade. Glenn Markoe cited similar studies at the smaller Phoenician town of Sarepta near Sidon which showed uninterrupted occupation, and identified a continuity of the economy, religion, language and culture during this time.[63] Nor has any evidence of destruction been found in other Phoenician cities across Lebanon.

In other words, the Phoenicians were untouched by the maelstrom of death and devastation that swirled around them. In clear contrast to this, the firestorm destroyed all their enemies: the ones who had made the Phoenicians refugees in their own land, stripped away the trade that was their life-blood, and pushed them to the edge of extinction at the feet of marching soldiers.

The Hittite empire and its previously unstoppable armies, which had taken the city of Arwad and stormed almost to the gates of Byblos, were now gone.

The Mycenaeans who had driven the Phoenicians out of Crete and taken away their Aegean trade had suffered a mortal wound. Within ninety years, they would pass into oblivion.

The city of Ugarit, which had taken much of the trade left to the Phoenicians after the loss of the Aegean, was now razed to the ground. It would never be rebuilt.

Egypt, which had put the Phoenicians under its thumb and attempted to rule it from the Nile, had lost all its territories on the east coast of the Mediterranean. The land of the pharaohs was so weakened that it would itself become ruled by a succession of foreign kings.

The opposite fortune befell the Phoenicians. For them, all things were now possible.

And their good relationship with the Sea Peoples did not end with the settling down of these migrants in their new lands. From this point forward—as we shall see—everywhere the Sea Peoples now lived in the Mediterranean, the Phoenicians were welcomed as friends. One well-documented example occurred at Sicily, where the Sicilians welcomed the Phoenicians and they lived side by side.[64] This special relationship had been forged in fire, and was remembered for many years.

In the final analysis, then, the cities of Lebanon which were once besieged by the Hittites on the north and east, by the Mycenaeans on the west, and by the Egyptians on the south, had felt the noose tightening around their neck. Now with a single stroke the rope had been cut, and they were free. Life's bountiful opportunities were open to them again.

Their second empire beckoned.

CHAPTER 13

CASTING BREAD UPON THE WATERS

A huge weight had been lifted from the people of Tyre, Sidon, Beirut and Byblos. No longer did an outside power lean on them and attempt to dictate their actions. No menacing army stood at their door. They were able once again to pursue the life they wanted, and they did exactly that.

Traders set out to visit new ports, and picked up the reins of trade dropped by fallen rivals. Woodworkers began to lay hulls for new ships that soon would be needed. Docks were expanded in the harbors of their port cities. Foundations for new houses were laid.

Those among them who had fled from the city of Arwad when it was captured by the Hittites were now able to return. Its island was reclaimed, and all was put back as it once had been. This was an especially high priority because the demise of Ugarit left a void in the sea trade that served Anatolia and the overland routes to Mesopotamia. Arwad immediately picked up significant amounts of that trade.

The same was true all across the Mediterranean. Before anyone else could step in to fill the gaping need for sea trade, the Phoenicians needed to get there. They urgently gathered their strength and moved outward.

After the Sea Peoples had fought their final battle with Egypt, their tribes put down roots where they were, or wherever they could find good land. The Phoenicians now began to call on them, re-establishing trade relationships and learning what goods were needed.

With so many large, prosperous cities changing to earthy, agrarian communities, it caused a radical change in the mercantile goods carried aboard ships. Plowshares, tools, food and raw materials were in demand. Fine cloths, delicate goldwork and jewelry were out of reach for almost all, and difficult to obtain in any event. But there was trade, and it was serviced.

The sense of urgency flowed to the shipbuilding yards in the Phoenician cities. This physically demanding craftsmanship once more became a major occupation for many people. Hewers of wood went up the mountainsides again in search of the best cedar, pine and oak, dragging huge logs down to the dry-docks beside the harbors. Woodworkers shaped them with sharp saws, adzes and the other tools of their trade. Craftsmen assembled the jigsaw puzzle of pieces into huge, watertight vessels and fitted them with the best oars and sails available. The demand for trade seemed endless, and the only limitation to meeting it was the ability to put decks of sturdy wood under the feet of young captains, so they could put to sea and claim their share.

It was a tumultuous, optimistic and exciting time. With the huge sources of trade in Egypt and the Aegean basically collapsed, life was difficult for a while. But soon enough good fortune and wealth began to flow, just as it had before.

Amid all the bustling activity in these cities on the Lebanese coast, there was also an awareness of their sometimes reckless new neighbors in the Sea People communities. This goaded a renewal of the deeply ingrained Phoenician desire to blend in as a means of seeking safety and self-preservation. As they had done with the Egyptians and Amorites, they now did with the Tjekers and Palestinians. They purposely began to reflect a more rustic tone in their cities and their personal appearance. In some cases they even gave their children names consistent with their Black Sea neighbors. The Phoenicians must have been acutely aware that the only coastal cities in the region which had been spared—with high walls unbroken, industry intact and creative culture flourishing—were those on the shores of Lebanon. The Sea Peoples' antipathy against cities and all they represented had been curbed as a reward for the assistance given, but there was no sense in provoking a reflex reaction to raid a provocative city.

They also did not forget the bitter lessons of the previous three hundred years. Trapped on a strip of coastal land, the Phoenicians had been easy prey for the land-based armies of the Egyptians, Amorites and Hittites. It was clear that they needed to spread their risk by opening new outposts abroad, as they had done long ago.

Returning to Crete was not really possible at that time. The Mycenaeans, though battered by the Sea Peoples and driven out of many port cities, still held strong inland positions on the mainland and Crete, and would so for several decades. So the Phoenicians had to look elsewhere.

They turned once more to Cyprus, their original first-choice so long ago. Recently stormed and taken by tribes of the Sea Peoples, it was as good a place as any to test their partnership with these newly arrived homesteaders. Those families had made their settlements mostly on the northern coast of the island, since that area was closest to the land from which they had come. And apparently they gave the answer the Phoenicians wanted to hear, for those sea traders began work immediately on establishing an outpost on the southeast corner of the island. There the port city of Kition had been destroyed by the fiery sword of the Sea Peoples in one of their intense attacks. The Phoenicians made repairs to the harbor, raised a trading house, and built a grand temple to Our Lady. Then put into operation their first major new outpost outside of Lebanon.

And what an excellent location it was. Cyprus remained one of the Mediterranean's most productive sources of copper, which was essential for making bronze tools, weapons and objects used in everyday living. It was always in demand, and having an outpost here put the Phoenicians at the center of the copper trade.

Not only that, the port of Kition was reasonably close to Byblos on a straight line across the sea. This was an ideal place of safety in the event that one or more of the Lebanese coastal cities should be attacked by an aggressive land power again.

And in terms of trade routes between Lebanon and the Aegean, it could not be better situated. Just as Tyre served as an excellent gathering-place for trade goods bound for Egypt on large merchant-man vessels, Cyprus was well-positioned to play this same role for

Fig. 65   Ancient Kition in Cyprus

westward trade. Small ships from Byblos, Arwad and Cilicia on the Anatolia coast could put into port at Kition with their trade goods, and the merchantmen could then take the cargo west.

In the Aegean the Phoenicians had to move carefully because the deeply wounded Mycenaeans were still staggering out on raids. On Crete, all the northern ports with which they were familiar were out of reach due to Mycenaean presence. Santorini was unavailable because it was still recovering from the deep mass of volcanic ash that covered it. On that once-beautiful island, small bushes and sprigs of green would sprout through cracks in the gray pumice. The land was populated now by massive numbers of brown swallows and sprinklings of other birds that came across the water to this quiet preserve. In time the land would heal and support significant towns again, but not yet.

Of the other available islands, the Phoenicians soon decided on Rhodes, an excellent choice for many reasons. It was the first island encountered when approaching the Aegean from Lebanon. It also had been a significant outpost of theirs during the days of the

Minoan civilization. That port had been lost when the Mycenaeans swept through the region, but was rendered neutral again by the fiery passage of the Sea Peoples. So it was a time for prosperous new beginnings on Rhodes, located as it was between Crete and the Anatolia mainland where large amounts of trade awaited.

That was an excellent starting place, but the Aegean was too large for a single outpost to serve it all. Santorini had been much more centrally located, and even then it had required Dia Island and other outposts. So from Rhodes the Phoenician traders headed west in the direction of Crete but avoided the heavily populated northern shore where Mycenaean presence was strongest. On the relatively less-populated southern shore, they found the former Minoan port city of Kommos available to them. Quietly they moved in and took possession of it. This gave them a toe-hold on trade lines into the vast interior of the island and the huge supply of foodstuffs, olive oil and other products produced there. In the future they might possibly do more, but for now the port at Kommos was enough to bring the rich resources of this island into their trading ships.

Farther west past Crete they came to the island of Cythera, also known as Cerigo, which stood just offshore from the Greek main-

Fig. 66 Kommos outpost on Crete

land. This worthy but frequently overlooked isle had also been oft-visited in Minoan times. It was in an excellent position to benefit from mainland trade while retaining the safety of an island location. Here they built a fine harbor outpost called Scandea.

These footholds in the Aegean gave the Phoenicians access to all the ports and markets on the islands, as well as the turbulent but large markets on the mainlands of Greece and Anatolia.

Just beyond Cythera lay the open sea, whose waters lapped on the shores of southern Italy and the island of Sicily. So the Phoenicians' quest to quickly bring all available trade routes into their hands naturally took them in that direction.

The Mediterranean Sea separated Africa from Europe along its whole length, and on average was roughly three hundred miles wide. Yet near the middle of this vast body of water, Europe reached down in the form of the Italian peninsula and Africa reached upward from the Tunisian headland. Between these two outcroppings spread the island of Sicily.

From Sicily to Tunisia was the short distance of ninety miles. From Sicily to Italy was only three miles across the Messina Strait. The island itself, 150 miles long, filled the rest of the distance between the two continents. The unique value of Sicily to the Phoenicians and to all the people of the mid-Mediterranean was this strategic position it held. And it was rendered even more valuable by being a fertile breadbasket of abundant crops. Sicily stood at the crossroads between Europe and Africa. And it separated the eastern Mediterranean from the western expanse of that sea.

Approaching Sicily from the east, the Phoenicians found an ideal site for their local outpost. It was the small island of Ortygia in the middle of a beautiful natural harbor on Sicily's eastern coast. Over the course of years, the city of Syracuse would come to stand upon that place. But at this time the land was deserted. Even though a tribe of the Sea Peoples had settled on Sicily and good relations could be expected with them, the conservative and prudent step was to take up a position on this island, with its natural advantage of having a "moat" of water around it.

Since their plan was to establish a trading post for the region and not to create a large and lavish city spreading across the land, no huge construction projects were undertaken. As with their other outposts, the traders did only the minimum amount needed to establish docks and a trading house. They kept a low profile, blended in with the rustic Sea Peoples on the island, and soon were hauling in rich shiploads of trade. Being experts at milking the cow of trade with a gentle but firm hand, they went about their work with a will.

South of Ortygia and Sicily, the Phoenicians returned to the island of Malta. After the tragic disappearance of the Maltese people during the building of the Great Pyramid, the Phoenicians had stayed away

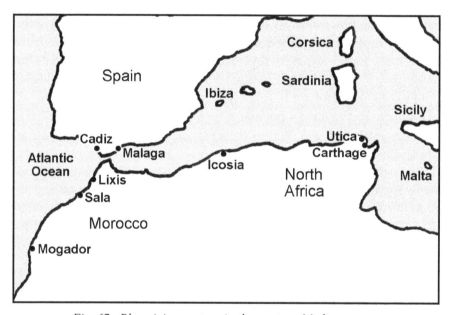

Fig. 67   Phoenician centers in the western Mediterranean

for many years. In time, though, the island of Malta and its smaller companion Gozo had once again become a place of quiet pilgrimage and reflection for them—a peaceful haven from the war-torn world.

Over the years, new settlers had arrived on Malta and established quiet villages. In some cases those people used the ancient temple sites for cremation practices, but by and large they left the temples undisturbed. Though the culture of the relatively recent settlers was different from that of the temple-builders, the isolation of these islands in the middle of the Mediterranean seemed to instill in them some of the peacefulness of those who had gone before. The Phoenician ship-captains, traders and sailors once more brought needed things to Malta as barter and as gifts, and paid their respects at the ruins on the ancient hills.

These sea-traders eventually obtained the right to put a small out-post on the island. The ideal location seemed to be the Grand Har-bour on Malta, one of the largest and most magnificent natural harbors in the entire Mediterranean. But there was also an attractive small island in nearby Marsamxett Harbour. The additional isolation it afforded was usually the Phoenicians' first choice when establish-

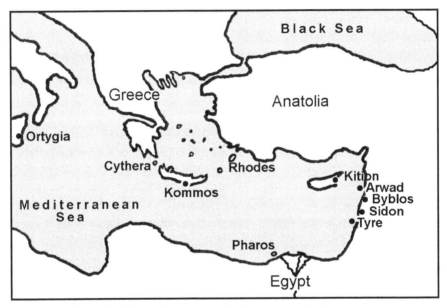

Fig. 68 Phoenician centers in the eastern Mediterranean

ing a trading post, due to the protection it afforded from warlike societies.

But that was not the case at Malta. The local people were relatively peaceful, and the Phoenicians enjoyed a renewed closeness with them. This was evidenced by the site finally chosen for the outpost on Malta: a place called Birgu in the Grand Harbour. It was a sign of their trust and comfort with the local people that the Phoenicians selected a place accessible by land from the local villages. Yet there was still a measure of inborn caution reflected in the fact that the outpost rested at the end of a particularly long peninsula. This finger of land protruded into the harbor and was surrounded on three sides by water. But there it was.

Unlike the other outposts they created at this time, Birgu was not primarily a trading post. The role of providing access to major sources of trade in the region was already being played by their settlement at Sicily, only eighty miles to the north. The port on Malta had an entirely different purpose, becoming the shipyard and dry-docks for the Phoenician trading fleets in the Mediterranean. It was a place where ships could be built and repaired in privacy, far away from the prying eyes of possible competitors. The sharp edge of secrecy they always carried had been honed to a fine edge by the recent ordeals which almost caused their extinction at the hands of powerful neighbors and competitors.

Malta also played an important role as the safety valve in this region for this trading empire the Phoenicians were quickly assembling across the Mediterranean. Good relations were still in place with the Sea Peoples on Sicily, but that situation could change. Those people's fighting capabilities made a violent surge onto the island of Ortygia a distinct possibility if some future leader galvanized them into action. The same was true for each of the other outposts being planted. Malta was their quiet refuge from those risks of violence—a haven in time of need.

Sailing west from Malta, the traders arrived at the promontory of North Africa. At the mouth of the Majardah River they planted a major trading post which would come to be known as Utica. From this settlement African goods flowed northward across the relatively short expanse of water to Sicily, and then passed to Italy and Europe. In the same way, European goods came down in return. Trade going south into Africa could be sent inland along the Majardah River or to the east or west along the coast. Hundreds of years later, another Phoenician city would be founded just twenty-five miles to the southeast and vastly surpass Utica. The new city would be the legendary Carthage. But that was another day.

From this strategic promontory on the coast of North Africa, Utica served as an essential trading center. It was a stop-over point for trading ships going to the western Mediterranean, including the shores of what would one day be Italy, France, Spain, Morocco, Algeria and Tunisia. In those early days after 1200 BC, tribes of people were scattered across all these lands and were gathered into different kingships as the ebb and flow of power and war dictated. Even Rome would not come into being on the coast of Italy until hundreds of years later. This was very much a frontier full of promise, and the Phoenicians set about establishing their contacts as broadly as possible.

Their exploration reached virtually every corner of the Mediterranean. In all that immense expanse of watery sea and wooded shore, it was clear there was actually too much opportunity and too many places where good trade might be obtained.

There was certainly no way they could conduct trade as they had done previously in the eastern Mediterranean, where they built port cities and harbors of stone blocks near their major customers. One clear reason for this was that they did not have the resources to do so. Another was that these western lands were not highly developed civilizations with major cities as gathering points for trade. They were countless small villages spread over vast areas.

This resulted in a rather amazing method of trade being developed by the Phoenicians which embraced the scattered villages in the West and reflected the sea-traders' well-established principles of privacy and international exchange. They found a way to trade with virtually anyone.

Herodotus talked with some of the Phoenician traders, and they described an example of this trading method to show how it worked. He reported it this way.

> They no sooner arrive but forthwith they unlade their wares, and having disposed them after an orderly fashion along the beach, leave them, and, returning aboard their ships, raise a great smoke. The natives, when they see the smoke, come down to the shore, and, laying out to view so much gold as they think the worth of the wares, withdraw to a distance. The [Phoenicians] upon this come ashore and look. If they think the gold enough, they take it and go their way; but if it does not seem to them sufficient, they go aboard ship once more and wait patiently. Then the others approach and add to their gold, till the [Phoenicians] are content. Neither party

deals unfairly by the other: for they themselves never touch the gold till it comes up to the worth of their goods, nor do the natives ever carry off the goods till the gold is taken away.

Herodotus 4:196

It is worthy of note that the Phoenicians off-loaded their goods and then pulled their ship back far enough from shore that no one on land could see how it was built nor reach it for any attack. Their risk, then, was limited to the goods on the beach and not the whole of their cargo, ship and crew. If their comings and goings with their ship seemed overcautious, it should be realized that it was a system born of unfortunate experiences at earlier times. It also kept their losses low enough that continued trading was not only possible but highly profitable.

The other remarkable aspect of the whole process was the high level of trust which developed between the two parties to the trade. In far too many cultures—in those days and today—goods left unattended would disappear with nothing left in exchange. But the Phoenicians carefully built up the necessary level of trust—not just in one place but across countless shores and villages. It became known by the local people that if they wanted these wonderful goods—which they could get no other way—they had to practice the self-discipline which made the system work.

In these exchanges and others over the years, the Phoenicians seem to have conducted themselves as though they wanted more than just a good bargain and trade on that current day. What they wanted were satisfied customers who would work to produce more goods and want to trade again at the next opportunity.

The Phoenicians' far-ranging trades and exploration took their ships not only to the ends of the Mediterranean but beyond. They passed through the Pillars of Hercules, which we know today as the Strait of Gibraltar, and emerged into the coastal waters of the Atlantic Ocean. For over two thousand years, since the days of early trade with Egypt, they had been building and improving their sturdy ships of solid cedar beams, and by this point their merchantmen were comparable in size to the three ships in which Columbus would sail across the Atlantic to America. The Phoenician ships were more than up to the task of sailing along the ocean shore, as their resulting outposts showed.

In fact, the Phoenicians found some of their greatest rewards on the Atlantic coast of Spain. Here were mines rich with silver and gold, plus other trade of great value. Mighty rivers brought these things from deep in the heartland out to the shore. All that was needed was a suitable place to establish their trading post. They found this on the islands at the mouth of the Guadalete River on the Atlantic coast of Spain. Here they created the outpost of Gadir. This would grow into the great city of Cadiz, which is still one of Spain's major shipping ports. Blessed with a beautiful natural harbor nestled between the islands and the mainland—and proximity to the Strait of Gibraltar for quick entry to the Mediterranean shipping lanes—this location was a perfect choice.

In many ways this city shaped the new Phoenician trading empire which was gradually coming together. By finding an exceedingly rich source at the far end of the Mediterranean, these sea-traders were virtually compelled to create and maintain a long string of outposts the entire length of the sea from east to west. At the same time, the glittering wealth that began to course back and forth along this network nourished these outposts, and caused the network to grow.

It also fueled interest in further exploration, causing ships to travel north to the coasts of Britain and Brittany—on opposite sides of the English Channel—bringing back precious tin and other goods.

Exploration south of Gibraltar along the Atlantic coast of Africa produced a similar, if slightly less spectacular result. An outpost was created at Lixis, not far south of the place that would become known as Tangier, Morocco. Having this vantage point, trade from the long African coast on the Atlantic could be gathered in one place which, again, was located close to the Strait of Gibraltar and the Mediterranean shipping lines.

With these trading posts established, the working outline of the new Phoenician empire had been drawn. The size of this far-flung territory, and the Phoenicians' limited resources in those days, meant it would take time to establish the tremendous infrastructure required to support such a vast trading empire.

The most visible result of this heavy demand on their resources was that their investment in construction was put into boat-building and not into land facilities. To think that a handful of cities in Lebanon, battered almost to the point of oblivion, could suddenly serve such an extensive new area as the entirety of the Mediterranean is somewhat staggering. Yet they seemed to feel compelled to do it lest their recently vanquished oppressors recover and take it themselves. The Phoenicians were adventurous enough to race to the far reaches of the Mediterranean, and self-confident enough to claim it all for themselves.

The miracle of this whole process was that they actually made it work. In time they would have major colonies and countless outposts extending from Lebanon all the way to the Atlantic coast of Spain and Morocco. But that required time, effort and materials, all of which were in short supply at the beginning.

So for their outposts, everything was kept minimal. Not only did the Phoenicians not have enough resources to send stonemasons and city-builders halfway across the known world, but this was also virgin territory and they had no certain knowledge that these would be the best locations. Some early camps were relocated to nearby sites or be abandoned in favor of other ports. And a very real problem was that there was no possible way to defend all of these outposts. Each one consisted of a few Phoenicians surrounded by hundreds of miles of wilderness and local villagers who exceedingly outnumbered them. One hot-headed native leader and a sufficient quantity of locals were more than enough to sweep over any of the Phoenician outposts in a single day. So how much of their few resources should they invest in a durable harbor and fine buildings for these outposts?

The answer was: no more than the minimal amount needed to do the job. The day would come for grand buildings, but not for a long time. The priority was placed on keeping cargoes aboard ships at sea rather than in exposed warehouses.

The Phoenicians were aided in this by their long-held preference for blending in and getting along with their neighbors wherever and whoever they might be. At each outpost they seem to have eaten local food, worn local clothing and eaten off local plates. Precious space on the too-few ships was not wasted on bringing luxury items to support an elevated "Phoenician" lifestyle in these places. By all indications, however, their lifestyle was not bad at all. Their share of the trades would have enabled them to live on a par with the best of the local families.

The net result of this was that there were no distinctive Phoenician cities being built overseas at this early time. Outposts were minimal, and the lifestyles being lived would have been similar to those of the local people. Historical records did, however, attest to the founding of many of these outposts at this time, and over the years some of them would grow to become powerful and famous cities.

Their second empire had been born.

CHAPTER 14

SOMETHING OLD, SOMETHING NEW

There was one exception to the Phoenician rule of not building grand cities at this time outside Lebanon, and it occurred at Cyprus. This large and resource-rich island strategically situated near the coastlines of Lebanon, Syria and Anatolia had always held a special place in the lives of the Phoenicians.

Long ago, around 3200 BC, the Phoenicians' first efforts to establish regular lines of sea-trade in the eastern Mediterranean had coincided with a change in the lives of the people on Cyprus. Those people had been simple farmers and shepherds for about a thousand years on their large but mountainous island. Then the young Phoenicians and other adventurers arrived seeking trade and learned of the rich deposits of copper which were plentiful on many parts of the island. Almost overnight, mining and metalworking became a major feature of life on Cyprus, and it would remain so from that time forward. With this trade came real prosperity for the islanders, and their humble homes began to include some larger estates among them.

Around 2400 BC, a new breed of people surged onto Cyprus from Anatolia bringing bronze weapons with them and imposing a different way of life. It was these new rulers of the island who rebuffed the Phoenicians' advances at that time and caused the sea traders to take the longer journey to Crete, giving rise to the Minoan empire. Throughout the five hundred years that followed, the Phoenicians and their related Minoan family dominated sea-trade to and from Cyprus. They were joined in those days by smaller traders such as Ugarit and Cilicia who took modest amounts of copper for their local markets. The people of Cyprus benefited from all these things.

Then the eruption of Santorini's volcano in 1628 BC brought sudden changes to this idyllic arrangement. The devastation of Phoenician and Minoan fleets caused their dominance and protection of the trade with Cyprus to disappear. Piracy and fighting on the island quickly ensued. A hundred years later, the Mycenaeans not only took Crete and the Aegean islands but—recognizing the value of having a rich source of copper for their bronze weapons—came to settle on the western side of Cyprus as well. Shortly thereafter, the Egyptians swept northward up the coast of the Levant and established their "protection" over the Phoenicians and Ugarit. This resulted in the painful but quasi-profitable relationship between those two competing cities.

The new relationship also caused two trading cities—Enkomi and Kition—to emerge on the eastern side of Cyprus, since that was the shore which faced the reluctant trading partners. With trade coming from Ugarit and the Phoenician cities, Enkomi grew to become the largest and richest city on the island, while Kition served more as a working port. When the Sea Peoples crashed onto the shores of the island, those two cities were essentially destroyed. That gave the Phoenicians an opportunity to choose which of those harbors to rebuild. They decided on the southern port of Kition. This was slightly closer to their cities on the mainland, and a bit farther from the Sea Peoples in the north of the island.

Though they were being economical with their development at the many new outposts they were creating, the Phoenicians made an exception for Cyprus. The port at Kition was well within reach from the Lebanese coast, so they could rally a large number of ships to its rescue if anyone should attack. That meant any investment they made in the harbor and buildings would be secure. And they *had* to build there. With copper as important as it was in Mediterranean trade, this was an essential center they had to have and hold. They wanted to keep the city and its prominent share of this trade no matter what attacks might come from unruly people on land or at sea. This meant the construction of stone buildings and thick, solid city walls.

So the construction began. As was traditional for Phoenician ports, maritime buildings were placed on a promontory of land that protruded into the coastal water. This created their usual north and south harbor arrangement. Immediately behind those buildings rose the acropolis of the city. There the trading house was placed beside the grand residences of the community's leading families, commanding a view of the bustling harbor and the blue waters that stretched beyond.

Before the coming of the Sea Peoples, when the Phoenicians had shared this working port with the local inhabitants and the traders from Ugarit, there had been a small sacred garden on the north slope of the acropolis with two small temples nestled on its grounds. Both buildings had been destroyed by the attacks that swept this land. The Phoenicians now re-dedicated the land to Our Lady and built a beautiful temple on the site in her name.

Fig. 69   Large foundation stones at Phoenician temple of Our Lady in Kition, Cyprus

The huge stones used for this temple and the spacious grounds around it clearly show that this must have been a dominant district of the city and an important part of the local society's festivities and life. The stones on the bottom course of the temple each stood roughly six feet high, six feet deep and nine feet long. The ashlar-cut stones fit perfectly side by side without need for mortar, which was typical of Phoenician craftsmanship by that time. The inside of this massive structure was laid out like a traditional Lebanese house, reflecting the ancient view that this was a home for Mother Nature. The entrance opened into a large central hall, with a row of rooms on the right-hand side of the hall, and another row of rooms along the left.

Just to the east of this large temple spread the sacred garden, with the ruins of the small, earlier chapels to the left and right of a path that led eastward across the grounds. The path then gave way to a broad paved roadway that continued east through the adjacent area where two more temples were later built. Immediately north of these grounds stood a thick city wall which the Phoenicians built at this time, reflecting the necessities of that turbulent era. To the east, the broad roadway between the temples reached a gate in the city wall, and beyond this gate the sea lapped at the shore.

Reverence for Mother Nature had been part of life on Cyprus since the musty, early days of its antiquity, as it had been for many of the lands around the Mediterranean. But the incursion of warlike settlers in 2400 BC had beaten her followers back to a few pockets in the hinterlands. Under the influence of Minoan traders from the west and Phoenician traders from the east, however, the worship of Our Lady slowly made a comeback over the ensuing years. This was in keeping with the deeply held beliefs of the native people on this island. After 1200 BC, Cyprus was ripe for full appreciation of her culture of love as an essential part of life. The beautiful temples built for her at Kition and other parts of the island were well received.

In one of those odd occurrences that seem to happen from time to time, archaeologists first identified the style of these temples as Near Eastern, referring to the Phoenicians and their neighbors. Yet researchers who came later, seeing the huge stones that were used in the temple construction, argued strongly that those stones meant the builders must have been Mycenaean. Now, of course, we understand how that misconception happened. The Phoenicians carried stone-building skills to Crete, which led to the huge Minoan palaces. The Mycenaeans inherited those palaces and skills when they took over Crete. As a result, the Mycenaean and Phoenician stone-building came to be similar in appearance. This makes it necessary to look beyond the large stones used in construction of the temples to understand who built them.

Doing this, it is noticed that other aspects of these temples to the goddess of love on Cyprus included the use of a sacred pool which the Phoenicians had adopted from the Egyptians many years earlier. It is also abundantly clear that reverence for this gentle goddess was central to the Phoenicians' beliefs, going back to their earliest days with the temple to Our Lady in Byblos. The same could not be said for the Mycenaeans. For these and similar reasons a better understanding of this temple at Kition is becoming accepted on Cyprus.

Several hundred years later when the classical Greeks adopted this goddess of love, they called her Aphrodite and gave her a special heritage. They recognized that she came from the sea to the Phoenician colony of Cythera and then to Cyprus. As told by the Greek poet Hesiod, this was her beginning: her unique birth arose from a dispute between Uranus—the father of the gods—and his son Chronos, who castrated him....

> The genitals, cut off with adamant
> And thrown from land into the stormy sea,
> Were carried for a long time on the waves.
> White foam surrounded the immortal flesh,
> And in it grew a girl. At first [she] touched
> On holy Cythera, from there [she] came
> To Cyprus, circled by the waves. And there
> The goddess came forth, lovely, much revered,
> And grass grew up beneath her delicate feet.
> Her name is Aphrodite among men
> And gods, because she grew up in the foam....

Hesiod
Theogony 185-195

As has often been noted, the war-oriented societies of that age took male gods as their dominant deities. In such a culture, as we saw happen with the Canaanites, the most significant goddess was basically changed from being a patron of love and fertility to being a patron of war. The Mycenaeans accorded male deities the highest honor. And when the classical Greeks ascended some time later, they did the same. The main Greek goddess arguably was Athena, whose magnificent statue resided inside her primary temple—the ageless Parthenon on the acropolis at Athens. In the Parthenon as in her other depictions, Athena stood wearing a helmet and holding her spear and her shield.

In contrast with this, Aphrodite was only involved with love and fertility. She was the clearest expression of Our Lady of the Phoenicians that has come down to us today. A picture of Aphrodite—whom the Romans would call Venus—was painted by Sandro Botticelli, showing her birth at sea and arrival upon Cyprus. It is instantly recognized today around the world.

Fig. 70   Aphrodite comes to Cyprus

With respect to the main Phoenician cities on the Lebanese coast, we were quite fortunate to have a remarkable picture of life at this time recorded for us. In an age when most written records were overtly self-aggrandizing inscriptions commissioned by kings and powerful people to assure their favorable image in the annals of history, this document stood out for its forthrightness and its view of life at not-so-grand a level. Written in 1075 BC on papyrus by a man named

Wenamun, the main body of the report has survived even though a portion of it was lost due to the brittle nature of the media on which it was written.

This intriguing view of a trading trip from Egypt to Byblos was particularly noteworthy because the writer was an Egyptian seeing the Phoenician people and cities with fresh eyes. He simply reported what he saw. As a priest from an Egyptian temple, Wenamun was in many ways an innocent going about his "important" mission. He was supposed to obtain a cedar boat from the builders at Byblos, to be used for ceremonies in his temple. He actually believed the ongoing image-building in Egypt which said the land of the Nile was the center of the universe and still dominated the east coast of the Mediterranean. This was believed even though the Sea Peoples had destroyed that arrangement more than a hundred years earlier.

Wenamun's account has proven to be remarkably accurate in all the historical details that can be confirmed. After Ramses III fought the Sea Peoples, eight Egyptian kings had come and gone inauspiciously. During the last of these reigns, the land had become divided between two rulers: Herihor who commanded the south, ruling from Thebes; and Smendes who ruled the north from Tanis in the delta. The Tjeker tribe of Sea Peoples held the coastline south of the Phoenicians, while Tyre, Sidon and Byblos thrived at the center of a growing sea-trade empire. This was a wonderful first-hand account of those times.

> Year 5, fourth month of summer, day 16, the day of departure of Wenamun, the Elder of the Portal of the Temple of Amun, Lord of Thrones-of-the-Two-Lands, to fetch timber for the great noble [riverboat] of Amen-Re, King of Gods, which is upon the river and (is called) Amen-user-he.
>
> On the day of my arrival at Tanis, the place where Smendes and Tentamun are, I gave them the dispatches of Amen-Re, King of Gods. They had them read out before them and they said: "I will do, I will do as Amen-Re, King of Gods, our lord has said."
>
> I stayed until the fourth month of summer in Tanis. Then Smendes and Tentamun sent me off with the ship's

captain Mengebet, and I went down upon the great sea of [Phoenicia. Within a month] I arrived at Dor, a Tjeker town; and Beder, its prince, had fifty loaves, one jug of wine, and one ox-haunch brought to me. Then a man of my ship fled after stealing one vessel of gold worth 5 *deben*, four jars of silver worth 20 *deben*, and a bag with 11 *deben* of silver; (total of what he stole): gold 5 *deben*, silver 31 *deben*.

That morning when I had risen, I went to where the prince was and said to him: "I have been robbed in your harbor. Now you are the prince of this land, you are the one who controls it. Search for my money! Indeed the money belongs to Amen-Re, King of Gods, the lord of the lands. It belongs to Smendes; it belongs to Herihor, my lord, and (to) the other magnates of Egypt. It belongs to you; it belongs to Weret; it belongs to Mekmer; it belongs to Tjekerbaal, the prince of Byblos!" He said to me: "Are you serious? Are you joking? Indeed I do not understand the demand you make to me. If it had been a thief belonging to my land who had gone down to your ship and had stolen your money, I would replace it for you from my storehouse, until your thief, whatever his name, had been found. But the thief who robbed you, he is yours, he belongs to your ship. Spend a few days here with me; I will search for him."

I stayed nine days moored in his harbor. Then I went to him and said to him: "Look, you have not found my money. (Let me depart) with the ship captains, with those who go to sea."

(The next eight lines are broken. Apparently the prince advises Wenamun to wait some more, but Wenamun departs. He passes Tyre and approaches Byblos. Then he seizes thirty deben of silver from a ship he has encountered which belongs to the Tjeker. He tells the owners that he will keep the money until his money has been found. Through this action he incurs the enmity of the Tjeker).

They departed and I celebrated (in) a tent on the shore of the sea in the harbor of Byblos. And (I made a

hiding place for) Amun-of-the-Road and placed his possessions in it. Then the prince of Byblos sent to me saying: "(Leave my) harbor!" I sent to him, saying: "Where
shall (I go)? ---------- If (you have a ship to carry me), let
me be taken back to Egypt." I spent twenty-nine days in
his harbor, and he spent time sending to me daily to say:
"Leave my harbor!"

Now while he was offering to his gods, the god took
hold of a young man (of) his young men and put him in
a trance. He said to him: "Bring (the) god up! Bring the
envoy who is carrying him! It is Amun who sent him. It
is he who made him come!" Now it was while the entranced one was entranced that night that I had found a
ship headed for Egypt. I had loaded all my belongings
into it and was watching for the darkness, saying: "When
it descends I will load the god so that no other eye shall
see him."

Then the harbor master came to me, saying: "Wait until morning, says the prince!" I said to him: "Was it not
you who daily took time to come to me, saying: 'Leave
my harbor'? Do you now say: 'Wait this night,' in order
to let the ship that I found depart, and then you will
come to say: 'Go away'?" He went and told it to the
prince. Then the prince sent to the captain of the ship,
saying: "Wait until morning, says the prince."

When morning came, he sent and brought me up,
while the god rested in the tent where he was on the
shore of the sea. I found him seated in his upper chamber
with his back against a window, and the waves of the
great sea of [Phoenicia] broke behind his head. I said to
him: "Blessings of Amun!" He said to me: "How long is
it to this day since you came from the place where Amun
is?" I said to him: "Five whole months till now." He said
to me: "If you are right, where is the dispatch of Amun
that was in your hand? Where is the letter of the High
Priest of Amun that was in your hand?" I said to him: "I
gave them to Smendes and Tentamun." Then he became
very angry and said to me: "Now then, dispatches, let-

ters you have none. Where is the ship of pinewood that Smendes gave you? Where is its [Phoenician] crew? Did he not entrust you to this foreign ship's captain in order to have him kill you and have them throw you into the sea? From whom would one then seek the god? And you, from whom would one seek you?" So he said to me.

I said to him: "Is it not an Egyptian ship? Those who sail under Smendes are Egyptian crews. He has no [Phoenician] crews." He said to me: "Are there not twenty ships here in my harbor that do business with Smendes? As for Sidon, that other (place) you passed, are there not another fifty ships there that do business with Werekter and haul to this house?"

I was silent in this great moment. Then he spoke to me, saying: "On what business have you come?" I said to him: "I have come in quest of timber for the great noble [riverboat] of Amen-Re, King of Gods. What your father did, what the father of your father did, you too will do it." So I said to him. He said to me: "True, they did it. If you pay me for doing it, I will do it. My relations carried out this business after Pharaoh had sent six ships laden with the goods of Egypt, and they had been unloaded into their storehouses. You, what have you brought for me?"

He had the daybook of his forefathers brought and had it read before me. They found entered in his book a thousand *deben* of silver and all sorts of things. He said to me: "If the ruler of Egypt were the lord of what is mine and I were his servant, he would not have sent silver and gold to say: 'Carry out the business of Amun.' It was not a royal gift that they gave to my father! I too, I am not your servant, nor am I the servant of him who sent you! If I shout aloud to the Lebanon, the sky opens and the logs lie here on the shore of the sea! Give me the sails you brought to move your ships, loaded with logs for (Egypt)! Give me the ropes you brought (to lash the pines) that I am to fell in order to make them for you. ---- --------- that I am to make for you for the sails of your ships; or the yards may be too heavy and may break, and you may die (in) the midst of the sea. For Amun makes thunder in the sky ever since he placed Seth beside him! Indeed, Amun has founded all the lands. He founded them after having first founded the land of Egypt from which you have come. Thus craftsmanship came from it in order to reach the place where I am! Thus learning came from it in order to reach the place where I am! What are these foolish travels they made you do?"

I said to him: "Wrong! These are not foolish travels that I am doing. There is no ship on the river that does not belong to Amun. His is the sea and his the Lebanon of which you say, 'It is mine.' It is a growing ground for Amen-user-he, the lord of every ship. Truly, it was Amen-Re, King of Gods, who said to Herihor, my master: 'Send me!' And he made me come with this great god. But look, you have let this great god spend these twenty-nine days moored in your harbor. Did you not know that he was here? Is he not he who he was? You are prepared to haggle over the Lebanon with Amun, its lord? As to your saying, the former kings sent silver and gold: If they had owned life and health, they would not have sent these things. It was in place of life and health that they sent these things to your fathers! But Amen-Re, King of Gods, he is the lord of life and health, and he was the lord of your fathers! They passed their lifetimes offering to Amun. You too, you are the servant of Amun!

"If you will say 'I will do' to Amun, and will carry out his business, you will live, you will prosper, you will be healthy; you will be beneficent to your whole land and your people. Do not desire what belongs to Amun-Re, King of Gods! Indeed, a lion loves his possessions! Have your scribe brought to me that I may send him to Smendes and Tentamun, the pillars Amun has set up for the north of his land; and they will send all that is needed. I will send him to them, saying 'Have it brought until I return to the south; then I shall refund you all your expenses.'" So I said to him.

He placed my letter in the hand of his messenger; and he loaded the keel, the prow-piece, and the stern-piece, together with four other hewn logs, seven in all, and sent them to Egypt. His messenger who had gone to Egypt returned to me in [Phoenicia] in the first month of winter, Smendes and Tentamun having sent: four jars and one *kakmen*-vessel of gold; five jars of silver; ten garments of royal linen; ten *hrd*-garments of fine linen; five hundred smooth linen mats; five hundred ox-hides; five hundred ropes; twenty sacks of lentils; and thirty baskets of fish. And she had sent to me: five garments of fine linen; five *hrd*-garments of fine linen; one sack of lentils; and five baskets of fish.

The prince rejoiced. He assigned three hundred men and three hundred oxen, and he set supervisors over them to have them fell the timbers. They were felled and they lay there during the winter. In the third month of summer they dragged them to the shore of the sea. The prince came out and stood by them, and he sent to me saying: "Come!" Now when I had been brought into his presence, the shadow of his sunshade fell on me. Then Penamun, a butler of his, intervened, saying "The shadow of Pharaoh, your lord, has fallen upon you." And he was angry with him and said: "Leave him alone."

As I stood before him, he addressed me, saying: "Look, the business my fathers did in the past, I have done it, although you did not do for me what your fathers did for mine. Look, the last of your timber has arrived and is ready. Do as I wish, and come to load it. For has it not been given to you? Do not come to look at the terror of the sea. For if you look at the terror of the sea, you will see my own! Indeed, I have not done to you what was done to the envoys of Khaemwese, after they had spent seventeen years in this land. They died on the spot." And he said to his butler: "Take him to see the tomb where they lie."

I said to him: "Do not make me see it. As for Khaemwese, the envoys he sent you were men and he himself was a man. You have not here one of his envoys, though you say: 'Go and see your companions.' Should you not rejoice and have a stela (made) for yourself, and say on it: 'Amen-Re, King of Gods, sent me Amun-of-the-Road, his envoy, together with Wenamun, his human envoy, in quest of timber for the great noble [riverboat] of Amen-Re, King of Gods. I felled it; I loaded it; I supplied my ships and my crews. I let them reach Egypt so as to beg for me from Amun fifty years of life over and above my allotted fate.' And if it comes to pass that in another day an envoy comes from the land of Egypt who knows writing and he reads out your name on the stela, you will receive water of the west like the gods who are there."

He said to me: "A great speech of admonition is what you have said to me." I said to him: "As to the many (things) you have said to me: if I reach the place where the High Priest of Amun is and he sees your accomplishment, it is your accomplishment that will draw profit to you."

I went off to the shore of the sea, to where the logs were lying. And I saw eleven ships that had come in from the sea and belonged to the Tjeker (who were) saying: "Arrest him! Let no ship of his leave for the land of Egypt!" Then I sat down and wept. And the secretary of the prince came out to me and said to me: "What is it?" I said to him: "Do you not see the migrant birds going down to Egypt a second time? Look at them traveling to the cool water! Until when shall I be left here? For do you not see those who have come to arrest me?"

He went and told it to the prince. And the prince began to weep on account of the words said to him, for they were painful. He sent his secretary out to me, bringing me two jugs of wine and a sheep. And he sent me Tentne, an Egyptian songstress who was with him, saying: "Sing for him! Do not let his heart be anxious." And he sent to me, saying: "Eat, drink; do not let your heart be anxious. You shall hear what I will say tomorrow."

When morning came, he had his assembly summoned. He stood in their midst and said to the Tjeker:
"What have you come for?" They said to him: "We have
come after the blasted ships that you are sending to
Egypt with our enemy." He said to them: "I cannot arrest
the envoy of Amun in my country. Let me send him off,
and you go after him to arrest him."

He had me board and sent me off from the harbor of
the sea. And the wind drove me to the land of [Cyprus].
Then the town's people came out against me to kill me.
But I forced my way through them to where Hatiba, the
princess of the town was. I met her coming from one of
her houses to enter another. I saluted her and said to the
people who stood around her: "Is there not one among
you who understands Egyptian?" And one among them
said: "I understand it." I said to him: "Tell my lady that I
have heard it said as far away as Thebes, the place where
Amun is: 'If wrong is done in every town, in the land of
[Cyprus] right is done.' Now is wrong done here too
every day?"

She said: "What is it you have said?" I said to her: "If
the sea rages and the wind drives me to the land where
you are, will you let me be received so as to kill me,
though I am the envoy of Amun? Look, as for me, they
would search for me till the end of time. As for this crew
of the prince of Byblos, whom they seek to kill, will not
their lord find ten crews of yours and kill them also?"
She had the people summoned and they were repri-
manded. She said to me: "Spend the night ------------------
[the story is broken here].[65]

Ancient Egyptian Literature

It may be recalled that in the earlier discussion of Khufu and the
building of his Great Pyramid, there were two cedar boats buried
beside that huge structure as part of his funeral rites. The boats were
stored in pieces, with each piece labeled and ready to be assembled.
If we did not already know the Phoenicians had produced those
boats, this report from Wenamun describing the reason for his

journey to Byblos would certainly have given that answer in great detail. The supplying of impressive cedar boats for Egyptian religious purposes was a service provided by the people of Lebanon in return for good payment.

The house of the "prince of Byblos" in which Wenamun's negotiations took place was almost certainly the trading house we examined at Byblos and whose lower level still stands today. Its main room—

Fig. 71   Trading house at Byblos (on right) with view of the Mediterranean

just off the central hall, on the northwest corner—does indeed afford an excellent view of the sea.

Another great building would also soon figure richly in Phoenician lore, and that was Solomon's Temple.

CHAPTER 15

A DOVE ALIGHTS UPON THE MOUNT

While trade prospered with distant lands, a new force came to life just south of the Lebanese cities. It had started growing five hundred years earlier when a new group of people quietly entered the cross-roads that was Canaan. These people followed the patriarch Abra-ham from the city of Ur in Mesopotamia to new homes in the land that was to become Israel.[66] They would be known as the Hebrew people. Upon first arriving they came to Shechem near current-day Nablus, before settling in Bethel, which was about ten miles north of the city of Salem. This latter city would become famous one day as Jerusalem.

When a series of droughts tortured the land, many of Abraham's descendants went to Egypt and settled near the Nile Delta, much as the Hyksos had done in prior years. Between the reigns of Ramses II and Ramses III, Egypt descended into a period of anarchy and rebellion. It is believed that around this time Moses led the by-then large number of Hebrew people out of Egypt and back to Canaan. It was in these days that long-lived Jericho was leveled and its thick walls fell down.

This was also the time that the Sea Peoples came southward through the Canaanite countryside, destroying the cities they found there and settling upon the land. While the Tjeker and the Peleset, who would become the Palestinians, took up positions near the coast, the Hebrews of Moses and Joshua settled inland on the long stretch of hills.

For over a hundred years an uneasy truce existed between the people of the coast and those of the hills. Then a man named Saul became king of the Hebrews during a time of troubles. The campaigns fought by Saul against the Palestinians and Canaanites enjoyed some modest success. However he was vastly outdone by his successor, a great leader and general who arose among the Hebrew people and came to be known as King David. The energetic David led his people into Jerusalem and made it their capital city. Assembling a large army he marched far and wide across the land, establishing a great kingdom for the tribes of Israel, as the groups of his extended family were known.

Finally, his campaigns moved northward to the lower reaches of Lebanon. It was at this point that King Abibaal of Tyre and his young son Hiram showered gifts on David and arranged a peace between them. Among those gifts was a palace to be built for David in Jerusalem. When Abibaal died shortly thereafter, his nineteen-year-old son Hiram was crowned king of Tyre. It then became Hiram's duty to deliver the palace as promised.

The events of these times made such a deep impact on the Hebrew people that their scribes recorded them in great detail. Those writings were then handed down from generation to generation until they came into our hands today. Known in Judaism as the Tanakh and in Christianity as the Old Testament, these words give us glimpses of some people and deeds from those ancient days.

It is true that documents from antiquity, particularly those which contain articles of faith, need to be compared with other sources to see which parts are historically accurate. But since we know Solomon's Temple existed and other aspects of building it have proven to be fairly accurate, then related events such as the following seem reasonable as well.

> And Hiram king of Tyre sent messengers to David, and cedar trees, and carpenters, and masons; and they built David a house.
>
> 2 Samuel 5:11

In these accounts, King David then spoke of erecting a great temple in Jerusalem, and Hiram lavished more gifts upon him in the form of valuable building materials. As years passed, however, these materials piled up in the capital unused. David disclosed the reason for this, saying a message had come to him from God declaring, "thou hast been a man of war, and hast shed blood."[67] Therefore he would not be allowed to build the temple of his dreams. This honor would fall to one of his sons.

This meant Hiram was free from any obligation to David about building a large temple in Jerusalem. So he threw himself into making Tyre a greater city than he had inherited.

Archaeological evidence shows Tyre originally stood on a reef some 1,650 feet long.[68] Hiram proceeded to build a causeway to the smaller island just east of Tyre, then built up both the old and new areas with artificial embankments. Altogether, he amassed perhaps forty acres for his growing city. Strabo tells us this maritime port was densely populated and that it resorted to multistory buildings to house its occupants on the small amount of precious land available.[69] This conjures up images of an ancient forerunner to the modern islands of Manhattan and Hong Kong.

On the acropolis in the southwestern part of the island-city of Tyre stood two regal temples: one dedicated to Our Lady and the other to her male consort, whom Herodotus knew as Hercules. However it is the *older* temple of Hercules that is of greater interest to us. Built on the small island that Hiram attached to the city, this temple was the one we saw Herodotus describe as being so rich in beauty, with "two pillars, one of pure gold, the other of emerald, shining with great brilliancy." It must have been an impressive sight to boats from distant lands as they approached Tyre by sea, just as it would have been when seen from shore.

King David finally passed away in 970 BC, causing his son Solomon to ascend the throne in Jerusalem. Finally the long-delayed project to build a magnificent temple for the Hebrew people was set in motion. When Solomon was ready, Hiram gathered his artisans and building materials and set them to work. It is worth noting that even when working on a magnificent creation such as Solomon's Temple, the Phoenicians made no claim for a share of the glory. Their legendary privacy was so entrenched and pervasive that they left no commemorative plaques or writings proudly asserting their accomplishment. Were it not for the remarkable work of archaeologists, historians, and Hebrew scribes, this Phoenician contribution would have completely faded from view.

We resume the unfolding of these events, as told in the Tanakh and Old Testament.

> And Solomon sent to Hiram, saying, "Thou knowest how that David my father could not build an house unto the name of the LORD his God for the wars which were about him on every side, until the LORD put them under the soles of his feet. But now the LORD my God hath given me rest on every side, so that there is neither adversary nor evil occurrent. And, behold, I purpose to build an house unto the name of the LORD my God, as the LORD spake unto David my father, saying, Thy son, whom I will set upon thy throne in thy room, he shall build an house unto my name. Now therefore command thou that they hew me cedar trees out of Lebanon; and my servants shall be with thy servants; and unto thee will I give hire for thy servants according to all that thou shalt appoint; for thou knowest that there is not among us any that can skill to hew timber like unto the Sidonians."
>
> And it came to pass, when Hiram heard the words of Solomon, that he rejoiced greatly, and said, "Blessed be the LORD this day, which hath given unto David a wise son over this great people."
>
> And Hiram sent to Solomon, saying, "I have considered the things which thou sentest to me for; and I will do all thy desire concerning timber of cedar, and concerning timber of fir. My servants shall bring them down from Lebanon unto the sea; and I will convey them by sea in floats unto the place that thou shalt appoint me, and will cause them to be discharged there, and thou shalt receive them; and thou shalt accomplish my desire, in giving food for my household."

So Hiram gave Solomon cedar trees and fir trees according to all his desire. And Solomon gave Hiram twenty thousand measures of wheat for food to his household, and twenty measures of pure oil; thus gave Solomon to Hiram year by year. And the LORD gave Solomon wisdom, as he promised him; and there was peace between Hiram and Solomon; and they two made a league together.

1 Kings 5:2-12

To honor King Solomon, his scribes then described him as performing all the work himself. In real life the artisans and laborers provided by the Phoenicians and Hebrews did the actual work, and they labored under the guidance of an architect. This brings up the intriguing question of whether the architect was Phoenician or Hebrew. It is significant because it has a bearing on whether the Phoenicians were simply suppliers and laborers or made a more essential contribution. Clearly, Solomon stood in the position we would today call the owner, and the work was done for him. As any owner would do, he surely had definite ideas of what he wanted, and asked for a design to match his desires. But how was it accomplished?

As mentioned earlier, the Hebrew people had recently converted from a nomadic, shepherd-based existence to being warriors who captured the sizable city of Jerusalem. They were in the throes of adjusting to the rigors of governing not only a large city but also a large kingdom. It turned out that they had never before built a temple.

Jewish tradition up to that time was to make offerings to God on a simple altar, often described as being outdoors—much as Abraham did when he offered up a ram in place of his son Isaac. Looking ahead for a moment—many years after the passing of Solomon's Temple—the Jewish faithful gathered in new places and called those meeting-places "synagogues." These relatively modest edifices were given this name because it was believed that there had been only one temple for the Jewish people: the one built by Solomon.

In Solomon's day the Hebrews' shortage of experience in this area was not a problem, however, because the Phoenicians had been supplying and assisting the Egyptians in temple-building for about 2,200 years at this point. They had also been building their own temples in cities such as Byblos, Kition and Tyre. In fact, the one described by Herodotus in Tyre has often been cited as the guide that was used to create this much-larger temple in Jerusalem. The Phoenicians provided the master craftsmen as well, one of whom was named and described in the Old Testament accounts.

All of this was a bit over-simplified by the scribes of the time who said, with many bows to the king, that Solomon did all the work.

> So Solomon built the house [of the LORD], and finished it. And he built the walls of the house within with boards of cedar, both the floor of the house, and the walls of the ceiling; and he covered them on the inside with wood, and covered the floor of the house with planks of fir. And he built twenty cubits on the sides of the house, both the floor and the walls with boards of cedar; he even built them for it within, even for the oracle [sanctuary], even for the most holy place.
>
> And the house, that is, the temple before it, was forty cubits long. And the cedar of the house within was carved with knops and open flowers; all was cedar; there was no stone seen. And the oracle he prepared in the house within, to set there the ark of the covenant of the LORD. And the oracle in the forepart was twenty cubits in length, and twenty cubits in breadth, and twenty cubits in the height thereof: and he overlaid it with pure gold; and so covered the altar which was of cedar.
>
> So Solomon overlaid the house within with pure gold; and he made a partition by the chains of gold before the oracle; and he overlaid it with gold. And the whole house he overlaid with gold, until he had finished all the house; also the whole altar that was by the oracle he overlaid with gold.
>
> In the fourth year [of Solomon's reign] was the foundation of the house of the LORD laid, in the month Zif. And in the eleventh year, in the month Bul, which is the eighth month, was the house finished throughout all the

parts thereof, and according to all the fashion of it. So was he seven years in building it.

1 Kings 6:14-22, 37-38

Interestingly, we are then given the name of the master craftsman in brasswork for this magnificent Temple. He was known as Hiram and came from Tyre, but was no relation to the king of that city. Among the many works he crafted for the Temple were two stunning pillars to stand in front of it. They were made of polished brass instead of jewels and gold, but were exceedingly impressive in their enormous size.

> And king Solomon sent and fetched Hiram out of Tyre. He was a widow's son of the tribe of Naphtali, and his father was a man of Tyre, a worker in brass; and he was filled with wisdom, and understanding, and cunning to work all works in brass. And he came to king Solomon, and wrought all his work.
>
> For he cast two pillars of brass, of eighteen cubits high apiece; and a line of twelve cubits did compass either of them about. And he made two chapiters [capitals] of molten brass, to set upon the tops of the pillars; the height of the one chapiter was five cubits, and the height of the other chapiter was five cubits. And nets of checker work, and wreaths of chain work, for the chapiters which were upon the top of the pillars; seven for the one chapiter, and seven for the other chapiter.
>
> And he set up the pillars in the porch of the temple; and he set up the right pillar, and called the name thereof Jachin; and he set up the left pillar, and called the name thereof Boaz. And upon the top of the pillars was lily work; so was the work of the pillars finished.
>
> And Hiram made the lavers, and the shovels, and the basons [basins]. So Hiram made an end of doing all the work that he made king Solomon for the house of the LORD.

1 Kings 7:13-17, 21-22, 40

After the seven years required to build the temple, a new project was begun. This was a spacious palace built for Solomon that he called his "cedar forest" for reasons that will quickly become apparent. This royal residence included a throne room where he would one day sit in judgment over two women who were fighting over a baby, an event that would help establish his reputation for wise judgment.

> But Solomon was building his own house [palace] thirteen years, and he finished all his house. He built also the house of the forest of Lebanon; the length thereof was an hundred cubits, and the breadth thereof fifty cubits, and the height thereof thirty cubits, upon four rows of cedar pillars, with cedar beams upon the pillars.
>
> And it was covered with cedar above upon the beams, that lay on forty five pillars, fifteen in a row. And there were windows in three rows, and light was against light in three ranks. And all the doors and posts were square, with the windows; and light was against light in three ranks.
>
> And he made a porch of pillars; the length thereof was fifty cubits, and the breadth thereof thirty cubits; and the porch was before them; and the other pillars and the thick beam were before them. Then he made a porch for the throne where he might judge, even the porch of judgment: and it was covered with cedar from one side of the floor to the other.
>
> 1 Kings 7:1-7

This great palace was believed to have stood near Solomon's Temple on Temple Mount, as the rocky Mount Moriah came to be known. The two structures were described as being of breathtaking beauty. The massive construction effort must have been successful because these buildings stood for almost four hundred years until conquest toppled them. Seventy years after its destruction, the Temple was built again on the same site and stood another five hundred years.

When the Temple and palace were fresh and new, the Phoenicians had invested twenty years of skilled labor and forests of cedar logs as

*Fig. 72 Western Wall in Jerusalem. Solomon's Temple
once stood near these trees*

well as other supplies. They were owed much more than the thousands of measures of wheat and oil that had been paid to them each year. So Solomon ceded to the Phoenicians extensive lands in the Upper Galilee and received a payment in gold to achieve a fair balance.

> Now Hiram the king of Tyre had furnished Solomon with cedar trees and fir trees, and with gold, according to all his desire—that then king Solomon gave Hiram twenty cities in the land of Galilee.
>
> And Hiram came out from Tyre to see the cities which Solomon had given him; and they pleased him not. And he said, "What cities are these which thou hast given me, my brother?" And he called them the land of Cabul unto this day.
>
> And Hiram sent to the king sixscore talents of gold.
>
> 1 Kings 9:11-14

It should be noted that the partnership created between Hiram, Solomon, and their respective peoples was not limited to constructing these massive structures. They also engaged in joint trading

ventures in which the Hebrews provided the strategic port of Ezion-
geber—today called Eilat—on the Red Sea and a portion of the
trading stock. The Phoenicians provided the ships, crews and trading
contacts in distant countries. Of course, Hebrew scribes portrayed the
arrangement as if the navy were Solomon's even though his people
were notoriously inexperienced sailors. But descriptions of that
nature were normal. This trade, by the way, was primarily with
Ophir, which is generally understood to be India. It made both
partners in these trading ventures exceedingly rich.

> And king Solomon made a navy of ships in Eziongeber,
> which is beside Eloth, on the shore of the Red sea, in the
> land of Edom.
>   And Hiram sent in the navy his servants, shipmen
> that had knowledge of the sea, with the servants of Sol-
> omon.
>   And they came to Ophir, and fetched from thence
> gold, four hundred and twenty talents, and brought it to
> king Solomon.
>   1 Kings 9:26-28

In all these things we have seen the Phoenician principles at work.
Consider for a moment how these events would have turned out
with almost any other society. And how much differently they
happened here.

The encounter began with the apparently unstoppable Hebrew
army sweeping all before it as it marched north to Lebanon. Most
societies would have immediately gone to war to defend their
homeland. This would almost certainly have resulted in Sidon,
Beirut, Byblos, and possibly Tyre being consumed by fire. The
kingdom of David would have been slightly larger, and the Phoenicians would have become a subjugated people if they did not disappear altogether.

Similarly, if the Phoenician cities were destroyed and the people
of Israel had to rely on their own devices to build their temple, it is
reasonable to expect that a much more modest edifice would have
been the result.

Going a step further, crushing the Phoenicians would have likewise crushed the joint trade ventures to Ophir that sprang up later. One often hears references to the riches of Solomon without giving any thought to the source of his wealth. Did it come from taxing his shepherd-soldiers, or the poor farmers they conquered? That was too weak a base to produce much wealth. When we see the massive amounts of gold that came to him from trade ventures with the Phoenicians, it begins to make more sense.

So if the initial clash between Israel and Lebanon had been bloody war and the Hebrews had emerged victorious, they would have been able to celebrate their victory in a modest temple in the middle of a poor country. And the Lebanese people would likewise have been brought down into suffering by the encounter.

Instead, this moment was met by the Phoenician principle of peaceful resolution of conflicts. Rich gifts and peaceful relations were offered and accepted.

The ever-present principle of privacy allowed the people of Lebanon to continue operating their highly profitable Mediterranean trading empire during this time without arousing greed among poor shepherd-soldiers in Israel. The thought of streams of gold and silver flowing into Tyre from Spain and other outposts might have been too much to bear, and swords might have come out of Hebrew scabbards.

Creating strong partnerships was a principle practiced avidly by Hiram, who became known thereby as a great admirer of David. He also became a partner with Solomon in two great ventures. The first and most famous partnership led to the building of the magnificent Temple, which has lived on in the hearts and imagination of Jewish people down to the present day. The second partnership involved foreign trade ventures that made them both rich.

Both of these partnerships were built upon the principle of international trade. Constructing the legendary temple was not just an exertion of labor. It involved the export of massive amounts of cedar, fir and brass. In return flowed mountains of wheat and oil, and even twenty cities in payment.

Into this international trade they also introduced the principle of equality and sharing the wealth. The Phoenicians were an older and well-established society, while the Hebrews were younger and a more powerful military force. Yet Hiram approached Solomon as king-to-king. He did not try to demand submissiveness from the younger nation, nor did he allow his resources to be taken without payment. The basis offered from the beginning was "equal exchange." Similarly, sharing the wealth from their joint foreign trade clearly had its desired effect, since the Hebrew scribes showed great satisfaction with the gold received.

Altogether, the sum of the Phoenician principles clearly affected the course of history which flowed through this event. Instead of dealing with the aftermath of destruction in Lebanon and poverty in Israel, the two countries thrived and enjoyed some of their best years.

Imagine what might happen if those principles were revived in the Middle East today. If countries were willing to let their neighbors have peace and prosperity, they might yet find greater peace and prosperity for themselves as well.

CHAPTER 16

LIGHTING THE FLAME

While those historical events were transpiring in Lebanon, the Phoenicians' trading ventures across the Mediterranean were also growing by leaps and bounds. Kition and other outposts were well established on Cyprus and shipping large amounts of copper to buyers in all directions. With Cyprus and the island of Arwad as jumping-off points, Phoenician traders had established excellent trading posts in Cilicia on the coast of Anatolia, an area that had been exceedingly difficult for them to work before. This entry point to all the trade of that subcontinent had previously been jealously guarded by the city of Ugarit as its major source of revenue. But that city had fallen and the way was open. Phoenician traders established themselves at the Cilician ports of Tarsus and Myriandros, and their ships bulged with goods as trade expanded.

In the Aegean Sea more trading posts were created on several islands. Phoenician crews now called on every available port from Crete in the south to Thrace in the north. The Greek mainland and islands had fallen into a "dark age" after the Sea People raids and the subsequent disintegration of the Mycenaeans. The arts, literature and social life created by the Minoans, and kept alive by the Mycenaeans, had faded away. It remained that way for several hundred years.

Now, during the ninth century BC, Greek cities were starting to take shape again on the mainland as well as on the islands, and even on the coast of Anatolia. One of the essentials that made this gradual revival possible was seaborne trade. The Phoenicians suffered no dark age after the Sea Peoples passed through. They remained literate and even experienced exuberant growth in their society and wealth since then.

Cautiously, the Phoenicians had only lightly touched the edges of the Aegean Sea until the Mycenaeans completely faded away. The painful memory of being evicted from those waters by the Mycenaeans had been too fresh. But after time passed, the Phoenicians came back and established new trading partnerships in the Aegean. With that, a measure of the former prosperity began to come back as well.

Cities began to grow around bustling marketplaces, and trade between the cities and islands multiplied also. The first tendrils of classical Greek society began to take form. These would soon poke above the ground like flowers in springtime, ready to bring forth its blooms in the form of fine arts and architecture. Those days were still a number of years away, but the seeds were beginning to sprout and be nourished.

Homer was believed to have lived at this time and to have assembled his stirring epics from the various verbal traditions which came down to him. Into these he stirred his own imagination and poetic mastery. Those epics so entranced his audiences that some inspired individuals became his apprentices, learning the long epics exactly as the master taught it. They then traveled from town to town and declaimed the powerful verses in exchange for reasonable compensation and a measure of celebrity.

Another gift also came to the Greeks from the Phoenicians at this time that would have a profound effect on the civilization they were about to create. This was the written alphabet. It would make possible the great literature of the Greek Golden Age, replete with the works of legendary philosophers such as Socrates and Plato, great playwrights Aeschylus and Euripides, and historians such as Herodotus and Thucydides.

The arrival of the alphabet in Greece was documented in legend as having been brought by a Phoenician named Cadmus who was a member of the leading family in Tyre. He was believed to have come to the land of Boeotia just west of Athens, where he founded a city called Thebes. Herodotus documented the contribution this way.

> Now the Phoenicians who came with Cadmus, and to whom the Gephyraei belonged, introduced into Greece upon their arrival a great variety of arts, among the rest that of writing, whereof the Greeks till then had, as I think, been ignorant. And originally they shaped their letters exactly like all the other Phoenicians, but afterwards, in the course of time, they changed by degrees their language, and together with it the form likewise of their characters. Now the Greeks who dwelt about those parts at that time were chiefly the Ionians. The Phoenician letters were accordingly adopted by them, but with some variation in the shape of a few, and so they arrived at the present use, still calling the letters Phoenician, as justice required, after the name of those who were the first to introduce them into Greece.
>
> Herodotus 5:58

In reality, of course, throwing out hieroglyphics and cuneiform writing to replace them with the alphabet was such a huge change that it would not have been introduced into Greece by one man. Rather it would have been transmitted through many Greek-Phoenician contacts at many places and gradually been adopted by all. But the legend at least acknowledged the direction from which it came.

Actually, the creation of writing was a much more fascinating story than even the stuff of legend. To tell it briefly: back in the days before writing existed, when shepherds or farmers wanted to record what they owned or what they were trading, they would use small clay tokens that represented the goods involved. For example, if baskets of grain were kept in the village's storage cellar, and a farmer put in three more baskets, he would be given three basket-tokens. He could then return at any time to trade one or more tokens for the corresponding amount of grain.

Around 4000 BC, these tokens began to be pressed into soft clay to record complex transactions. A sheep token could be pressed into the clay eight times to denote eight sheep and, if this was a trade, many other items might be listed as given in exchange for the sheep. Other pictures also began to be drawn on the clay to represent head, foot, sun, woman, and so on—becoming the first crude pictograph writing. The clay was then hardened to make a permanent record of this trade, which was now complete or which had been promised for the future. It is worthy of note that the trading and handling of goods were what made this pictographic writing necessary.

To avoid having to draw intricate pictures or carry tokens, the people of Mesopotamia replaced these pictures by using wedge-shaped pen marks to represent them. For example, a wooden pen pressed into the clay four times in a particular pattern became the new symbol for "woman." This writing was called cuneiform and was then used for several thousand years.

At the same time, however, a completely different system was being used in Egypt. These people continued to use the original pictures but made a tremendous breakthrough by letting each picture represent a syllable. For example Narmer, the first king of the first dynasty, had his name shown as a picture of a catfish (*nar*) followed by a chisel (*mer*). This style of writing was called hieroglyphics, and was also used for several thousand years. Eventually, hieroglyphic pictures began to be used to represent particular sounds, which was a half-step in the direction of an alphabet.

One serious problem with hieroglyphic and cuneiform writing was that there were hundreds or thousands of symbols, making them extremely difficult to learn. As a result, only a small number of individuals ever learned to write, and almost all of those people worked for the king, high priest or a trader. It was a very exclusive club.

The other problem was the complexity involved with having to write different languages when traveling. Recording all of the changes of words and sounds in different lands by using picture-based writing like hieroglyphics or cuneiform was a nightmare. Most people of those times solved the problem by never traveling outside their own country or by using the age-old practice of requiring everyone who came into their country to speak their language. Even in the relatively enlightened classical age of Socrates, the Greeks called outsiders barbarians because they thought those people's languages just sounded like bar-bar-bar. Since most people just stayed in one country, their world was quite simple.

But if you were a trader whose livelihood depended on traveling from country to country, this was a serious problem. The Phoenicians were in just such a predicament, and they were highly receptive to any way out of this dilemma.

The solution arrived around 1400 BC in the form of the Phoenician alphabet. It was not clear whether this breakthrough was created by someone sitting at a table in Tyre tearing his hair out until he came up with this brilliant solution, or whether some woman in the desert cobbled it together for her own use. Nor did it really matter. The crucial Phoenician contribution was the fact that they incorporated it into the world of trade and introduced it everywhere. They made it the new standard used throughout the known world. As a result, it has been known as the Phoenician alphabet from that day to the present. And virtually every linguistic expert in the world agrees that all the other alphabets were derived from this one.

The concept was amazingly simple. One symbol was assigned to each consonant sound. That was all there was to it. Every language was spoken, so it was made up of sounds. The writer need only listen to the speaker and write down the sounds. Later, a reader could say out loud the sounds written, and know exactly what had been recorded, just as if the original speaker were talking.

Any language that existed could be written using this alphabet. It was able to immediately travel anywhere in the world. And best of all, the Phoenician alphabet had only twenty-two letters. Anyone could master this alphabet.

Every Phoenician trader would have had to learn this alphabet. To say it was a necessity in their life would be an understatement. They were inveterate record-keepers, as witnessed by the book shown to Wenamun in the Byblos trading-house, and by the huge piles of clay tablets found in Minoan palaces with business transactions recorded on them. It also made sense. From the beginning of their existence the Phoenicians had shared the profits of their ventures in one way or another. No doubt some participants—such as the ship's captain— were deemed to have put in something of greater value than others. He reasonably would have been promised some larger share of the proceeds. To avoid arguments later, the agreement before the voyage

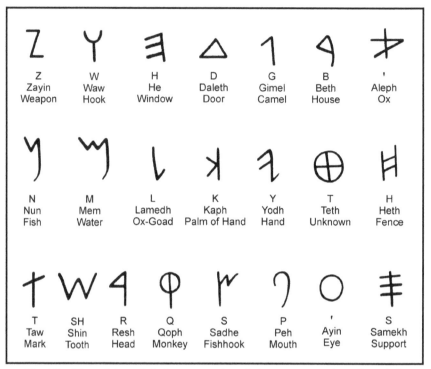

Fig. 73 Phoenician alphabet—note that their writing reads right to left, and that some symbols were later re-used and made into vowels

would be recorded when possible—and the captain would certainly want a copy of it. Upon successful conclusion of the voyage, all would be paid out according to that agreement.

And what were the profits that were being divided? They were the difference between the value of the cargo placed in the ship before it left port, compared to the value when it returned. The beginning cargo value would be carefully recorded—as well as the source from which it came—so that its value could be properly returned to the owner along with that individual's share of the profit. Records were also kept of actual trades, which was invaluable later in determining the value of various goods. The ship's holds were limited in size. For each destination, putting on board only the goods most highly desired at that location would lead to higher profits. Note that the records at Byblos were kept in considerable detail in a daybook, and that prior trades could be looked up when needed. [70]

But the traders were not alone in this desire. Their customers likewise were highly motivated to learn how to record these trades. For most local people the trades they made were the difference between bare subsistence and a comfortable life. Many business dealings were done by contract; and if only the Phoenicians could read and write while the local person could not, that was a severe disadvantage. So local people learned to write. Individuals with great wealth also needed writing to track their revenue-earning affairs. Having a simple system that they and their steward could master suited their needs exactly.

This marriage of the alphabet to wealth-building was what made the new creation so incredibly popular. It was as if a bookish bride had married a wealthy trader and suddenly discovered she had many new friends. In this case the bride was radiant, and she went on the arm of the Phoenician to every port and city in the known world.

A number of ports in Greece were just beginning to emerge from their dark period into a time of growing prosperity. They readily adopted the Phoenician alphabet, and much to their credit, they were not passive participants in the process. They took the 22-consonant alphabet and added several vowels, making it more robust. Then they began to spread this democratic and easy-to-learn system of writing throughout their society. Even though the days of great writers such as Euripides and Plato were still several hundred years away, the foundation of widespread education and writing was being established.

As the Greeks did these things, their preferred method of writing became the use of ink on papyrus. So they began to purchase this papyrus from the Phoenicians in large quantity to support their new addiction, and the sea-traders gladly obliged. Of course, those traders bought it in turn from Egypt where the papyrus was grown, but the Greeks seemed not to be aware of that simple fact. This suggested that the Phoenicians had finally managed to re-establish themselves as the central point of trade in the Mediterranean. In keeping with their principle of privacy, they traditionally kept their sources confidential—whether they were important or minor. Of course this also meant their trades were shielded from historical records, so we do not know many of the details about their trading partners—unless that partner decided to keep specific records.

Since the Greeks were writing now, they were soon recording many things. In these documents they gave names to cities and lands outside their own without paying too much attention to what the people of those places had named them. One cannot be too critical of this, since many other countries have done the same. And the Greeks received as much ill treatment in this regard as they gave. They once called their country Hellas and now call it Ellas—yet westerners still insist it be called Greece. That is the world we live in.

Another example of this was that the Greeks gave Byblos its name. The Phoenicians had always referred to this city as *gbl*, which was pronounced Gebail. This original name is preserved in the current Lebanese name for this city which is Jbail. The Greeks attached so much importance to their writing and to the papyrus they received from this port that they gave this city the name of "book" which is βίβλος (Byblos). Outside of Lebanon, the city is still most frequently recognized as Byblos.

In fact, the Greeks assigned the name "Phoenicians" to the people of this land, an appellation that became their predominant name over the years. Almost certainly these people referred to themselves in some way, even if it was only as Our People or Our Society. But the practice of privacy seemed to apply to this also, so we may never know the expression used. Instead, the Greek-given name of Phoenicians continues to be used around the world.

The meaning of that name was actually quite flattering. It was believed to refer to the royal-purple color associated with the tremendously luxurious dyed cloth the Phoenicians produced. This was made through a secret process using an exotic dye extracted drop by drop from murex shells. This beautiful purple cloth was so valuable and rare that it was used almost exclusively by royalty and the wealthiest families around the Mediterranean. To be known by that name was quite a compliment, all things considered.

With the aid of rising trade and a written alphabet, the Greeks began to emerge from their dark days and enjoy a measure of prosperity. The sea-traders from Lebanon likewise benefited from this trade through their growing number of outposts in the Aegean. These now included Rhodes, Cythera, Kommos on Crete, Thebes, the island of Aegina just south of Athens, and many others. Everyone prospered, so it was a win-win situation.

The same robust growth was happening beyond the Aegean.

At Sicily, the Phoenicians spread outward from their Ortygia settlement on the east coast and established a presence all around the outside of the island. In the northeast part of the land—in the shadow of Mount Etna and within sight of Italy across the water—another significant outpost began taking shape at a good anchorage which would one day be known as Naxos. The Phoenicians were welcomed by the local Sicilian population, but those sons and daughters of Sea Peoples were still quite feisty and protective of the inland parts of the island, so the traders kept mostly to the shore. In this way good relations were maintained and everyone prospered.

Malta was, as always, a special case. On this small island south of Sicily, the Phoenicians approached the local people like long-lost cousins and were received in that same vein. In addition to the shipyards they built beside Birgu, the sea-traders started a small settlement much deeper into the Grand Harbour at a place called Marsa. This put them much closer to the Maltese towns on the nearby flatlands. If this seemed unusual for the Phoenicians to leave the protection of their peninsula compound to live among the local people, it definitely was. But they did not stop there. They moved into many places in the interior of the island and lived among the Maltese as if they were all part of the same family. They lived in the south at Marsaxlokk Bay and built a small temple there. They lived at Mdina in the central highlands, and also far to the north. They even settled in the port town of Mgarr on the diminutive neighboring island of Gozo. They shared the life of the local people, repaired their ships, and regained their health and energy for the long voyages east and west. Malta was not a center of trade nor a place of negotiations. It was a place of rest before going back to uncertain fate on the seas and foreign shores.

Traveling westward from that island brought the Phoenician crews to Utica on the north shore of Africa. After two hundred years, it was still a frontier outpost at the mouth of the Majardah River, but an influential one, given its position astride the trade routes. From this vantage point, ships sailed north to the next major island in the Phoenician chain—Sardinia. There a spacious bay awaited with its thriving outposts at Nora and Karalis, which is today called Cagliari. This island had been known to trade since Minoan times, and was re-established by the Phoenicians after the passage of the Sea Peoples. Its major contribution was the copper, iron, lead and some silver that was mined from its hills. From there began the long voyage to Spain.

Across the south of Spain other outposts such as Malaga were established, which were somewhat modest at first, but were useful rest stops as well as places to conduct limited trade. Their importance would grow over time and eventually yield fine cities along this languid Costa del Sol. Another small post was established at Gibraltar, the last point of land before ships left the Mediterranean. A cave grotto was found here where Phoenician seamen left a vast number of small glass bottles and other offerings for good luck and safety as they were about to venture out into the ocean.

While those outposts were still young, the senior settlement of Cadiz on the Atlantic side of the Iberian peninsula was already an important city. This reflected the fact that Spain was now the crown jewel in the Phoenicians' western empire of trade. Rich in silver, gold and many other natural resources, it was also the linchpin in the critical tin trade that was needed in the making of bronze. Raw blocks of this valuable metal were brought down the Atlantic coast of Europe from Cornwall and Brittany to Cadiz. There it was put on huge merchantman ships for the long haul across the Mediterranean to waiting bronze-makers in the east.

This central role in the Phoenicians' richest trade earned Cadiz the distinction of being one of the first western outposts to earn major development into a full-fledged city. Carpenters and builders set to work constructing semi-permanent buildings and dock facilities, though the solid stone structures which would last through the ages were yet to come. The trade port stood on the northernmost isle known as Erytheia, which is today where the Old City remains. A small channel separated it from the long, narrow island called Kotinoussa, which ran southeast toward the shore. There, another channel divided it from the mainland. Over the years sand has filled in these channels, and today the city of Cadiz stretches all along this narrow stretch of land and is fully accessible from the mainland. All of this was put in motion by builders in the ninth century BC.

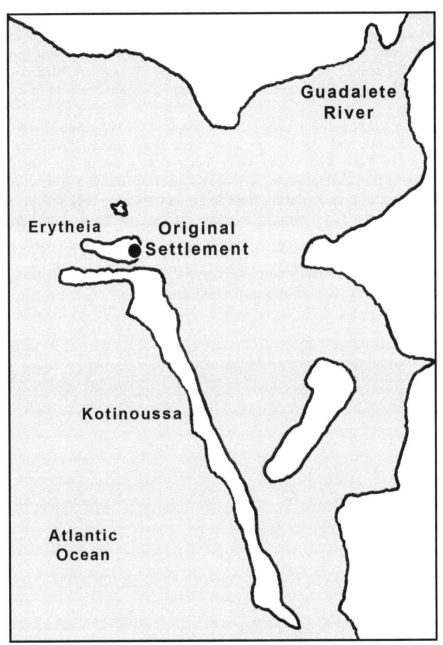

Fig. 74 Ancient Cadiz in Spain

Southward past the Strait of Gibraltar, the outpost of Lixis in Morocco was doing well. Though the traders there could not possibly hope to compete with the riches of Spain, they were nevertheless able to expand southward to the small post of Sala farther down the Atlantic coast. They also established a post in northern Morocco directly on the strait called Tingis, which has come down to us as Tangier.

The return path for trade from the Strait of Gibraltar passed eastern Morocco and Algeria, which became dotted with small outposts. Some of those would fade away, while others would last. Their primary purpose, however, was not so much to add to the flow of trade but to keep it moving from Spain and Morocco back to Utica. From there it sailed onward to other outposts on the way back to Lebanon.

Life was good for the Phoenician people in their flourishing Lebanese cities and the many outposts scattered across the Mediterranean. But there were storm clouds on the horizon.

CHAPTER 17

LIKE A CANDLE IN THE WIND

All this good fortune for the Phoenician people had the unintended effect of bringing a long-simmering problem to the fore. The great prosperity and many footholds on lands across the Mediterranean stirred old memories of the idyllic life their forebears once enjoyed on Crete. They remembered the spacious villas filled with fine furniture and works of art. They recalled the images of second-story rooms with doorways leading out to balconies from which extensive lands could be seen rolling over the nearby hills. Their olive trees, vineyards and tilled fields had been surrounded by lush forests, and the view of picturesque villages adorned distant hills. This was a life that still appealed to many.

In Lebanon the initial crush of too many refugees from Crete being squeezed into cities and islands too small to accommodate them had long since been addressed. Many homes had been built. Some of them were quite large and luxurious, even if the land each commanded was only a narrow walkway around the house. A small town along the coast between Tyre and Sidon now grew into a city called Sarepta—modern Sarafand. This allowed additional living space. The problem was eased further by producing more ships and acquiring distant outposts, for these caused many people to be sent outward to handle the much-welcomed explosion of trade.

For the majority of Phoenicians at this time, having a villa and all that went with it was far from the most important thing in their life. What they seemed to treasure most was their freedom and their unique society. They were rich not just in terms of valuable goods — though the maritime ventures in which they were engaged certainly brought those in great quantity — but in other ways as well. They had the luxury of knowing they benefited from and were protected by the efforts of other members of their community. They were rich in the peacefulness that pervaded their community and family life. They were also rich in the arts and in exposure to exotic cultures. They had the ability to travel beyond the horizon to new lands, meet new people, and return home a little wiser, inspired, and eager to do something with their lives.

The strong desires behind these two passionate views — changing to the Minoan lifestyle or preserving the one they had — finally became too strong to resist. It began to rip the fabric of their society. In the past an occasional king of a Phoenician city had felt he had the power to go his own way. In each such case, the council and society had won the high ground and persevered because of unwavering support from the people.

Now, in 820 BC, the dispute involved more than a king. A strong dissident group wanted to re-establish the landed estates of the Minoan lifestyle, and tensions began to run high. The matter came to a head when the king of Tyre, Mattan I, died and left his two children as possible successors. The choice was up to the council, as was normal Phoenician practice, but the council was unfortunately split. The late king's brother, Acherbas, led a group supporting the older child, Mattan's daughter Elissa, who leaned toward establishing large, landed estates. However the majority favored her younger brother Pygmalion — who was only eleven years old at the time — and wanted to maintain the traditional values of their sea-going society. In a compromise, the young boy became king of Tyre, and leader of all the Phoenician cities — but at a price.

It was normal for the king to also be the high priest, but the compromise gave that honor to his uncle Acherbas. The uncle was apparently an ambitious man, for he had already married his niece — the young king's sister Elissa — with the expectation that she would get the throne. Instead, he received only the position of high priest.

This clearly was not a religious position but a powerful administrative one, in keeping with the tradition established at Byblos in 2000 BC. The boy-king still stood between him and the crown.

One or more of the king's supporters evidently realized the youth's life was in danger, because action was immediately taken. It was Acherbas who died suddenly and quietly.

For six years, young Pygmalion ruled while the divisive issue of landed estates festered. Finally, in a dramatic break with Phoenician tradition, the families favoring landed estates—including many of the richest in this highly affluent society—refused to abide by majority rule. In defiance they suddenly set sail with all their wealth and possessions in a large armada of ships. They made their way quickly to Cyprus where a sympathetic and powerful local leader let them use a protected harbor while they decided on their next course of action. Elissa had sailed with them, and they acknowledged her as their leader. It was a role for which she seemed naturally suited.

They knew that the seas were controlled by Phoenician ships loyal to her brother, the king of Tyre, and that any venturing out from the Cyprus harbor would produce a disastrous confrontation. So Elissa fell back on her society's principle of peacefully resolving conflicts, and tried negotiation instead. The leaders of Tyre, seeing the genie was out of the bottle and could not be put in again, came to accept that concessions had to be made. Rather than lose these people completely, the council at Tyre apparently agreed to the demand that they have a new city of their own—but with certain conditions. Laws in the new city could allow landed estates and related concerns, but beyond that the residents of that city would have to abide by the traditional Phoenician statutes. These included recognizing the supreme position of the king of Tyre and the Phoenician council, making an annual payment of a share of their profits to Tyre, and maintaining strict confidentiality of all Phoenician affairs.

As their subsequent actions would show, the dissident families were not anti-Phoenician in any way. They just wanted the freedom to enjoy the fruits of their labors, including the villas and vineyards of their dreams. The proposed conditions were acceptable. So the only question was: where?

Elissa and the leaders of the families who had followed her on this exodus realized the lands beyond Sicily were a great new frontier.

The wealth of Spain and other western lands beckoned. And much of that countryside was uncultivated, ripe for new ownership. North Africa just beyond the end of Sicily seemed especially attractive.

Of course there was already a Phoenician colony in that area, Utica, which was growing into a major player in the region's trade. But Elissa's people showed no interest in joining that city. They wanted a fresh start. And they found it twenty-five miles down the coast.

Legend has it that she negotiated with the local people for a small piece of land which could be covered by a cowhide. Then her people cut the cowhide into many small strips which they tied end-to-end, and used the resulting knotted cord to mark out a large hill for their use. The hill on which they settled was called Byrsa, which meant "cowhide." The new city itself was called Kart-hadasht, which literally meant "new city." It is known today by its more famous name of Carthage.

The most defining aspect of this city was that it was built on Byrsa Hill, well back from the shore. This broke with the long-established Phoenician tradition of building each city on an island if it was available or, if not, then on a promontory extending into the water. This tradition, of course, reflected their deeply held orientation to the sea. It placed the highest importance on closeness to the harbor and to their escape route across the water in case of attack. The people of Carthage began with a clear statement that they were choosing a high ground from which they could defend their surrounding lands.

Nor was this the only way their settlement differed from the other colonies. This was not a modest handful of traders with a few ships. They had no intention of creating a crude port which would require several hundred years to grow into a significant city. Instead, they put shipload after shipload of colonists ashore at Carthage on the first day. And the colonists were outrageously rich. Together they brought a significant portion of the whole wealth of Tyre, the greatest Phoenician city of that time. This new community on the coast of North Africa burst into prominence immediately after it was founded. So it quickly eclipsed neighboring Utica up the coast. That older city remained significant but definitely secondary to this powerful young player in the western Mediterranean.

The impressive beginning of this legendary city was artfully captured by J. M. W. Turner in his acclaimed painting with the rambling

Fig. 75   Elissa Building Carthage

title, "Dido [Elissa] Building Carthage, or, the Rise of the Carthaginian Empire," which now resides at the National Gallery in London.

It was only natural, of course, that legends sprang up around the
founding of this great city and the commercial empire it would
eventually lead. As always, those legends mixed some facts with a bit
of mythology, and became entertaining stories that only grew more
dramatic as time went on. These legends revolved around Elissa—
who was also called Dido ("the wanderer") because of her indirect
voyage from Tyre to Carthage. The earliest known account of her
adventures was written by Timaeus of Sicily between 356-200 BC; and
though it has since been lost, it was used and referenced by others.
He dated the founding of Carthage to 814 BC, which has come to be
the commonly accepted date.

The story of Elissa, and Carthage's early days, was most famously
told by the Roman poet Virgil in his masterwork *Aeneid*. Early in this
epic the hero Aeneas came to the shore of North Africa where
Aphrodite told him Elissa's background—after which the traveling
warrior and the leading lady of Carthage had a romantic interlude.
Since the story was told from a Roman perspective, Roman names

were used for major people and places: Aphrodite was called Venus, Elissa was Dido, Acherbas was Sychaeus, and African was Libyan.

> Weariedly struggle the men of Aeneas to pilot their vessels
> Each to the nearest shore, and are turned to the Libyan sea-
> coast.
> Deep in a bay is an isle, enclosing a harbor, and stretching
> Wide its protecting arms, whereon each wave rolling in-
> ward
> Breaks, and divides itself into refluent curves; and beyond
> it,
> Rising to right and left, tall cliffs and twin peaks threaten
> Heaven,
> Under whose sentinel heights the plain of the water is
> peaceful
> Far and wide; then rises a scene of glimmering woodland,
> While a dark forest impends from above with bristling
> shadows.
> Under the opposite brow, in the beetling cliff, is a grotto;
> Seats in the living rock are there, and crystalline waters,
> Home of the nymphs; no chains are there needed for wave-
> wearied vessels,
> Nor with curving beak need ever an anchor restrain them.
> From the whole number of ships but seven remain, and Ae-
> neas
> Steals hither with these....

> Venus replied [to Aeneas]: ....
> This that thou seest is [Carthaginian] land, by Tyrians peo-
> pled;
> Here is Agenor's town; fierce Libyans harass our borders;
> Dido is queen of the realm; she abandoned her Tyrian city
> Fleeing her brother; —but long are her woes, too long their
> recital;
> Nevertheless, in its broader lines, I will follow her story.
> She was the bride of Sychaeus, a man who was counted the
> richest
> Owner of land in Tyre, and devotedly loved by poor Dido,

Whom in her maidenly bloom, her father had pledged in be-
   trothal:
Omens of marriage were bright; but over the Tyrian people
Reigned her own brother Pygmalion as king, —a monster of
   evil.
Bitter dissension arose in the home, and by avarice blinded,
Disregarding his sister's love, and defiant of Heaven,
Even at the altar he stealthily slew unwatchful Sychaeus.
Long he concealed the deed, and, imagining many a pretext,
Basely deceived and encouraged the hope of his heart-
   broken sister.
But in her slumbers the spirit itself of her husband unburied
Came, and uplifting a face of strange and unnatural pallor,
Showed her the blood-stained shrine, and his breast trans-
   fixed by the dagger,
Plainly disclosing the secret disgrace of her home and her
   brother.
Then he adjured her to hasten her flight, and escape from
   the country,
Telling of treasure long hid in the earth, to aid her depar-
   ture,
Gold unreckoned in weight, and silver unmeasured in val-
   ue.
Dido, alarmed by the dream, made ready her flight and her
   comrades;
Gathered all those to her side who detested the merciless ty-
   rant,
All who were moved by fear. Then, a vessel that chanced in
   the harbor
Seizing, they freighted with gold, and sordid Pygmalion's
   treasure
Floated away on the sea; —and this was the deed of a woman!
Down to this place they came, where soon you will see the
   majestic
Walls and rising towers of the new-born city of Carthage.
Next they purchased a site, called Byrsa because of their
   bargain;

> Only so much could be bought as their wit could surround
> by a bull's hide.

Virgil, *Aeneid* 1.157-1.170, 1.335-1.368

It was unfortunate that the Phoenicians did not preserve for us their own writings. What we have is simply the stories written by their adversaries—in this case written by the Romans against whom they fought the Punic Wars. Some of the elements in this tale were certainly factual, such as the king of Tyre being Pygmalion who reigned from 820 to 772 BC. That was the same time that Carthage was founded. But he came to that throne at eleven years of age. Could a young teenager do all the things portrayed in this tale? Yet it made an entertaining story when it was written, more than five hundred years after the event.

Meanwhile, a storm was brewing to the east of the Phoenician cities of Tyre, Sidon, Beirut and Byblos. It was coming at them from the land of Assyria. That slowly growing power in Mesopotamia had first come into being around 1900 BC after the fall of the old empire of Sumer and Akkad. At that time, Babylon had risen to prominence in the southern part of the old empire and Assyria arose in the north. Originally a confederation of the cities of Ashur, Nineveh and Arbel on the Tigris River, Assyria then began to acquire local lands but was blocked by the Hittites from marching westward. With the coming of the Sea Peoples, that obstacle was removed. As a result, the Assyrian king Tiglath-Pileser I successfully led his army to the Mediterranean around 1100 BC. There he received gifts from the Phoenicians at Arwad. After that, he returned to his own lands and nothing more was heard from him.

Many generations later, another strong Assyrian leader, Ashur-nasirpal II, turned his attention away from internal fighting in Mesopotamia long enough to make a campaign west to the sea in 870 BC. Once there he received lavish gifts from the Phoenicians, as did his son when he came to the throne two years later. After those two incursions, the Assyrians mounted campaigns in other directions and were no more trouble to the people of Lebanon.

A hundred years later, however, it was a different matter altogether. Tiglath-Pileser III ascended the Assyrian throne and immediately sent out his armies to annex more lands to his kingdom. By 738 BC he had won large parts of Syria, including the northern coast above Byblos. Arwad was taken, but subsequently received a degree of autonomy. The Phoenician cities from Byblos to Tyre were required to pay tribute to the Assyrians, and the nearby kingdoms of Damascus and Israel were compelled to do the same.

Though Tyre and the other Phoenician cities kept their self-government and a fair amount of independence from Assyria, they were heavily taxed and required to pay massive tribute. This serious-

Fig. 76   Phoenician gifts to Ashurnasirpal II included these two monkeys

ly reduced the rich quality of their lifestyle. But to be fair, they still were left with more than most of the people of their day. When the Egyptians had done this to the Phoenicians almost eight hundred years earlier, it was the first time they had experienced it. At that time they had no idea how to remedy the situation. As a result their cities suffered patiently for three hundred years under that foreign overlordship before a loose alliance with the Sea Peoples brought them freedom once more. Though they were slow to learn the first time, they were quick to apply it when the heavy Assyrian hand was laid upon them.

The moment Tiglath-Pileser turned his attention to his northeastern boundaries, the Phoenicians formed an alliance with Damascus and Israel to jointly oppose the invader. The Hebrews had two kingdoms at this time: the northern being Israel and the southern being Judah. Tiglath-Pileser was outraged at this rebellion and returned with a vengeance. He swiftly retook Arwad. After that proof of his determination, the king of Tyre, Hiram II, sued for peace on behalf of all the Phoenician cities. After he paid the Assyrian king a rich quantity of tribute, Hiram and his cities received a pardon. Damascus was not as fortunate and was directly annexed into the Assyrian kingdom. Within ten years, the kingdom of Israel was also absorbed into Assyria.

The Phoenicians received favored treatment from the Assyrians in this regard because they managed to keep themselves valuable to their powerful neighbors through their sea-borne trade. The subtle message was that their many mysterious sources had to be worked by Phoenician hands; for without those hands, the eastern empire's much-desired participation in this wealth-building process would disappear. This well-practiced persuasion had been used on many others before the Assyrians and had been developed into an art form. Not too surprisingly, more latitude was granted to the Phoenicians by the Assyrians and other powers throughout history than was accorded to their neighbors.

Having tried alliance and rebellion and been unsuccessful, the Phoenicians now bided their time and plied their trade actively. This work lined their own pockets in addition to those of the Assyrians—thereby justifying the leniency with which they were treated. But the Phoenicians had not given up.

Thirty years later, when the Assyrian king Sennacherib imposed more frequent demands for tribute, King Luli of Tyre did not comply and the Assyrians invaded the coastal land belonging to Tyre. When Luli fled to Cyprus, Sennacherib was satisfied. What happened next showed that he, like many others in antiquity, had no understanding of the strength of the bond between the Phoenician people regardless of the city in which they lived. The Phoenician principle of maintaining a degree of secrecy over their internal affairs was rewarded in difficult situations like these. Sennacherib punished Tyre by awarding all their mainland properties to a Phoenician in Sidon named Ithobaal who had shown himself to be an admirer of the Assyrians, and arranged for the man to be declared king of Sidon.

By the time Sennacherib died, Sidon was led by a new king, Abdi-Milkuti. The young Sidonian seized this opportunity to form an alliance between the Phoenicians and the Cilicians, then announced the rejection of Assyrian rule. Many outsiders were shocked. But it was not a surprise to anyone who knew that the Phoenicians were ruled by their councils, whose members served at the will of the people. Their choice for Ithobaal's successor would necessarily have been someone who reflected the desires of the Phoenician people. The Assyrians could have overridden their choice by force, but that does not seem to have happened in this case.

Unfortunately the new Assyrian king Esarhaddon proved to be a capable general, and he attacked Sidon in 677 BC. The Phoenicians resorted to their usual response—given that they were not military people and could not hope to successfully defend a city on the mainland—and evacuated by sea what people and wealth they could manage. Shortly thereafter Esarhaddon overran the city, tore down its walls, took what booty was there, and deported the remaining population.

His next action was a tribute to how much the people of those times valued the Phoenicians' skills and wealth-making ability. Despite all that had happened, the Assyrian king now attempted to befriend Tyre by giving it all of Sidon's southern lands.

Following the consistent Phoenician policy toward Assyria, Tyre immediately formed a new alliance to evict the occupiers and recover the rest of Sidon. It was joined in this by the kingdom of Judah, many Syrian cities, Cyprus and Egypt. Esarhaddon countered this by attacking and defeating Egypt. He then occupied the Lebanese mainland opposite the island of Tyre. The king of that city sued for peace and paid the excessive demands for tribute. After that Tyre was—quite remarkably—allowed to maintain its independence. Sidon remained in the possession of the Assyrians for a while, but the other Phoenician cities, including Byblos and Arwad, kept their independence as well.

To give some appreciation for how committed the Phoenicians were to their desire to be free of foreign oversight, consider that when the next Assyrian king came to the throne the Lebanese people once again allied themselves with Egypt and rebelled. And once more, the Assyrian king defeated Egypt. He then turned to face Tyre, which again chose to capitulate to the armed forces on its mainland. This was, however, Assyria's last campaign to the Mediterranean. It would soon fall victim to the new Babylonian empire which was rising in Mesopotamia.

When that event occurred, the Phoenicians took advantage and recovered Sidon, restored that city's culture, and returned it to prosperity as an active trading center. Lebanon was free again.

Yet even during all those years of domination by an outside power in Lebanon, the Phoenicians' world kept moving steadily ahead. The international trade at their Mediterranean outposts—many of which were now becoming actual cities—continued to thrive. And all of this had been kept largely invisible to the Assyrians. Only the small amount of goods that actually touched Lebanese ports was seen and taxed.

Yet all those cities owed a tithe that was paid to Tyre for the benefit of all the Phoenicians in Lebanon. This payment was kept "off the books" and not taxed because of the device shown earlier at Byblos. Incoming payments were called a religious tithe and were paid to the temple of Melqart at Tyre. By coincidence, the king of Tyre was the high priest of this temple. By further coincidence, the name Melqart in Phoenician meant "king of the city." But neither the Assyrians nor any other oppressor on the land ever figured out this riddle. The only one who might have seen through it was Alexander the Great. This temple of Melqart on the island of Tyre was the one he insisted upon visiting. It was the one that would have contained all of Tyre's records and gold payments. Rather than allow him to "pray" in the temple, they let him besiege the city—with dire consequences. Such was the value of the contents of this temple. But that was all in the future.

In addition to the trade coursing through their foreign outposts, commerce in the Lebanese cities also remained quite high during these days despite the Assyrian attacks from time to time. In fact, the Phoenicians used this trade to build a feeling of mutual support with their local partners, who became their allies in attempting to oust the Assyrians. In the lull after the Assyrian hold on Lebanon was broken, trade and prosperity multiplied.

Unfortunately, their erstwhile allies in Egypt seemed to take advantage of the power vacuum by stepping in and making demands which infringed on the well-known Phoenician privacy and secrets. Around 605 BC, pharaoh Necho II was working on an ambitious canal to link the Mediterranean Sea with the Red Sea. To do this, he had crews digging eastward from the Nile toward the Suez area of the Red Sea. When advisors told him that the canal was in serious danger of being taken over and used by the growing military power of Persia, he gave it up. And then the pharaoh urgently looked for some other way to improve his trade routes between the seas.

He knew the Phoenicians were sailing out of the Mediterranean and down the Atlantic coast of Africa. And he seemed to believe they knew more than they were telling about a possible southern route around Africa. So he ordered them to take a handful of his officers on a voyage around the African continent. If successful, he could not only turn the route to his own profit, but also achieve his original goal of linking trade between the Red Sea and the Mediterranean. This was how Herodotus described that voyage.

> As for Libya [Africa], we know it to be washed on all sides by the sea, except where it is attached to Asia. This discovery was first made by [Necho], the Egyptian king, who on desisting from the canal which he had begun between the Nile and the Arabian [Suez] Gulf, sent to sea a number of ships manned by Phoenicians, with orders to make for the Pillars of Hercules, and return to Egypt through them, and by the Mediterranean. The Phoenicians took their departure from Egypt by way of the

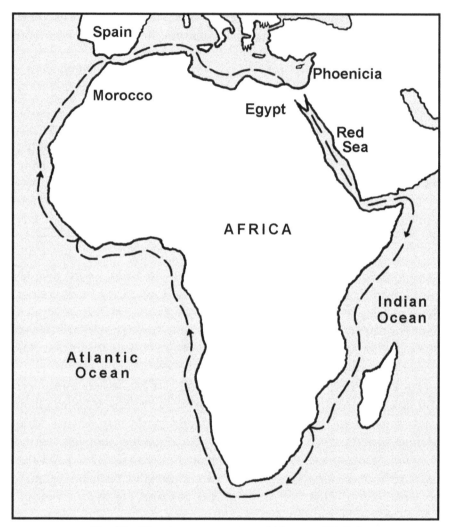

Fig. 77   The circumnavigation of Africa in 600 BC

Erythraean [Red] Sea, and so sailed into the southern
ocean. When autumn came, they went ashore, wherever
they might happen to be, and having sown a tract of land
with corn, waited until the grain was fit to cut. Having
reaped it, they again set sail; and thus it came to pass
that two whole years went by, and it was not till the
third year that they doubled the Pillars of Hercules, and
made good their voyage home. On their return, they de-

clared—I for my part do not believe them, but perhaps others may—that in sailing round Libya they had the sun upon their right hand. In this way was the extent of Libya first discovered.

Herodotus 4:42

This voyage took so long to complete that the Egyptians lost interest and never pursued it further. In fact, no one other than the Phoenicians ever completed the circumnavigation again until Vasco da Gama in 1497 AD—over two thousand years later.

The Phoenician voyage was such an amazing accomplishment that many said they did not believe it. Yet in his account, Herodotus gave clear proof that it was true. It was not proof to the people of that age but it is to us, with the benefit of modern geography. It is based on the simple fact that, although the sun moved slightly north and south of the equator as the seasons changed, it never went farther north than a line called the Tropic of Cancer. All of the Mediterranean Sea and its surrounding population centers were north of the Tropic of Cancer. This meant that no matter what the season, the midday sun was always in the south. Herodotus and all Egyptians knew that a ship going east to west in the Mediterranean would have the sun only on its left side every day. The ship that circumnavigated Africa was also traveling from east to west—*yet it had the sun on its right side*. We know today that this was only possible if the ship had passed south of the Tropic of Cancer and south of the equator—which it would have had to do on a successful circumnavigation.

Should such an accomplishment have been surprising to us? The Phoenicians had been sailing to Lixis on the Atlantic coast of Africa—and beyond on trading ventures—for about five hundred years by the time this circumnavigation was reported. And the record of the voyage noted no terrible deaths due to scurvy or malnutrition, nor a ship torn by reefs or battered by rocks. It was the kind of uneventful voyage made by sailors when they were familiar with a route.

And note that the Egyptians did not abandon this route because of any difficulty in doing it. The trip simply took too long. It was reported on this trip that the Phoenicians stopped each Egyptian autumn—springtime south of the equator—to plant food and wait several months for it to grow. On all their other reported voyages, the

Phoenicians foraged for food or traded with natives for it, and then
went on their way. This voyage seemed to be purposefully made
much longer than necessary by stopping to plant crops and, if so, it
had the desired effect. The Egyptians and others stayed home
thereafter. And the Phoenicians retained the African seas as their
private domain.

In 604 BC, the Babylonians finally came west under the able leadership of Nebuchadnezzar II. There they received tribute from the
former Assyrian "protectorates," including the Phoenicians. Being
equally as impressed with the new overseers as they were with the
old, the Phoenician people again formed alliances with Judah and a
number of Syrian cities and promptly rebelled. Nebuchadnezzar
responded by destroying Jerusalem and beginning his famous
thirteen-year siege of Tyre. This island city, well supplied by boats
coming to their seaward side, had never fallen to a foreign attacker
and did not fall this time. The Babylonians held the mainland shore
that faced the island, but this time the people of Tyre decided to wait
them out. When Nebuchadnezzar finally wearied of the futile effort,
he allowed Tyre to keep its independence. The foreign king retired
with a payment of tribute as compensation and face-saving grace.

The short-lived Babylonian empire did not much outlive Nebuchadnezzar. In 539 BC, it fell to the Persians under Cyrus the Great.
The Phoenician people, never giving up, once again tried their
traditional approach to dealing with a neighboring land power. They
offered Cyrus rich gifts and cooperation.[71] This time they met with
much better success. While the Assyrians and Babylonians had been
domineering and sometimes brutal, the Persians seemed to immediately understand the value of the people they found in Lebanon.
They were being offered the services of a great sea power—which
they realized was of immense value to an ambitious and distant land
power such as themselves.

So it was that the Phoenicians and Persians came to enjoy a relationship in which they were essentially partners—though one of
them was clearly the senior partner. This would prove to be of
tremendous value for the Phoenician people in Lebanon, as well as
for their daughter city at Carthage.

Yet these cumulative intrusions from the East were beginning to force the sea-traders' city in North Africa to take on greater responsibility for the quickly growing Phoenician empire overseas.

CHAPTER 18

A GRECIAN SPRINGTIME

Much had happened to the people of Carthage while their brethren chafed in Lebanon under the rough hands of the Assyrians and Babylonians. The strong infusion of population and wealth Elissa's people had brought onto the North African coast allowed Carthage to take over as the main gathering point for the Phoenicians' western Mediterranean trade headed east. In so doing, its people immediately benefited from the trade routes already bringing gold, silver and other valuable commodities from Spain, Morocco and the Atlantic coast. They also acquired the key trade route northward to the most significant land-based power in the region, the Etruscans of north-central Italy.

The Etruscans had arrived on the Italian peninsula perhaps a hundred years before the founding of Carthage, and rapidly spread over the region from the Arno river in the north to the Tiber in the south. Below the Tiber was a scattering of Latin villages down the coast, there being no Rome at the time. Where the Etruscans came from is not known exactly, other than that they brought with them a well-developed civilization with Greek attributes. Sculpture, painting and artistic expression were prominent in the cities they created. Yet they also had a strong military orientation, which enabled them to dominate the surrounding villages.

They put the rustic local people to work on Etruscan estates doing the farming, shepherding, weaving and other manual tasks. This in turn freed the Etruscans to develop the culture and arts that they manifested. The cities they formed were initially independent and each was ruled by its own king. However they soon banded together into a confederation of cities for mutual protection and for forming pacts with others. Almost from its inception, Carthage created trade agreements with the Etruscans which were apparently quite profitable for both parties. This relationship between the Etruscans and Phoenicians remained warm for many years.

Shortly thereafter, a Latin village near the Tiber began to grow. It would eventually become known as the city of Rome. Its legendary founding date was 753 BC on the low hills beside the river, and it would mature over the centuries to become the great and powerful capital of a widespread empire. But in these early days it was a village growing in the shadow of the Etruscans and absorbing aspects of those well-established people's culture and civilization.

Carthage's other main trade initiative during the eighth century BC was to Spain. In addition to long-established Cadiz on the Atlantic coast, they now added a series of trading cities along Spain's southern coast which faced the Mediterranean. These included Cero del Villar, Toscanos, Almeria and a growing Malaga, each of which had an attractive pair of attributes. They were located near rivers that gave access to the interior of the Iberian peninsula for trade, and they had fertile agricultural land which produced an abundance of food and other crops.

The creation of settlements in these places—and the expanding of buildings at Cadiz into larger and more permanent structures of stone—reflected a significant shift away from traditional Phoenician practices and toward the more land-based orientation of Carthage. The emphasis on permanent land settlements and the attendant need for higher food production echoed the same issues that caused the original exodus to North Africa. The people of Carthage wanted to be a land power as well as a sea power. And for better or worse, that orientation would continue to shape all of their actions.

A significant port-of-call came into being about this time just off the Spanish coast: the trading post on the island of Ibiza. It stood exactly astride the approach to Spain from Sardinia and, like that island, offered an excellent rest stop on the long voyage from east to west. Originally called *'ybsm* in Phoenician, which meant "isle of balsam," it was named after the fragrant trees which covered the island. But besides being an ideal place to recover from long sea voyages, Ibiza played another key role as well.

As an island, it was protected from the risk of land-based raids against the coastal outposts. While relations with the indigenous Iberian people were quite good overall, occasional outbreaks from the wilder interior of this vast land could never be ruled out. So Ibiza became a place of safekeeping for goods being traded in the region, and gradually took on a significant role for servicing trading ships from all over this part of the Mediterranean.

Crossing the Strait of Gibraltar to Morocco, it could be seen that the trading posts at Lixis and Tangier were also becoming better established on the land at this point. And Sala in the south (modern-day Rabat), was doing particularly well serving as a steppingstone to another colony 250 miles farther south at Mogador (today's Essaoui-ra). This last outpost was an island strategically placed to collect trade from farther down the coast. It also would have served as the supply point for any trips to the large Canary Islands, which lay farther offshore. Those islands became famous many years later

Fig. 78   Ancient site of Sala, Morocco

when Columbus and others used them as the jumping-off point for voyages to the New World. But in the eighth century BC this *was* the New World and the Phoenicians were exploring and developing it with a great deal of energy.

Returning to the Strait of Gibraltar and continuing eastward along the coast of Africa, they added another outpost at Melilla on the Mediterranean side of Morocco. Further east in what is now known as Algeria they established colonies at Les Andalouses, Rachgoun and Icosium—which was later called Algiers. Near Carthage, the coastline of Tunisia eventually became dotted with many more settlements.

Yet it was directly northeast of Carthage, on the island of Sicily, where the great tug-of-war for mastery of the central Mediterranean was about to begin. It was a gut-wrenching and strenuous procession of events which would eventually decide the fate of many countries and peoples, including the Phoenicians. It all began innocently enough.

The newly rejuvenated Greek cities emerging from the Hellenistic dark age had become so successful and prosperous that their populations were overflowing the city walls. Rather than simply expand outside those walls into the difficult, rocky countryside which often surrounded them, many individuals chose to gather large groups of fellow citizens around them and relocate to new settlements where the soil was rich and opportunities were greater. The older cities sponsored them on condition that some of their new resources be sent back to the home city as repayment for the colonizing effort, or simply as trade. The colonies thus generated began to spread across the Aegean islands and to the western coast of Anatolia. They also spread across the Greek mainland itself, and eventually to the east coast of Italy and Sicily.

When the Greeks arrived at Sicily, however, they found the Phoenicians well established and holding outposts all around the island. The sea-traders were peacefully engaged in active trade with the Sicilians who lived on the coasts and in the interior. The Greeks, however, soon made it clear that they had no intention of living quietly alongside the locals. They proceeded to take the land needed for their colonies by force of arms. The Phoenicians simply withdrew

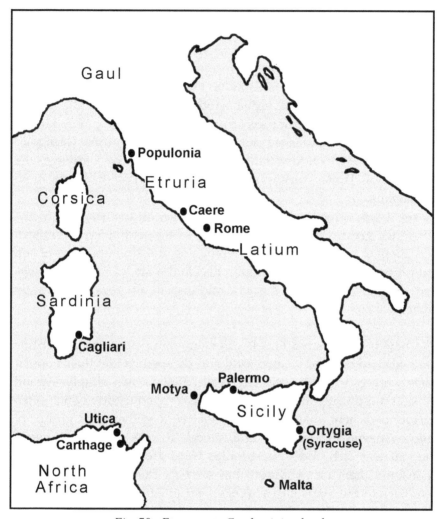

Fig. 79   Etruscan to Carthaginian lands

from eastern Sicily in the face of the overwhelming numbers of arriving Greeks. They even gave up the island of Ortygia, which appeared to be their trading center on Sicily. After being acquired by Greek colonists, this port went on to greater glory as the city of Syracuse. The Sicilians, unlike the Phoenicians, were well versed in warfare and were defending their homeland. They fought, and had to be driven out by force.

In his famous work *The History of the Peloponnesian War,* Greek historian Thucydides recounted these events for us in some detail. After describing earlier migrations of people onto Sicily, he then related:

> There were also Phoenicians living all round Sicily, who had occupied promontories upon the sea coasts and the islets adjacent for the purpose of trading with the Sicels. But when the Hellenes [Greeks] began to arrive in considerable numbers by sea, the Phoenicians abandoned most of their stations, and took up their abode in Motye, Soloeis, and Panormus, near the Elymi [local people], with whom they united, confiding in their alliance, and also because this is the nearest point for the voyage between Carthage and Sicily.
>
> These were the barbarians in Sicily, settled as I have said. Of the Hellenes, the first to arrive were Chalcidians from Euboea with Thucles, their founder. They founded Naxos and built the altar to Apollo Archegetes, which now stands outside the town, and upon which the deputies for the games sacrifice before sailing from Sicily. Syracuse was founded the year afterwards by Archias, one of the Heraclids from Corinth, who began by driving out the Sicels from the island upon which the inner city now stands. . . .
>
> Thucydides 6:2-3

Historical and archaeological evidence bears out these ancient observations, giving the founding of Naxos as 734 BC and Syracuse as 733 BC. The city of Motya—founded by the Phoenicians as their new center on western Sicily after being driven out of Ortygia—has been placed in the neighborhood of 720 BC. The port town of Panormus, which was also started by the Phoenicians at this time, has come down to us with the better-known name of Palermo.

The most important end result of this populous relocation of Greeks to Sicily was that the Phoenicians were now face-to-face with the people who were heirs to the Mycenaeans—the ones who had driven the Phoenicians from Crete and ended the Minoan society. But this time the Phoenicians did not leave the island. While they yielded the eastern half to Greek colonists for the moment, they dug in and resolved to hold the western half, postponing a final resolution until a later date.

They took this new tack because the Phoenicians' interests in Sicily were now represented by the people of Carthage. These were the same people whose insistence upon landed estates had driven them to create their colony in North Africa, and whose first act on arrival had been to settle on a defensible hill that they could hold against any attackers. This new approach was vastly different from the one which had guided their society for over 2,400 years at that point.

Prior to these events on Sicily, Phoenician cities had occasionally put up resistance when attacked—but their main recourse was inevitably the use of gifts-and-negotiation, or temporary withdrawal by sea from the afflicted city. The goal was always to save the people and the society. The houses and buildings of the city were left to be taken and burned by the invaders. Then after the invaders departed, the homes and buildings were rapidly rebuilt—because the people and their resources had always survived. Historians and other observers were often in awe at how quickly a destroyed Phoenician city sprang back to life. Now it is evident how and why that happened.[72]

But the people of Carthage were changing the rules. Though they still abided by most of the Phoenician traditions—especially as related to sea trade—their emphasis on holding land and fighting to defend it was new. This deviation was small at first. They did, after all, go along with the withdrawal from Sicily's east coast to other parts of that island before digging in. But it was a deviation which would widen over time.

The most immediate response to this Greek entry into the Phoenician-held middle of the Mediterranean was a new emphasis on permanent Phoenician colonies at every place where their interests were involved. Efforts were redoubled to develop colonies across the southern coast of Europe, which reportedly included a settlement made as a joint venture with the Gauls in France where the city of Marseilles would one day stand. The Phoenicians also quickly embedded additional settlements along the north coast of Africa. But the most visible and closest point of prolific expansion was on the neighboring island of Sardinia.

The long-standing Phoenician outposts at Nora and Cagliari near the southern tip of the island—and the harbor on the isle of Sulci just off the southwestern coast—were now reinforced. They were also joined by a plethora of new settlements across the whole southern half of the island.[73] Over the next hundred years, this colonization spread not just along the shores but also deep into the interior. The Phoenicians left no room for easy incursions onto this key island which lay between Sicily and Spain—not by the Greeks or anyone else.

This strong focus on acquiring land was not the only way in which the people of Carthage began to modify the long-standing Phoenician practices. Since the earliest days, each member of Phoenician society had a say in the governing of his or her city and in the trade it conducted. They did through their representatives on the city councils, the king who was chosen to lead the city, and the large meetings of all the people when appropriate and necessary. Carthage kept alive this principle of equality and government by the people, but added its own variations.

This Phoenician approach to governing, which allowed people to manage their own affairs, was highly unusual in the ancient world. This was especially true during the centuries before Greece and Rome rose to prominence—a time when lands were usually taken by force and thereafter ruled by kings having absolute power. It was so unusual that the Greek philosopher Aristotle held up the constitution of Carthage as a model of good governance. In the course of doing so, he gave us a wonderfully detailed look inside this part of Phoenician society and the Phoenician way of life, as we see here:

> The Carthaginians are also considered to have an excellent form of government, which differs from that of any other state in several respects, though it is in some [respects] very like the [Spartan]. Indeed, all three states— the [Spartan], the Cretan, and the Carthaginian—nearly resemble one another, and are very different from any others. Many of the Carthaginian institutions are excel-

lent. The superiority of their constitution is proved by
the fact that, although containing an element of democracy, it has been lasting; the Carthaginians have never
had any rebellion worth speaking of, and have never
been under the rule of a tyrant.

Among the points in which the Carthaginian constitution resembles the [Spartan] are the following: The common tables of the clubs answer to the Spartan *phiditia*,
and their magistracy of the 104 to the Ephors; but,
whereas the Ephors are any chance persons, the magis-
trates of the Carthaginians are elected according to mer-
it—this is an improvement. They have also their kings
and their *gerousia*, or council of elders, who correspond
to the kings and elders of Sparta. Their kings, unlike the
Spartan, are not always of the same family, whatever
that may happen to be, but if there is some distinguished
family they are selected out of it and not appointed by
seniority—this is far better. Such officers have great
power, and therefore, if they are persons of little worth,
do a great deal of harm, and they have already done
harm at [Sparta].

Most of the defects or deviations from the perfect
state, for which the Carthaginian constitution would be
censured, apply equally to all the forms of government
which we have mentioned. But of the deflections from
aristocracy and constitutional government, some incline
more to democracy and some to oligarchy. The kings and
elders, if unanimous, may determine whether they will
or will not bring a matter before the people, but when
they are not unanimous, the people may decide whether
or not the matter shall be brought forward. And whatever the kings and elders bring before the people is not only heard but also determined by them, and any one who
likes may oppose it; now this is not permitted in Sparta
and Crete.

Aristotle
The Politics 2:11.1-6

From what we now know about the involvement of the Phoenicians on Crete, it should come as no surprise that the people of that island continued to govern themselves according to the same principles practiced by the Phoenicians. Very soon in these pages we will see why Sparta went this way as well.

Carthage meanwhile also carried on another Phoenician tradition—exploration and the renewal of trade routes. Being located on the northern coast of Africa, the people of this city naturally had significant interest in that continent and the wealth it produced. Following their circumnavigation of Africa in 605 BC with Egyptian passengers on board, the Phoenicians now made additional explorations going in the opposite direction. Within fifty years of the earlier voyage, Hanno set out from Carthage to found several additional colonies on the Moroccan coast. He then continued down the western shore of Africa until he either reached the region of Gabon or circumnavigated the continent by coming up its eastern side to the Red Sea. While the Phoenicians clearly sailed the Atlantic coast of Africa many times over the years, this trip was made memorable by the fact that a summary of the trip was placed in one of Carthage's temples in public view.

The cautionary part of this narrative which needs to be pointed out is that the Phoenicians virtually *never* allowed any of their documents to fall into the hands of outsiders. The few bits of information that they did allow others to receive were usually along the lines of horrific tales of what would happen to anyone who should venture outside the Pillars of Hercules. This disinformation was clearly designed to keep outsiders away from the lucrative trade routes that the Phoenicians maintained in the Atlantic Ocean.

Careful analysis of Hanno's report on his voyage immediately reveals many inaccuracies that an even halfway responsible account would not have had. Its many references to country of fire and streams of fire also sound more like the disinformation accounts that were purposefully put out for people to see. Yet it also contains the first known description of gorillas, so it does have some value.

The Voyage of Hanno, commander of the Carthaginians, round the parts of Libya [Africa] beyond the Pillars of

Hercules [Strait of Gibraltar], which he deposited in the temple of Saturn [Baal Shamem].

It was decreed by the Carthaginians, that Hanno should undertake a voyage beyond the Pillars of Hercules, and found Liby-Phoenician cities. He sailed accordingly with sixty ships of fifty oars each, and a body of men and women to the number of thirty thousand, and provisions and other necessaries.

When we had passed the Pillars on our voyage, and had sailed beyond them for two days, we founded the first city, which we named Thymiaterium. Below it lay an extensive plain. Proceeding thence towards the west, we came to Soloeis, a promontory of Libya, a place thickly covered with trees, where we erected a temple to Neptune; and again proceeded for the space of half a day towards the east, until we arrived at a lake lying not far from the sea, and filled with abundance of large reeds. Here elephants, and a great number of other wild beasts, were feeding.

Having passed the lake about a day's sail, we founded cities near the sea, called Cariconticos, and Gytte, and Acra, and Melitta, and Arambys. Thence we came to the great river Lixus, which flows from Libya. On its banks the Lixitae, a shepherd tribe, were feeding flocks, amongst whom we continued some time on friendly terms. [Note the Phoenician city of Lixis, hundreds of years old by that time, whose remains are still visible today, was not mentioned. That might have made the land seem too safe.] Beyond the Lixitae dwelt the inhospitable Ethiopians, who pasture a wild country intersected by large mountains, from which they say the river Lixus flows. In the neighbourhood of the mountains lived the Troglodytae, men of various appearances, whom the Lixitae described as swifter in running than horses.

Having procured interpreters from them, we coasted along a desert country towards the south two days. Thence we proceeded towards the east the course of a day. Here we found in a recess of a certain bay a small island, containing a circle of five stadia, where we settled a colony, and called it Cerne. We judged from our voyage that this place lay in a direct line with Carthage; for the length of our voyage from Carthage to the Pillars was equal to that from the Pillars to Cerne.

We then came to a lake, which we reached by sailing up a large river called Chretes. This lake had three islands, larger than Cerne; from which proceeding a day's sail, we came to the extremity of the lake, that was overhung by large mountains, inhabited by savage men, clothed in skins of wild beasts, who drove us away by throwing stones, and hindered us from landing. Sailing thence we came to another river, that was large and broad, and full of crocodiles and river horses; whence returning back we came again to Cerne.

Thence we sailed towards the south twelve days, coasting the shore, the whole of which is inhabited by Ethiopians, who would not wait our approach, but fled from us. Their language was not intelligible even to the Lixitae, who were with us. Towards the last day we approached some large mountains covered with trees, the wood of which was sweet-scented and variegated. Having sailed by these mountains for two days, we came to an immense opening of the sea; on each side of which, towards the continent, was a plain; from which we saw by night fire arising at intervals in all directions, either more or less.

Having taken in water there, we sailed forwards five days near the land, until we came to a large bay, which our interpreters informed us was called the Western Horn. In this was a large island, and in the island a saltwater lake, and in this another island, where, when we had landed, we could discover nothing in the day-time except trees; but in the night we saw many fires burning, and heard the sound of pipes, cymbals, drums, and confused shouts. We were then afraid, and our diviners ordered us to abandon the island. Sailing quickly away thence we passed a country burning with fires and perfumes; and streams of fire supplied from it fell into the sea. The country was impassable on account of the heat. We sailed quickly thence, being much terrified; and passing on for four days, we discovered at night a country full of fire. In the middle was a lofty fire, larger than the rest, which seemed to touch the stars. When day came we discovered it to be a large hill, called the Chariot of the Gods. On the third day after our departure thence, having sailed by those streams of fire, we arrived at a bay called the Southern Horn; at the bottom of which lay an island like the former, having a lake, and in this lake another island, full of savage people, the greater part of whom were women, whose bodies were hairy, and whom our interpreters called Gorillae. Though we pursued the men we could not seize any of them; but all fled from us, escaping over the precipices, and defending themselves with stones. Three women were however taken; but they attacked their conductors with their teeth and hands, and could not be prevailed upon to accompany us. Having killed them, we flayed them, and brought their skins with us to Carthage. We did not sail farther on, our provisions failing us.[74]

> From: *Historical researches into the politics, intercourse and trade of the Carthaginians, Ethiopians, and Egyptians*

Pliny the Elder was a Roman author who seemed to have access to additional information about Hanno's journey. He stated that the voyage was not cut short (as suggested in the public account above) but actually went much farther. Since he criticized several other stories related to Hanno's trip as being false, he apparently felt the following statement to be well supported because he presented it as fact rather than dismissing it as he had done with the others.

> When the power of Carthage flourished, Hanno sailed round from Cádiz to the extremity of Arabia, and published a memoir of his voyage, as did Himilco when he

was dispatched at the same date to explore the outer coasts of Europe.

Pliny the Elder
Natural History 2.169a

As Pliny noted, another voyage of exploration was led by a man named Himilco at approximately this same time. Himilco sailed into the Atlantic Ocean as his compatriot had done, but then turned northward. Although the original report written by Himilco has been lost, portions of it are referred to by others, including the Roman author Rufus Festus Avienus. Even more so than in Hanno's account, this northern report seemed to convey wildly inaccurate information and a litany of terrible afflictions in the Atlantic. They were said to have been without wind. Seaweed impeded movement. There were sandbars. There was fog. Even monsters! All these things suggest that Himilco's report fell deeply into the category of disinformation released to the public to keep competitors out of the ocean's realm.

In the real world, the Phoenicians had many colonies on the Atlantic coast of Morocco, Spain and even Portugal for hundreds of years by the time these documents were written. On a regular basis their merchants sailed between these ports and brought huge quantities of silver, gold, tin and other goods into the Mediterranean from those lands and beyond. That their desire for privacy and competitive advantage should keep them from revealing these things—and instead to report monsters and perilous hazards—is actually quite reasonable.

The Greeks were also going through significant changes at this time, just like the Phoenicians. On the Peloponnesus in the southern part of Greece, the city of Sparta overflowed its city walls and annexed lands belonging to its neighbor, Messenia. This provided the people of Sparta with fertile fields and much-needed food. It also gave them a large number of unhappy people from Messenia living under their dominion. When those people revolted in 640 BC, the Spartans were faced with a severe crisis that they barely survived. Their path out of this predicament was to create their famed military state. In some ways they now came to reflect the Phoenician form of governance in that all members of the society were part of the city's business.

Unfortunately, in this case the business was war. Nevertheless they all shared in the profits of war, and each had a say in the city's major decisions.

The Spartans, as it turned out, were exceptionally good at fighting battles. Having found their calling, they began to attack and conquer their surrounding neighbors with great success. They were helped in these campaigns by the lessons learned from their near-disaster at Messenia. It became their practice after each conquest to allow the defeated city to stay independent if they would accept an obligation to send soldiers and supplies when needed for future campaigns against others. Given the horrible conditions that usually followed the military defeat of a city in those days—including burning, rape, death, slavery, and grueling taxation—the Spartan conditions seemed outrageously generous. And they were universally accepted. The result was a vast number of allies who marched behind the Spartan banner. Sparta quickly became the major power in all of Greece.

About one hundred miles northeast of Sparta lay the small city of Athens. It was not particularly notable yet—simply a modestly prosperous trading center due to its olive oil production and a nearby harbor. A few powerful families ruled the city, while large numbers of common people suffered from poor farmland and crushing debt. This social and economic divide created a great deal of resentment and there was threatening talk of rebellion. The situation deteriorated until 594 BC, when the increasingly anxious aristocratic families finally turned over leadership of the city to a brilliant man named Solon. Under his leadership a series of much-needed reforms were launched. It took almost a hundred years for these reforms to eventually result in the Athenian democracy, but it did happen. It was this democracy that was famously passed down to us through the writings of many classical historians and philosophers.

This was also a time when Athens and other Greek cities began to make inroads into Egyptian trade. This cut into the rich flow of goods that the Phoenicians had maintained ever since the violent migration by the Sea Peoples had put it back into their hands. Even so, the Phoenician position in Egypt was fairly strong because the land of the Nile had long-since ceased to be a serious sea-going threat.

Having had many opportunities to take a stronger maritime role, the Egyptians had invariably dabbled for a while and then relied again upon the Phoenicians to do the hard daily work upon the seas. As a result, the Phoenicians became confident enough in their position that they began to set up dry-docks for ship repairs in the city of Memphis. Alongside these were warehouses, trading facilities and housing. In fact, a significant area in this city that was sometimes the capital of Egypt was designated as the Phoenician district. The prominent position of these sea-traders was well established.

Into this world then, came the Greeks. Through the use of influence and perhaps a few well-placed gifts, the Phoenicians managed to keep these encroachers away from Memphis and its key location at the head of the long river which wound through the rich interior of the land. So the Greeks had to satisfy themselves with a separate enclave in the delta at Naukratis. From that city their goods seeped into the huge market that was Egypt. It was a modest start, but they were in—and would stay in—from that day forward.

Returning to the Greek mainland, changes were seen there as well. While the many islands of the Aegean Sea were populated by Greek-speaking people, each isle seemed to have its own variety of Greek culture. The islands were also highly independent, with each acting as if it were a separate city-state—or island-state if they were too small to have a city.

However on the eastern side of the sea, along the coast of Anatolia, some of the city-states were losing their freedom and independence. This happened because a new power had arrived on the scene. The new-comer would aggravate and motivate Greece throughout its classical period, coloring its development of the arts against a backdrop of war. This power was Persia.

Due east of Greece—in in the mountains of Anatolia and what is today known as Iran—Cyrus the Great was transforming a small Persian kingdom into a great empire. He managed to accomplish this by shrewdly making a series of alliances when possible, and swift war when it was not. By aggressively following this policy, he quickly swept westward through what we know as Turkey until he came to the western end of Anatolia. There he found the kingdom of Lydia, which encompassed considerable land and a handful of islands in the Aegean. The kingdom was so prosperous that the name of its wealthy king, Croesus, has come down to us in the once-popular expression "rich as Croesus." Cyrus approached the Lydian king with his usual offer: Croesus could remain as king if he would put his lands into the Persian empire. When Croesus refused, it took only two weeks for the Persian army to sack the Lydian capital of Sardis and take the lands by force. With that war complete, the Persians possessed all of Anatolia and looked out across the Aegean Sea at the Greek islands and distant mainland.

For the moment, however, Cyrus had gone as far west as he wanted to go. Now he turned his attention to a rival power much closer to home: the mighty and well-established Babylonians. Those warlike people held all of the lands to the south of his new Persian empire, including dominion over the Phoenician cities and all the lands from Egypt to Mesopotamia. Despite the vast size and entrenched position of his adversary, Cyrus was able to march victoriously into the city of Babylon in 539 BC.

This astounding victory by the Persians had the unwitting effect of setting free the Phoenician cities and all the other people of the eastern Mediterranean lands. Given this breath of fresh air for the first time in several hundred years, the Phoenicians took a moment to enjoy it. Then they turned their attention back to the west.

In the middle of the Mediterranean Sea, a new power was growing on the Italian peninsula. The city of Rome, which lay just to the south of the Etruscans' domain, had been increasing its size and power by gradually bringing together thirty Latin clans. It was ruled by a king in those days, but Rome also had a weak Senate made up of clan leaders, and an Assembly in which all male citizens participated.

In the sixth century BC, as Rome grew through conquest and recruitment, it provoked serious concern among the Etruscans about the city's intentions. To allay their fears, the Etruscans sent an army south and simply took over the growing city and its surrounding lands. They placed an Etruscan on the throne at Rome, and that is where matters rested for the next fifty years. This might have been the end of Rome's independence and ambitions except for an unfortunate but historically significant event which happened in 509 BC. A son of the Etruscan king who governed Rome raped a woman named Lucretia. That act was especially incendiary because she belonged to one of Rome's leading families. The outraged populace immediately took to the streets, threw out the Etruscan king, and regained their independence.

Still bitter over their experience with kings, the Romans did not go back to their monarchy. Instead they created what they called a republic. The Senate and Assembly remained, and each year they elected two consuls who exercised the power of the former kings. With this, Rome had almost all of the essentials it would need to grow into the classical imperium that was its future. It lacked only one thing: the riches of trade to fuel its growth.

To emerge from the Etruscan shadow in this regard, the Romans negotiated a treaty with Carthage in the same year they formally became a republic: 509 BC.[75] Carthage was the major broker of sea trade in the region, as reflected in their long-standing treaties with

Fig. 80   Phoenician gold and silver bowl found in Italy

the Etruscans. As a sign of the economic strength of the metropolitan city in North Africa compared to the younger Italian city, Rome had to agree not to trade with Sicily or Sardinia—leaving those to Carthage—in order to win access to a share of the remaining rich flow of Italian trade.

Significantly, this treaty was signed not only by Rome and Carthage, but also by Tyre as the senior authority among the Phoenicians. Some people have conjectured that Carthage was completely independent of the other Phoenician cities at this time or—even more astonishingly—that it might have come to dominate the cities in Lebanon. As this treaty and other events clearly show, however, neither of those conditions occurred. The cities in Lebanon and those overseas remained part of the larger Phoenician society.

In fact, the Phoenicians were busy establishing a beneficial relationship with the rising power in the East as well—the king of Persia.

CHAPTER 19

FLOWERS UPON THE BATTLEFIELD

After his great victory over the Babylonians, Persian king Cyrus declared all the lands of that empire to be his. But he also took special notice of the generous presents bestowed upon him by the Phoenicians. In return for those things freely given, and for the accompanying pledges of cooperation, he allowed these sea-traders to pursue their own affairs. And pursue them they did. Other than setting aside a piece of property for Persian representatives, the Phoenician cities purged themselves of unwanted signs of foreign rule. They built warehouses to handle the rapidly increasing trade, and the influence of their cities spread out farther into the hinterland of Lebanon.

The king of Tyre judiciously continued to disguise the rich flow of incoming foreign profits as tithes to his temple of Melqart. And to further protect that flow from outsiders' prying eyes, the city of Sidon was offered as the focal point for all contacts with the Persians. To sweeten that offer, a great parkland was created at Sidon, with luxurious villas for the use of Persian officials.

Right away the Phoenician cities of Arwad and Sidon benefited from the Persians' control of Anatolia and the eastern Aegean because it vastly increased their sea-trade routes to those areas. Trade with Cyprus and Egypt remained difficult, however, due to Greek competition. Direct trade with the Greek mainland was especially challenging because those cities continued their persistent struggle to capture pieces of sea commerce from what the Phoenicians already held. In contrast with this, the routes to Carthage and beyond were open and clear. So considerable resources were poured into increasing this pipeline—to the great benefit of the people in Lebanon and their colonies around the Mediterranean.

When Cyrus' son Cambyses came to the Persian throne and announced his intention of bringing Egypt into his empire, the king of Sidon—on behalf of all the Phoenicians—astutely offered to help him with a vast number of ships. This not only earned the trust and respect of the Persian ruler, it enabled him to sweep to victory in Egypt.

Heady with the euphoria of his triumph, Cambyses declared his intention of continuing westward to attack Carthage. This immediately placed the Phoenicians in an extremely difficult position. Putting their newly forged partnership on the line, the Phoenicians refused.[76]

They told the Persian king they could not attack this city they had created—and with which they had strong mutual obligations. It was a measure of the true depth of this new relationship between these two countries that Cambyses yielded and canceled his planned campaign against Carthage. Most hot-blooded conquerors would have sent demands and a fierce army to the shore opposite Tyre, but the Persians were more enlightened, and it served them well. There were many other campaigns they wanted to wage, and now they had the respect and unstinting support of the Phoenicians for what lay ahead.

The Persians also wanted to assure themselves of an ongoing supply of Lebanese cedar for their palaces and temples. This, in turn, led to a momentous change for the Phoenician people. The Bekaa Valley had long reverberated with the sound of marching feet as armies went north and south on their many campaigns of conquest. Canaanites, Amorites, Hittites, Egyptians, Mitanni—the list went on, seemingly without end. But the Phoenicians had no army of their own, and did not participate in those deadly games. They were content to control the forested lands from the Lebanon Mountains to the sea. Yet now the Persians had done what the Phoenicians could not do—they conquered and held the Bekaa Valley against all challengers. This

Fig. 81   Lebanese Coast and the Bekaa Valley

expanse of land between the Lebanon and Anti-Lebanon Mountains
(the eastern range that separated the valley from the desert beyond)
was largely a place of farms and villages, but that was not what the
Persians desired.

They wanted the tall, straight and fragrant cedars which grew on
the mountainsides. And they wanted as many of them as they could

get. To satisfy this need, they apparently gave control of this wide valley to the Phoenicians with the stipulation that large quantities of this timber be harvested from the Lebanon Mountains. These logs were then brought down to the Bekaa Valley and carried by river and slipchutes northward to a place where portage to the Euphrates River could be accomplished. From there, the logs were floated downriver to Babylon and other cities for the greater glory of the Persian king.

And so it was done. During the years that followed, vast amounts of lumber came down the mountain slopes to the valley and made their way north, to the enrichment of all involved. But something else happened also. Intermarriage between the Phoenicians and local people of Canaanite-Sea People heritage began to create a new community in the valley. In time the society of the local villages became indistinguishable from the larger Phoenician community. They joined in the logging of cedars and other woods on both ranges of the Lebanon Mountains and sent the valuable timber off for trade. With the prosperity this brought, the villages became large towns, with Zahlé, Baalbek and others beginning to thrive. As a result, a larger Lebanon came into being. This was the Lebanon whose borders would remain almost identical down to the present day. Despite the comings and goings of kings and rulers, these borders have endured for 2,500 years.

Several years after the conquest of Egypt, a new Persian king ascended the throne. This was Darius the Great, who quickly recognized the value of Egypt and his partnership with the Phoenicians. When he heard of the earlier project by pharaoh Necho to build a canal from the Nile River to the Red Sea, he resolved to continue the project. This would open a valuable sea route from Persia directly to the Mediterranean and connect the two ends of his empire. To accomplish this monumental task, he seems to have turned to the people who had an unparalleled reputation for maritime projects—the Phoenicians.

Their combination of seamanship and stone-working skills had proven to be extremely useful when building the Phoenicians' celebrated two-harbor ports and other projects involving waterways. As we have seen, the Phoenicians had come into possession of this stone-working ability in a natural and straightforward manner. Their friendship with the original people on Malta exposed them to large temples made of carefully cut stones placed almost seamlessly beside each other. The Phoenicians then supplied the Egyptians while this craft was taken to an even higher level. It was a highly educational experience. Thereafter, the Phoenicians were masters of breakwaters, canals and harborworks utilizing their abilities with ashlar stones.

When his canal from the Nile to the Red Sea was complete, Darius erected a series of red granite markers along the path to celebrate this remarkable accomplishment. The canal was then opened to shipboard commerce and was used for hundreds of years. Over two thousand years later, the Suez Canal was built to serve this same essential function, though it followed a more northerly route to the Mediterranean.

After that event, trade and relations settled into a comfortable status quo until 498 BC, when Athens made an exceedingly ill-advised move. One of its fellow Greek city-states in Anatolia was living under Persian rule, and now made an appeal for help. Gallantly and recklessly, Athens joined with other allies to launch a quick strike. With twenty ships transporting soldiers, they captured the city of Sardis which was home to the Persians' regional government. The other Greek cities in Anatolia celebrated and joined the rebellion. For some reason, Athens then decided its job was done and withdrew its military force. The Persian king regrouped his troops, called upon the Phoenicians for naval support, and swiftly retook control of the region. But that was not enough to satisfy his anger. Athens had stung him and would have to pay.

So in 490 BC, Darius sent an army of retribution to the Greek mainland with orders to march on Athens. These events began what the Greeks would call the Persian Wars.

Darius' invading troops landed safely on the shore, but to get to Athens they had to pass through Marathon. Here the Greeks met them in an epic battle upon which it could be reasonably said the future of their civilization depended. Had they lost, it is entirely possible that classical Greece and the Hellenic Golden Age would never have come into being. But on that particular day the Greeks prevailed, and Phidippides was said to have run twenty-six miles to Athens to deliver word of the great victory, dying after he delivered the joyful news. For the people of Athens, this battle of Marathon became their defining moment. From that day forward, they seemed to see themselves as the center of Greek culture and power, and acted on that belief.

Noting the success of its twenty ships in the raid on Sardis, Athens began to invest heavily in warships against the day of the Persians' expected return. Through this effort they eventually amassed an imposing fleet of two hundred vessels.

Nine years after Marathon, the next Persian king, Xerxes, gathered a great army and set out to complete the work of his predecessor. He fielded a daunting land force of over 150,000 soldiers. It was accompanied by over six hundred ships drawn from the Phoenicians, Cyprus and Cilicia, all serving under the direction of the Phoenician Admiral Tetamnestros. The Greeks pulled themselves together under the leadership of Sparta—still the greatest land power in Greece—with supporting roles being played by Corinth and Athens.

Great valor was shown by the Greeks, including a stand by three hundred Spartans at the pass of Thermopylae which seriously delayed the invading army. Even so, the Persians eventually marched into Athens and burned the ancient wooden buildings on the Acropolis. However in a naval battle at the island of Salamis just outside the port of Athens, the Greeks managed to sustain a victory in waters familiar to them. The Persian forces lost two hundred ships while the Athenians lost only forty.

This in itself would not have been a significant problem since the Persians had many more ships than the Greeks and could afford the loss. But Xerxes blundered by executing a number of Phoenician captains as scapegoats—whereupon all the Phoenician ships set sail for home followed by many of the others. This left the Persians without the necessary sea support. Chagrined, Xerxes was forced to withdraw his army to the city of Sardis in Anatolia, leaving only a small force at Plataea, one of the captured Greek cities. When the Spartans subsequently overran Plataea, the second wave of the Persian Wars was over.

But not all of the altercations were taking place in the Aegean. To the west, the confrontation that began when Greek settlers evicted Phoenician traders from the eastern half of Sicily continued to cause friction. The leaders of Carthage, intent on protecting their lands in Sicily, formed a land army for the first time in Phoenician history. By 550 BC, General Mago had led this force into action on Sicily and

Sardinia. In 520 BC, a land campaign was launched against the Greek city of Acragas, now known as Agrigento on the south coast of Sicily, in retaliation for claimed aggressions. To the Phoenicians in Lebanon, this action by their daughter city was shocking. For 2,700 years they had lived by their firm set of principles, and one of the strongest was the peaceful resolution of differences. They had never employed force through a military campaign. Over the years these principles had made them wealthy and enabled them to survive—even when empires around them crumbled into dust. Yet here was Carthage on the precipice of land war.

In 480 BC, a decisive moment came when Carthage's reliance upon military actions was put to the test. Just as the Persian army under

Fig. 82   Sites of Carthage's campaigns in Sicily

Xerxes was invading the Greek mainland, Carthage struck the Greek cities on Sicily. Whether the two moves were coordinated was hard to say. At the very least it made sense for Carthage to choose that moment for action because the local cities could not count on help from Athens or Sparta. And this was a *major* campaign.

The Carthaginian general Hamilcar, a descendant of Mago, assembled a land army of 300,000 men from all of the western colonies: from North Africa, Morocco, Spain, Gaul, Sardinia and Sicily.[77] The troops flooded in by sea to the Phoenician city of Palermo in northwestern Sicily and began their march. Syracuse and the other Greek cities raised a lesser but still significant force and girded for war. The two combatants met head-to-head at Himera where a fateful battle was fought. Despite the immense size of Hamilcar's army, Carthage's relative lack of military training and experience showed through, and the war was lost.[78]

The minority of people in Carthage who had argued in favor of the old traditions and against the war now carried the day. The city's flirtation with generals was ended, at least for a while. The status quo in Sicily was left alone, with a Greek east and a Phoenician west. Carthage humbly rejoined the rest of the Phoenicians in taking as their main priority the increasing of trade and prosperity for their people.

While addressing unusual practices at Carthage, some mention should be made about the ongoing debate surrounding child sacrifice. Several classical sources such as Diodorus and Cleitarchus asserted child sacrifice occurred at Carthage. And some burial sites, called *tophets* have been found in which the bodies of pre-natal and newborn children were found. They had apparently been burned and placed in urns alongside stone tablets with prayers to the gods. So an argument could be made that the unsavory charge was supported.

But a number of facts have come to light which cast doubt on that assertion.

Among these, we see the practice of child sacrifice was first documented in the Hebrew Tanakh, also known as the Old Testament. It acknowledged that some Israelites and Canaanites in the Topheth area of Jerusalem caused children to "pass through the fire," which has been interpreted as meaning child sacrifice. The Israelites tried to outlaw this practice, but it would not go away. That writing was the source of the name "tophet." And this same source even associated Abraham with the practice of human sacrifice, because he set out one day to offer up his son Isaac as a sign of his loyalty to God.

> Then he reached out his hand and took the knife to slay his son. But the angel of the Lord called out to him from heaven, "Abraham! Abraham!"
>
>   "Here I am," he replied.
>
>   "Do not lay a hand on the boy," he said. "Do not do anything to him. Now I know that you fear God, because

you have not withheld from me your son, your only son."

Abraham looked up and there in a thicket he saw a ram caught by its horns. He went over and took the ram and sacrificed it as a burnt offering instead of his son.

Genesis 22:10-13

Over the years, allegations of child sacrifice have been made against ancient Egyptians, Greeks, Romans and Phoenicians as well as the Israelites. So it would seem likely that a small number of individuals in almost all the societies of those days engaged in that practice. But only the Phoenicians have been singled out for blame as if this were some major part of their religion. Why?

Jeffrey H. Schwartz led an international team of researchers who examined in detail the contents of burial urns from the tophet at Carthage. They published their findings in 2010 and noted, among other things, that the ancient accusers belonged to societies harboring anti-Carthaginian leanings. But the primary thrust of this team's work was scientific in nature. While there was no way to determine which of the young-child burials might have been from sacrifice or natural causes, the quantity of burials appeared to be consistent with normal infant mortality rates in those days. Other findings in their report showed:

> Two types of cemeteries occur at Punic Carthage and other Carthaginian settlements: one centrally situated housing the remains of older children through adults, and another at the periphery of the settlement (the "Tophet") yielding small urns containing the cremated skeletal remains of very young animals and humans....
>
> Here we present the first rigorous analysis of the largest sample of cremated human skeletal remains (348 burial urns, N=540 individuals) from the Carthaginian Tophet....
>
> In sum, while the Carthaginians may occasionally have practiced human sacrifice, as did other circum-Mediterranean societies, our analyses do not support the

contention that all humans interred in the Tophet had been sacrificed. Rather, it would appear that the Carthaginian Tophet, and by extension Tophets at Carthaginian settlements in general, were cemeteries for the remains of human prenates and infants who died from a variety of causes and [were] then cremated....[79]

A second team of experts led by Patricia Smith studied the same group of urns from Carthage. But they arrived at the completely opposite conclusion.

The recent article on the Carthage Tophet infants by Schwartz et al. (2012) takes issue with our paper (Smith et al. 2011) that claims the Carthaginians practiced infant sacrifice. Both studies were carried out on the same sample of cremated infant remains excavated by the ASOR Punic project between 1975 and 1980 (Stager 1982). We examined the contents of 334 urns while Schwartz et al. (2012) examined the same sample plus an additional fourteen urns (N = 348). We differed, however, in our conclusions regarding the age distribution of the infants and the extent to which it supported or refuted claims that Tophet infants were sacrificed. This note explains why we think that Schwartz et al. (2012) erred in their age assessments and introduces additional evidence to show that the age distribution of the Tophet infants supports our contention of infant sacrifice.[80]

Despite their disagreements, both teams mentioned many lambs and other small animals were also buried in the tophet. Smith et al believed that if the animals were sacrificed, then the children there must have been sacrificed as well.

So, is that reasonable? Consider that in the present day, owners of pets suffering infirmity or painful disease sometimes choose to have the animal put down. Yet there are no widespread reports of parents having their suffering children put down. The two are not treated in the same manner.

The other team drew no major conclusion from the presence of animals in the tophet.

Stepping back from those differences of opinion, what if the truth lies somewhere between the two opposite camps? If child sacrifice was a small practice in many societies at that time, then it would be reasonable to say it was practiced to at least a modest degree among Carthaginians also. On the other hand, if infants were not being buried among adults, those who died of infant-mortality diseases had to be buried somewhere—which is to say, in the tophet. That would tend to support the non-sacrifice argument.

But judging from inscriptions on the many stone steles, something else was happening as well. Those inscriptions suggest it was a relatively common practice at that time to offer a prayer to the gods for something really important—and to pledge the life of one's next child if the prayer was granted. Just as in the case of Abraham, the promise of a parent to sacrifice a loved one showed how deeply committed they were to the matter at hand. If the desperate prayer was answered and their child died before birth or from normal infant mortality, the parent was off the hook. The remains were sent to the tophet, a stele was placed, and they had honored their pledge.

But if their child lived, they had a problem. Even so, there was a way out. They could follow the example of Abraham and find a lamb or other animal to sacrifice instead of their child.[81] Then the animal would be buried with full ceremony and stone stele. If that were the case, it would reconcile the unusual combination of findings discovered in these ancient tophets.

Even so, that pattern of social practice is only a possibility.

As we can see from the two respected teams who studied the same tophet samples and came up with opposite conclusions, more facts and evidence are needed before any conclusive finding on child sacrifice can be made.

On the distant coast of Lebanon, the city of Sidon was going through its own struggles trying to find its place in the world. It was Sidon to which Persian officials had been drawn, and the local leaders attempted to present an impressive face on behalf of the Phoenician people. As a result, the families of Sidon began to engage in a much more ostentatious display of wealth than in other Phoenician cities,

Fig. 83   Gold mask from Sidon

even though it could be argued that Tyre had the more crucial role in generating trade.

Throughout this time the Phoenicians viewed themselves as voluntary participants in the Persian empire. It was generally understood that if they did not offer their cooperation, they would almost certainly be compelled by force to give it; but having come forward on their own made that a moot point. And membership had its privileges. The Persians seemed intent upon beating back the Greeks, and whatever they achieved in this regard benefited the Phoenician traders. Instead of losing more markets to the encroaching Greeks, they were winning back some that had been lost. So, as was their custom, the Phoenician people welcomed the Persians and adopted visible signs of commonality with them.

Nowhere was this more evident than at Sidon with its extensive parkland—called a paradise by the Persians—and grand residences for the Persian representatives. Displays of opulence in the city may in some ways have been mirroring the Persian court, which would make it more understandable—if not still highly unusual—among the Phoenicians. Gold coinage was produced at Sidon; and while the other cities produced coinage also, only Sidon struck the largest and most prestigious unit of currency: the double stater.

Fig. 84   Temple of Eshmoun and temple of Our Lady

This city was now also a center for exquisite glassworks, which became famous all around the Mediterranean. Among its most popular creations were small glass bottles of incredibly pure clarity that had a wide variety of colors and shapes. These were often used to hold perfumes, unguents, cosmetics and exotic oils of great value. Besides the royal-purple cloth and objects of gold and silver, these glassworks held a highly respected place in the trade goods of Lebanese merchants.

Just outside of Sidon a beautiful temple complex was built about this time dedicated to Eshmoun, one of the names by which the male consort of Our Lady was known. On the grounds of the complex there was a temple to Our Lady directly beside the one to Eshmoun. The empty throne where she would sit is clearly visible today. Eshmoun was believed to have been a healer, and this whole collection of buildings and facilities was interlaced with water channels and wash basins much as one might expect in a health spa. When visitors washed here in the presence of Eshmoun, it was said that great cures were sometimes wrought. The Greek god of healing and medical arts, Asklepios, was often associated with him. In fact temples similar to this one were later dedicated to healing and to Asklepios all across Greece in the fourth century BC. The temple of Eshmoun near Sidon remained a place of pilgrimage for almost nine hundred years.

The Greek people, meanwhile, were not resting on their laurels. With the Persians still holding a commanding presence in Anatolia, they knew it would be only a matter of time before the confrontation with that foreign power erupted again. Fresh in the minds of Greeks living on all the islands spread across the Aegean was that Sparta had commanded their combined forces in the recent fighting and was a great land power. But on the other hand, it was the naval victory achieved by Athens that had saved the day. And as island dwellers they needed protection by sea, not by land. So at a meeting held on the island of Delos, they asked Athens to lead their newly formed Delian League and protect them from the Persians. This league soon included most of the Greek islands and a number of mainland cities.

Each of the members of the Delian League paid annual commitments to support this work. Athens, as their leader, spent most of these funds on enhancing the navy. It also sponsored highly selective raids on individual Greek islands and cities still held by the Persians, with the optimistic objective of setting them free. Surprisingly enough, this chipping away at the solid Persian presence was quite successful—mainly due to Xerxes being preoccupied with more critical problems in other parts of his vast empire. And so it was that by 467 BC, Athens and the Delian League had freed almost all of the Greek islands and cities along the coast of Anatolia.

Six years later a charismatic leader named Pericles was chosen to lead Athens. Under his guidance the Golden Age of Greece came into full flower. At peace for the time being—and having no war with Persia on which to spend the annual contributions of Delian League members—Pericles redirected the rich flow of funds to the arts. He spent freely in and around Athens for almost any endeavor that would bring greater glory to Greece and especially to Athens.

Since the Persians had destroyed the old temple and defenses atop the Acropolis, he had a clean slate with which to work. A magnificent statue of Athena, the patron goddess of the city, was created by Phidias, the greatest sculptor of the day. The goddess was housed in a beautiful temple known as the Parthenon, which was built at this time on the most prominent part of the Acropolis.

Fig. 85 The Parthenon

The theater of Dionysius at the foot of the sloping hillside below the Acropolis was the site of regular competitions where classical playwrights Aeschylus, Sophocles and Euripides created and presented their greatest works. The esteemed philosopher Socrates practiced his craft and presented his dialogues to students in the Agoura and to wealthy patrons at dinners in the best private homes of the city. His student Plato carried on the master's work and added creations of his own at his Academy in the outlying part of Athens.

The "father of history," Herodotus, was believed to have lived in the city for several years at this time before emigrating to the Athenian colony of Thurii and writing his seminal work *The Histories*. Thucydides lived most of his life in Athens during these heady, creative days and wrote his *History of the Peloponnesian War* amidst its bustling society.

Meanwhile Sparta, ever the leading land power in Greece, became jealous of these glories with which Athens covered itself. It also harbored suspicions regarding the expanding circle of alliances the Athenians were making. In response to these "provocations" Sparta launched the First Peloponnesian War against that city. In the beginning of this internecine struggle, Athens had the upper hand. However the city of classics stubbed its toe when it endured a disastrous defeat in Egypt fighting the Persians, who still enjoyed the benefit of strong Phoenician support. The Athenian navy was decimated, and that proud city had no choice but to sue for peace with Sparta and the Persians. Both of those pacts were arranged by 449 BC.

Over the next thirty-four years, the Greeks continued to be alternately at peace and at war with each other. This did not significantly affect outsiders until Athens decided to attack the Greek cities in Sicily, attempting to bring them under its control. That proved to be a disaster, with most of the Athenian navy being destroyed in the harbor of Syracuse and its army was captured on the coast. Athens had rendered itself seriously weak by this Greek-against-Greek enterprise, and its adversaries immediately took advantage.

The Persian king made an alliance with Sparta, promising its new ally support from the Phoenician fleets. Still, when Sparta attacked, the Athenians managed to eke out some early victories. But after the rest of its navy was destroyed in 405 BC, Athens was eventually starved out of its resistance and forced to surrender. Sparta tore down the walls of Athens, and the Golden Age was over.

What happened next foreshadowed events that would seriously impact the Mediterranean world several decades later, though it seemed innocent enough at the time. Sparta entered into a conspiracy with Cyrus, the brother of the Persian king, to place him on the throne of Persia. The conspirators' combined forces carried them from victory to victory. Their march went from Anatolia all the way to Mesopotamia. When Cyrus unexpectedly died in battle, the

Spartans were left with no claim to the throne, and so they withdrew. But they had shown that the Persians could be taken, and how to do it. The lesson would not be lost on a young king who would soon come to power in Greek Macedonia: Alexander the Great.

In the inevitable cycle of reprisals that seemed to ensnare those who fought wars in these times, the Persians carried the battle to Sparta a few years later. As also often happened, the Greeks were fighting amongst themselves again. As a result Sparta was unable to mount a complete defense against the renewed attack. The Persians, almost certainly with the Phoenician fleets in the vanguard, shredded and sank the Spartans' vessels and their remnants of sea power.

From that time onward the Greeks descended into more internal fighting, and ceased to be a significant factor in the Mediterranean for many years. Their loss was the Phoenicians' gain. The unlimited bounty of sea trade the people of Lebanon had enjoyed before the emergence of the Greeks seemed to be theirs once more. This left only one obstacle in their way: the Persians.

Though their relationship with the eastern empire had been mostly cordial during the 145 years of its existence, Persia was still a foreign power that had to be paid huge sums each year to keep those relations cordial. And then there was the burning memory of Phoenician captains being executed by the Persians after losing the naval battle of Salamis to the Greeks. This illustrated clearly what the Persians seemed to feel was their right—and the Phoenicians' place. And having Persians on Lebanese soil was a constant reminder that local actions could be vetoed at any time. This relationship was no substitute for complete independence.

In addition, the Persians no longer seemed to be the invincible power they once were. Internal fights for succession to the Persian throne had almost become institutionalized. A long series of assassinations and revolts accompanied those changes. Egypt had revolted successfully against Persian rule and now stood outside the empire, free again. It was a powerful image of what could be.

When the Persians launched a campaign in 373 BC to retake Egypt, they requested the usual support of the Phoenician fleets. The support was given, but so half-heartedly that it had the desired effect of frustrating the Persian advance. After many delays off the Egyptian coast, the Persians finally withdrew.

Turning the tables, the Egyptian pharaoh Tachos decided to go on the offensive and take advantage of the Persians' apparent weakness. He quickly gained the overt support of the Greek city-states and the covert support of the Phoenicians led by Abdashtart, the king of Sidon. The Phoenician king could make no public declaration to that effect since there were still Persian troops posted in his city, so all was done quietly. The Egyptian campaign into Phoenician territory seemed to be the beginning of a bright new day—when dark clouds of circumstance ruined it.

Internal dissention among the Egyptians led to a sudden scuttling of the campaign. Tachos, already on Phoenician soil, was given shelter by Abdashtart in Sidon. This harboring of an enemy of the empire was a brazen challenge to the Persian king's authority and did not go unnoticed. Even though the pharaoh ultimately "defected" to the Persians and ended the standoff, the Persians were not mollified. Sidon was immediately occupied by a larger number of Persian troops, and the Phoenicians' "independence" was revoked. They were placed under the Persian governor of Syria and Cilicia.

Four years later, the Phoenician autonomy was re-instituted. This was a clear recognition of the great importance placed by Persians on the Lebanese sea trade and navy. But in return they demanded that a new king, favorable to Persian interests, sit on the throne at Sidon. Their preferred candidate was a man named Tennes, who was subsequently given that position. The foreign troops also stayed. And the oversight by Persian officials seemed to become even more harsh and demanding than before.

Nor had the Persians given up on their ambitions toward Egypt. In 351 BC, they ordered the Phoenicians to prepare for another assault on that kingdom to the south, and now treated their former partners roughly, as if they were servants.

In Egypt the Persian army met with complete defeat. Encouraged by this sign of the empire's growing weakness, the Phoenicians went into revolt. They had formed a city in the north of Lebanon composed primarily of contingents from the cities of Tyre, Sidon and Arwad—and so it became known as Tripoli (three cities). Tripoli stood in a largely undeveloped area at the foot of the long Qadisha Valley, which extended far up the side of the Lebanon Mountains. This

Fig. 86 Qadisha Valley in the Lebanon Mountains

valley provided an excellent line of retreat to a place of safety in the event of attack.

Here the Phoenicians planned their revolt far from Persian eyes. When Egypt pledged its support to this rebellion, the formerly pro-Persian Tennes changed his allegiance and led an attack on the Persian officials in Sidon who had been oppressing the people there. Diodorus described how this happened.

> He [the Persian king] began to make war also on the Phoenicians for the following reasons. In Phoenicia there is an important city called Tripolis, whose name is appropriate to its nature, for there are in it three cities, at a distance of a stade from one another, and the names by which these are called are the city of the Aradians, of the Sidonians, and of the Tyrians. This city enjoys the highest repute amongst the cities of Phoenicia, for there, as it happens, the Phoenicians held their common council and deliberated on matters of supreme importance.
>
> Now since the King's satraps and generals dwelt in the city of the Sidonians and behaved in an outrageous

and high-handed fashion toward the Sidonians in ordering things to be done, the victims of this treatment, aggrieved by their insolence, decided to revolt from the Persians.

Having persuaded the rest of the Phoenicians to make a bid for their independence, they sent ambassadors to the Egyptian king Nectanebos, who was an enemy of the Persians, and after persuading him to accept them as allies they began to make preparations for the war.

Inasmuch as Sidon was distinguished for its wealth and its private citizens had amassed great riches from its shipping, many triremes were quickly outfitted and a multitude of mercenaries gathered, and, besides, arms, missiles, food, and all other materials useful in war were provided with dispatch.

The first hostile act was the cutting down and destroying of the royal park in which the Persian Kings were wont to take their recreation; the second was the burning of the fodder for the horses which had been stored up by the satraps for the war; last of all they arrested such Persians as had committed the acts of insolence and wreaked vengeance upon them.

Such was the beginning of the war with the Phoenicians, and Artaxerxes [the Persian king], being apprised of the rash acts of the insurgents, issued threatening warnings to all the Phoenicians and in particular to the people of Sidon.

Diodorus 16:41.1-6

It has been said that the "vengeance" wreaked upon the Persian officials was their summary execution. If so, this action would have been completely out of character for the Phoenicians—since it obviously destroyed any future negotiating position they might have wanted to take. There would need to have been some reason for it. As the tense confrontation with the Persians played out, it became apparent that the problem was Tennes, the completely unethical person who was made king of Sidon at the insistence of the Persians.

He would betray both sides before these dangerous events were done, and killing envoys was in line with his other actions.

Using Greek mercenaries hired for the purpose, the Phoenicians succeeded in beating back the first Persian attack. Given their peaceful, nonmilitary background, this was an accomplishment the Phoenicians could not have achieved without these highly skilled mercenaries. Hearing of this success, Cyprus likewise went into rebellion and declared its independence. But the joy did not last.

Realizing the immense size and still considerable power of their opponent, the people of Sidon prepared for the coming confrontation. Following the normal Phoenician practice when faced with imminent attack, they evacuated by ship as many members of their families and as much of their wealth as could reasonably be moved. Those who remained were physically able and personally willing to endure siege if necessary. Also remaining in the city were the non-Phoenician workers and slaves who lived there. It should be mentioned that slavery was a common practice in the Mediterranean at this time, and most of the people in this situation were from Europe and Asia, pressed into servitude by the frequent wars.

It was reported that the Phoenician population in Carthage saw an increase at this time. That would have been consistent with the removal of family members from Sidon.

The Persians, realizing they risked the loss of their entire western empire, gathered and marched to the Mediterranean coast a staggering force of 300,000 men. Tennes, once more the opportunist, switched sides again and betrayed Sidon in exchange for a personal pardon. That sealed the fate of the people remaining in the city. With the news of slain Persian officials and the embarrassing defeat of the previous imperial force still fresh in their minds, the Persians descended on the city with a fury unmatched in the 2,900 years of Phoenician history.

Six hundred of Sidon's leading citizens, coming forward with olive branches in their hands to negotiate, were killed outside the city gate. As the enraged army stormed through the city streets many were killed and fires were set. Diodorus believed the Sidonians burned themselves in their homes to avoid being taken. Anything was possible, but that would be so unlike the Phoenician philosophy of life and unlike anything they had done before, that it must be taken with a grain of salt. In any event more than forty thousand were reported to have died in this catastrophe. The surviving population was deported and sold into slavery. And despite having delivered the city, Tennes was executed. There were no winners.

The remaining Phoenician cities surrendered, and in 345 BC their independence was once more revoked. They were again placed under the governor of Syria and Cilicia. Their brief taste of complete freedom, the first in hundreds of years, was washed away by bitter bile from the battlefield. Nor was there to be peace thereafter. In a different land to the north another army was being gathered—and its heavy footsteps would soon be heard on the coastal road that led to Byblos and the other Phoenician cities.

CHAPTER 20

BY THE HAND OF ALEXANDER

When Sidon fell, Philip of Macedonia had been king of his provincial country in northern Greece for fourteen years. Showing much of the flair that his son, Alexander the Great, would exhibit later in life, Philip was a brilliant general and a great leader of men. He made peace with the wild European tribes to his north, and then turned south toward the center of Greece on a march of conquest. By 338 BC, he managed to take all of Greece except for Sparta at its southern tip. For all intents and purposes, he became the king of Greece as well as Macedonia.

Not satisfied with that significant accomplishment, Philip announced his next campaign: the conquest of Persia. When he suddenly died at the hand of an assassin, it appeared that his planned campaign would never happen. But he had left a worthy heir to follow him.

In the pivotal battle Philip had fought to win control of Greece—which took place at Chaeronea in Boeotia north of Athens—his eighteen-year-old son Alexander had led the cavalry charge that won the day. Three years later, after his father's sudden death, Alexander was ready, willing and able to take up his father's sword. He immediately declared his intention to launch the planned campaign against Persia. After making necessary preparations, he set out on his quest with a meager forty thousand men. The force was small because he had to leave much of his army to control the newly conquered and still restive Greek lands. In comparison with the massive armies that had seemingly become normal in those days, he was like David going forth with a slingshot.

Alexander crossed over into Persian-held Anatolia and secured a few small but sure victories, enough to gain some gold and supplies.

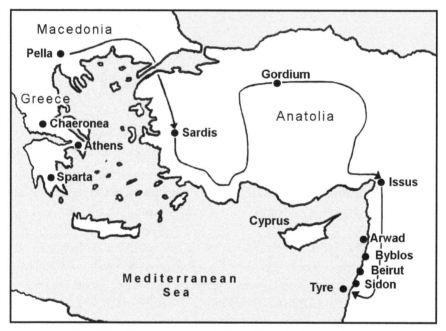

Fig. 87   Alexander's march from Macedonia to Lebanon

This also raised the morale and battle skills of his men, honing them into a weapon as sharp as their swords. With his momentum building, he moved faster and faster through Anatolia, sweeping all before him. The Persian king Darius III became aware of this small but fierce menace to his empire, and raised a force of his own. The Persian came westward with hundreds of thousands of fighting men—vastly outnumbering Alexander's meager army—and confronted the young Macedonian at Issus in Cilicia. This was the place where Anatolia touched Syria, at the northeast corner of the Mediterranean Sea. In this famous battle, Alexander brilliantly and bravely defeated Darius

Fig. 88 Alexander the Great

and his much larger force, sending them from the battlefield in a rout.

For now, Alexander let the fleeing king go. As a capable general he knew the eastern Mediterranean had to be won and securely held, or his back would not be protected when he charged inland. So he turned to face the two recognized powers along this Mediterranean coastline who were dangerous if left loose and valuable if held. These were the ships of the Phoenicians and the vast number of fighting men in Egypt. With that decided he celebrated the victory at Issus, refreshed his troops, and headed south along the coast toward Lebanon.

The Phoenicians no doubt received word of the Persian army's defeat with great deal of joy. Yet that elation changed to dread once it was realized that Alexander's direction was not east after the Persians, but south toward their own cities. Drawing from their past experience, a simple but sensible strategy was hastily put into effect.

The land-based Lebanese cities could not possibly survive an onslaught by Alexander's seemingly invincible army. So it was decided that those cities had to surrender to the advancing troops. That included the city of Sidon which—shortly after it was destroyed— had already sprung back to life with the return of its citizens and their portable wealth.

The goal was to have one Phoenician city remain free and independent. Then—after the army was past—figure out how to pull the other cities free also. There were two Phoenician island-cities, but to defend both would dangerously split their resources. Since Arwad had fallen before to hostile invaders, it was given up in surrender also.

That left Tyre free. In the more than two thousand years of its existence, the island-city of Tyre had never fallen. The powerful Assyrians besieged it for thirteen years and were unable to take it. Indomitable Tyre had ended each of the previous sieges by negotiation, in which they agreed to pay tribute and retained a large degree of freedom. The gamble now was that Alexander would be foiled by his youth and impatience. It was unimaginable that he could camp for thirteen years in front of Tyre in order to negotiate a settlement. He surely would become frustrated long before that and go away, leaving Tyre outside whatever empire he was intent upon creating.

Unfortunately, Alexander was not like other generals or kings.

He accepted the surrender of the other Phoenician cities along the coast, and came directly to Tyre. There the confrontation began in earnest. At first he could do nothing against the solid walls of the city, which rose high above the sea and stood a half-mile from the mainland shore. But he did not give up. Alexander had reaped a decent navy by taking the other Phoenician cities, which accomplished part of his goal. But if he walked away from Tyre, the city would be a gap in the back of his armor where he might be stabbed when he went after Darius. So he persisted.

In fact, he pressed the ship captains from the other cities into an extremely difficult position. He ordered them to blockade Tyre by sea while his troops attacked from shore. The captains did not really have a choice. The populations of their cities were held hostage, and the memory of what happened to Sidon at the hands of the Persians twelve years earlier was still fresh in their minds. So their blockade began. But it turned out to be quite porous and allowed necessary supplies to still get through for some reason.

The key element of Alexander's ingenious strategy at Tyre was to create a pier or causeway of stones and earth from the shore all the way across the half-mile of sea to the island. Yet the building of this structure was not only laborious, it was also lethal for many of the workers. Archers high on the walls of the city were able to pick off the men below with great ease. Attacks and counterattacks went on, but the work continued to move forward.

To be fair, this plan of attack was brilliant, but not all of Alexander's doing. He had been a good student in his early years and was taught by some of the best in Greece—including the great gatherer of knowledge, Aristotle. Nothing was too good for the son of a king. Among his lessons from those teachers and from his military-minded father must certainly have been the Greek victory at Motya.

On Sicily, where the Greek cities and Carthage's troops continued to attack each other in fits and starts over the years, the principal base for Carthage had become the island of Motya. That secure city was located just off the west coast of Sicily. No matter what battles were fought on the Sicilian countryside, Motya on its island was impregnable. But it had one weakness: a narrow causeway which ran from the mainland out to the island.

Knowing this, the Phoenicians destroyed the causeway when the Greeks approached. But the Greek general rebuilt the causeway and sent his troops storming across it to sack the city. This lesson had apparently not been lost on Alexander. He now stood before Tyre and brought forward a similar plan, hoping for the same result.

But the Phoenicians had also learned from the experience at Sicily. The walls of Tyre were said to be 150 feet high at their tallest point, and were incredibly thick. Even after Alexander arduously complet-

Fig. 89   The line of Alexander's causeway at Tyre

ed his causeway to the city, the solid walls held and the battle raged back and forth. The ongoing delay at this one city gave Alexander even more reasons to pull away and go about the business of creating his much desired empire. But he had never lost a battle to this point in his life and seemed grimly determined not to lose this one. He redoubled his efforts.

Finally, a weakness was found in the city walls, and the Macedonian soldiers poured in. It was said that during the siege, Greek negotiators had been sent by Alexander into the city, and in insolent defiance those men were thrown from the city walls to their death. It would have been extremely improbable for this to happen without any provocation. Not only was it completely out of character for Phoenicians to do such a thing, they also had the fresh memory of forty thousand people killed after a similar rash act at Sidon a dozen years earlier. Yet the Greek reports from this time say that it happened without provocation and no other version of this story survived the encounter.

After the Macedonians stormed the city, there was a grim reckoning. Because of those killings and because Tyre had put up resistance which delayed the young king, a total of eight thousand people were killed and thirty thousand were sold into slavery. In a show of generosity the rest were allowed to survive, and the city endured.[82]

In the past some historians thought the fact that other Phoenician cities were compelled by Alexander to join his siege of Tyre meant the cities had turned against each other. Now that we understand what happened, we see this was not the case. They put up appearances because they had no choice. How fiercely did the other cities attack Tyre? Quintus Curtius Rufus told us what happened when they stormed through the city's broken walls alongside the Macedonians.

> Young boys and girls had filled the temples, but the men all stood in the vestibules of their own homes ready to face the fury of their enemy.
>
> Many, however, found safety with the Sidonians among the Macedonian troops. Although these had entered the city with the conquerors, they remained aware that they were related to the Tyrians...and so they secret-

ly gave many of them protection and took them to their boats, on which they were hidden and transported to Sidon. Fifteen thousand were rescued from a violent death by such subterfuge.

Quintus Curtius Rufus
The History of Alexander 4.4

In any country, aiding the enemy during a battle would earn the death penalty. By their actions the people of Sidon revealed the strong ties of brotherhood that bound the Phoenicians.

But the die had been cast, and the game was lost. With this tragic event, Tyre and all the other Phoenician cities in Lebanon were now part of the Greek empire created by Alexander. The month of July in 332 BC was traditionally regarded as the end of the Phoenician society in the east, along with its trading empire in that part of the Mediterranean.

Soon we will return to the Phoenician people in Lebanon to see how they dealt with their reversal of fortune, for they still had more life in front of them. But for now let us look westward.

CHAPTER 21

CARTHAGE AT ITS HEIGHT

In contrast to those terrible events on the Lebanese shore, the Phoenician cities in North Africa, Sicily, Sardinia, Spain and Morocco were still free, and their trading empire still flourished.

In fact these were glory days for the people of Carthage. Their city had become even more important as troubles beset their fellow Phoenicians, and they were taking in many of the families exiled from Lebanon. The population of Carthage swelled to over half a million people. It became the largest city in the world.

Even so, they had once again been called away from their internal affairs when the town of Segesta in Sicily was attacked in 409 BC by the Greek city of Syracuse. Carthage quickly came to the aid of its small Sicilian ally, but this was not completely a mission of mercy. A faction within Carthage had been chafing for an opportunity to re-open the former campaign on that large, strategic island.

Once there in support of Segesta, Carthage's large army moved from defense to offense and took the Greek city of Selinus. (*See map of Sicily, Fig. 82*). After that it sacked Himera, the site of its former defeat. In reprisal for the loss of its general Hamilcar who had died in the earlier effort, three thousand were killed and the city was razed to the ground. One often hears of people who engage in violence being seduced by the dark side of human nature, and this unfortunate occurrence at Himera seemed a clear case of that coming to pass. The more success Carthage achieved with its army, the more it behaved like the other land forces of its day.

In three years' time, the young army managed to take all of Sicily except for Syracuse. That city had now grown large and prosperous, amassing perhaps 250,000 people inside and outside its walls. So it was not going to give up without a fight. In 397 BC, Syracuse counterattacked boldly, reaching all the way across Sicily to the west coast and attacking Carthage's island-city of Motya. This was the moment mentioned earlier when the Greeks successfully crossed a causeway to this strategic island and took it. That proved to be a turning point in the war. It was now Syracuse's turn to go on the offensive.

Twenty-three more years of battles back and forth finally resulted in a peace agreement that gave Carthage control of a significant amount of Sicily. It now held everything west of the Halycus river, with Syracuse retaining the remainder.

In the course of this war, Carthage gained more than some acres of real estate. All manner of beautiful artwork—especially marble sculptures—were appropriated from formerly Greek cities in Sicily and brought to adorn Carthage's public places. Despite their long adversarial relationship, the people of Carthage developed a deep appreciation for the masterful artistic ability of their Greek counterparts. This feeling of competition-but-appreciation seemed to spread throughout the Phoenician trading empire.

Unfortunately, there was little sign of that respect being returned. Although the Greeks had obtained from the Phoenicians the alphabet used for their much-lauded writing, along with rolls of papyrus on which to write it, and numerous other benefits to their society, any public display of Greek competition-but-appreciation for the Phoenicians was unfortunately rare.

As for trade voyages across the western reaches of the Mediterranean—from Sardinia to the lands beyond the Strait of Gibraltar—the waves belonged almost exclusively to the Phoenicians. Carthage led the cities scattered over this wide area, but a number of other ports also came into a degree of prominence and wealth as well. Palermo on Sicily seemed to have taken the lead after the fall of Motya. Cagliari on Sardinia presided over a large number of towns and metalworking centers scattered across the island. Ibiza had come into full flower as the major shipping center in the far western Mediterranean. Cadiz was a flourishing city growing in size and stature on the Atlantic coast of Spain. This city drew silver, gold and other riches from deep in the interior of Iberia, as well as from further up the Atlantic coast in lands that would one day be Portugal, France, England and Ireland. In Morocco no single city seemed to dominate all the others, but it was said that the Phoenicians planted "hundreds" of outposts far down the Atlantic coast of Africa. North Africa likewise became congested with small trading towns serving mighty Carthage and its patient understudy Utica.

While the Greek intrusion into these waters was small, it was nevertheless felt. This was especially true on the southern coast of France. The small Phoenician outpost near the mouth of the Rhone river had already been displaced by large numbers of Greek settlers and became a significant city by this time. This paved the way for Marseilles, which would one day surround that same harbor. Greek ships plying the waters between Sicily and Marseilles attempted to make inroads on the island of Sardinia several times, but were rebuffed by the Phoenicians living there. The Greeks also attempted to settle on the next island, Corsica, but were turned back by the Etruscans who controlled it, with naval support from their Phoenician allies.

This relationship between the Etruscans and Phoenicians remained strong throughout these tumultuous times. For hundreds of years Caere—the leading Etruscan city—along with Carthage and Syracuse had decided between them the outcome of major events in this region.

But in their midst a new power was rising. And that was the city of Rome.

While the relationship between Carthage and Syracuse was spelled out in a peace treaty made necessary by war, the Phoenician city's relationships with Caere and Rome were delineated in commercial trade treaties. Each of these trade agreements was formally negotiated and signed. As the strength and interests of the parties shifted, new agreements were reached. This avoided any need for armed conflict between them and assured the parties involved in each treaty that they would receive an uninterrupted flow of rich trade. This process had grown out of the Phoenician principles of

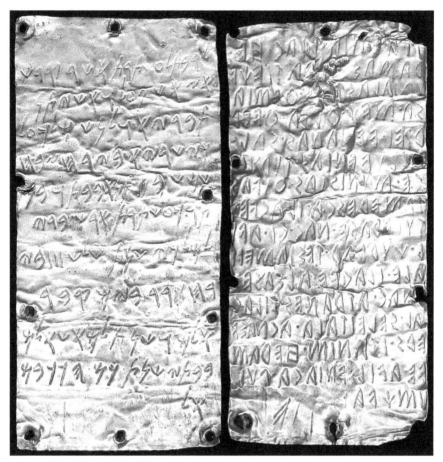

Fig. 90   Gold tablets containing the same dedicatory message in Phoenician (left) and Etruscan (right), found in Pyrgi, Italy, near Caere.

peaceful resolution of differences, creating strong partnerships, and pursuing international trade. It worked remarkably well.

In 348 BC, Carthage negotiated new trade treaties with Caere and Rome which acknowledged the fading strength of the Etruscans in favor of their growing southern neighbors at Rome. But Carthage still seemed to hold the stronger position in both cases.

The travails suffered by the Phoenicians in Lebanon were bittersweet for the people of Carthage. There was sympathy for the suffering there. Yet Carthage also benefited tremendously. When the Persians attacked Sidon in 345 BC, there was a surge of immigration to Carthage of highly capable seamen and traders who brought shiploads of gold, silver, jewelry, and other forms of wealth prudently removed from the city before it fell. The same events played out a dozen years later with Tyre. These dire tragedies in Lebanon were a boon for Carthage.

Throughout these extremely difficult times the Phoenicians in Carthage remained loyal to their larger society—not only by serving as a much-needed escape route but also by faithfully paying their full share of profits owed to Tyre each year. Even though it was bountifully obvious that the beleaguered city in Lebanon could not enforce the debt, it was paid anyway. In fact, ships from Carthage were said to have been approaching Tyre to deliver their annual tithe when Alexander sacked the city.

Tyre's disaster was not a complete surprise because Carthage had already absorbed many people from there as Alexander approached. Yet it was still hoped that the displacement was only temporary. In the case of Sidon, even with the brutal burning and butchering that occurred at the hands of the Persians twelve years earlier, most of the people and wealth had returned to rebuild that city.

For a long time, historians were surprised at how quickly Sidon was rebuilt. It was always assumed that this city was similar to almost all the others at that time: having treaties and relationships, but no one truly there for them in time of need. People also believed the picture Phoenicians presented to outsiders, in which they claimed to be small, separate cities and no danger to anyone. In reality we have seen many events where these cities were there for each other, as would happen in a true society.

In those days, when a city was burned to the ground it often just disappeared. A few were rebuilt, but that work was done by local people who had only scorched stones and farms as capital. Their restoration efforts might take them a century or more to achieve a return to prominence. Cities like Ugarit fell and never rose again.

But the destruction of any Phoenician city—even totally and savagely as happened at Sidon—was only a temporary setback. Each was completely rebuilt and thriving after only a few years. This happened because the other Phoenician cities sheltered their people and wealth during times of distress. The Phoenicians looked out for each other, regardless of the city in which they lived. That seemed to be important to them.

So, what was it like to be one of the people arriving at Carthage during this disruptive time? The first impression would have been one of immensity, given the vast size of this metropolis. The urban sprawl covered an extensive promontory which pointed like an arrow toward Sicily and then Italy across the blue water.

Approaching Carthage from the sea one saw huge walls built right to the shoreline. These could be as much as 43 feet high and 32 feet thick. And there were tall towers spaced along the solid walls at intervals. Beyond that barrier, packed buildings could be seen flowing up to the top of Byrsa Hill. Then those habitations followed the rise and fall of lower hilltops trailing off to the right.

The entrance to Carthage's vast harbor was on the left, so as ships drew closer the massive wall loomed above them, much higher than their masts and sails. Reaching that southeastern corner of the city, the nearby seawall suddenly ended at a solid tower and the extensive harbor became visible. A short channel of water about 65 feet wide exposed arriving ships to solid defensive positions on each side, before giving way to the wider commercial harbor.

On the left side of the water channel the solid city wall proceeded westward across dry land. This fortification was equally as impressive as the seawall, and separated the metropolis from sand-filled land outside. On that sandy soil were ramshackle buildings of all types where local boats could dock at rude wharfs to deliver their wares or just pull up on the shore. Once unloaded, the local craft would be re-filled with foreign goods acquired in exchange. A nearby gate in the city wall would allow the flow of goods to and from the more luxurious docks on the inner side, where huge international ships were safely berthed.

An arriving boat sailing through the entrance channel into the harbor would see quiet water stretching between rocky land under the massive wall on the right, and the opposite bank filled with warehouses. This harbor was an impressive 1170 feet wide and 1500 feet in length. Countless ships rested against wooden docks at water's edge, or were on their way in or out laden with rich cargoes.

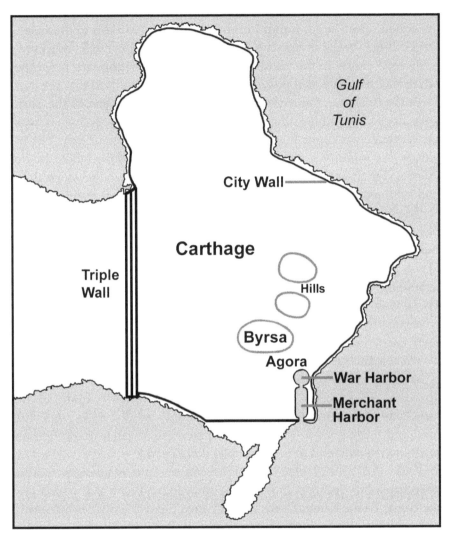

Fig. 91 Map of Carthage.

The arriving vessel would pass round-hulled merchantman ships moored at the docks, then find its own appropriate berth. Once the craft was lashed to the wharf with strong cables, a passenger could disembark and walk northward toward the heart of the city. Passing the loading and unloading boats, one came to the end of the harbor where warships were lodged.

In the not-too-distant future this terminus of the harbor would be expanded into a large, round harbor of its own, 1070 feet in diameter, with military ships occupying 220 berths around the circle. A round, multi-level house in the middle would serve as a headquarters for the admiral of the fleet, as reported by classical writers

But at this time, the warships simply occupied the end of the port, with docks not unlike those of the commercial vessels. Yet it was immediately apparent that these ships were completely different in nature. As military craft, they were narrower in width which made them faster than the merchantmen, and also much taller since they had between two and five rows of oars protruding from their sides.

These galleys also had sails, but their primary propulsion came from their many rowers. This was especially critical in combat when fighting vessels had to turn quickly and surge forward at high speed to catch or ram an opposing craft. To distinguish between them, the galleys with two rows of oars on each side were called biremes. Those with three rows were triremes. The taller ones with four rows were quadriremes, and those with five rows were quinqueremes. They each had their own position and responsibilities when the fleet was at sea. But here in port they fit wherever there was space.

Walking northward from the harbor, the busy agora of Carthage appeared. This was the hectic central marketplace where many of the hundreds of thousands of people in the city would have come for food and trade goods—though of course many smaller marketplaces must have developed to meet simple, daily needs.

From this central place, other businesses and residences would have spread to the right as far as the seawall, and forward, parallel to the coast. To the left and backward toward the city walls on the south and west was the industrial area where craftsmen worked with gold, silver, leather, fine cloth and all manner of exotic materials to make valuable goods for the marketplace and the outward-bound ships.

To the left and forward was the rising slope of Byrsa Hill. This was the ancient heart of the city, where the first settlers from Tyre established themselves. So naturally, this was where their first temples were built for worship and healing. Other civic buildings for debate, voting, administration and judicial matters would have stretched from there to the agora. A secondary wall surrounded the hilltop, creating the equivalent of an acropolis. When the Romans

Fig. 92 A grand home in ancient Carthage

attacked, this was Carthage's last line of defense. Unfortunately the Romans did such a thorough job destroying everything they found here that only scattered pieces of Carthaginian habitation remain.

But in those days around the year 300 BC when Phoenician emigrants came here fleeing the depredations of Alexander's troops in Lebanon, it would have been possible to stand among the magnificent temples and other buildings on the top of Byrsa Hill and look out over the far-flung city which stretched almost to the horizon in all directions.

In the distance, the massive city walls could be seen extending from the harbor westward to a fortified corner. There it turned northward in a truly daunting triple wall which would never be breached during the entire life of the city. The wall then followed the shoreline again, eventually turning eastward and then south again. After many twists and turns it came back to the harbor again. Altogether, the massive wall traversed about 21 miles.

Outside those walls were fields of fertile farmland, well watered by the rivers and streams coursing among them on their way to the sea. Simple farms stood side-by-side with fine villas adorned with vineyards, olive orchards and crop-bearing fields.[83]

And no farmer or master of a grand country estate had to worry about being able to sell their crops. Other people in many parts of the Mediterranean lived on rocky soil and were anxious to import food. So cargo ships departed from Carthage's harbor every hour laden with all the food crops and other goods they could carry.

Within those extensive city walls, its half-a-million people lived their lives and earned their livings. And a rich living it was. The constant stream of trade from all over the Mediterranean which entered its harbor not only brought wealth, but also gave its citizens first choice to pick from the most artistic and exotic goods which passed before their eyes.

Carthage was a model of beautiful public buildings, sculpture, elegant neighborhoods and, of course, busy harbors. The dream that Elissa and her followers had sought five hundred years earlier had at last come true—perhaps even on a grander scale than she could have imagined.

Life was good for these Phoenicians on the coast of North Africa. But around them the world continued to boil with troubles. And those challenges were starting to overflow onto them, willing or not.

CHAPTER 22

ROME AND THE PUNIC WARS

Carthage's influence and power were now felt far to the east and west across the Mediterranean. So it was able to provide strong support for the struggling cities of Lebanon during this time. It served as their pot of gold at the end of the rainbow. Yet in the midst of Carthage's prosperity, there was one significant problem. And it came in the form of a city called Rome.

Ever since these Latin people expelled the Etruscan king who ruled their city, the Romans had been expanding. They steadily worked their way northward, taking lands which once belonged to the highly civilized Etruscans. They kept going until they reached the northern border of those lands. There they met the Gauls, a Celtic people who lived in the alpine region of northern Italy as well as in the land that would become France. The Gauls were upset at this thrust upward into their borderlands, and descended en masse across the Alps. In 387 BC they crushed the Roman army. Then they pushed onward to Rome and took that city. Seizing all the gold and wealth this city had acquired from the Etruscans, they burned Rome to the ground. Having been well-rewarded for their efforts, they retired to their homeland.

The weakened people of Rome were left exposed on all sides to the cities and tribes they had previously conquered. They were confronted not only by revolt within the confines of the city but also by small armies marching on the remains of their territory. It is to the great credit of the Roman people that their city somehow survived. Not only that, the Romans managed to regain their strength and re-exerted their influence. It took fifty years, but they restored Rome and became masters of a wide swath of countryside surrounding it.

In an attempt to finish what they had started before disaster struck, the Romans pressed northward again in 295 BC. Over the course of fifteen years they confronted the last of the Etruscans and those people's allies from the Apennine mountains and Gaul. Upon the completion of this decisive Roman campaign, the Etruscan civilization was no more. Rome now had sole possession of the middle of the Italian peninsula.

At last they could turn their attention southward where many Greek cities were spread across the lower part of the Italian "boot." With their army now well-trained and larger than before, the Romans swept from success to success. By 265 BC they controlled all the lands south of Rome. This brought them victorious and celebrating to the toe of the Italian boot at the southernmost extent of the European continent. They stood separated by only a couple of miles of water from the large island of Sicily. From the mainland they could easily see the city of Messina as well as the hills and fields of this land that was held by the Phoenicians and Greeks. What they saw became their desire and their next objective. Nor did they have long to wait for an opportunity to march.

As fortune would have it, the independent city of Messina on Sicily was suddenly attacked by Greeks from Syracuse.[84] Its leaders promptly appealed to Carthage for help. In response the Carthaginian fleet arrived, and the soldiers from Syracuse were quickly driven away. In repayment for having come to their aid, Carthage sought rights and privileges at Messina in terms of trade. The people of that city, hoping to avoid any such concession, appealed to Rome to drive out the Carthaginians. This was the moment for which the Romans had been waiting. They swept in and took the city.

Only then, with the Roman wolf upon the land of Sicily, did the Phoenicians and Greeks realize the most dangerous enemy they faced was not each other. It was the legions whose banners now flapped in the wind at Messina.

Hasty negotiations led to a joint siege by Carthage and Syracuse on the Roman position at Messina. But the timely arrival of fresh reinforcements from Rome was enough to break the siege and bring relief to the city. The stronger Romans then chased the Greeks back to Syracuse and forced them to sue for peace. A quickly drafted peace treaty left the leaders of Syracuse with only the city itself and thirty miles of land. With this, the Greeks bowed out of the war for Sicily, leaving it to Carthage and Rome to fight over this valuable jewel of an island which lay between their two lands.

Thus began the First Punic War, which was fought for possession of Sicily. It is interesting to note that the Romans were highly aware of Carthage's Phoenician heritage, and in fact called them by that name. In Greek the Phoenicians were called *Phoínikes*. In Latin this name was shortened to *Poeni*. That is why the Romans called these confrontations the Punic Wars, which to them meant the Phoenician Wars.

For twenty-three years these pitched battles raged forward and back across the Sicilian countryside. General Hamilcar led the Carthaginian forces against a series of Roman commanders. Yet the war's most remarkable aspect was not the individual battles but a critical shift in how they were fought. The Romans reportedly captured some Phoenician ships and had them carefully taken apart to learn how they were built.[85] This was made necessary by the fact that the Roman legions were highly disciplined and extremely capable land forces—but they had virtually no sea support. None had ever been needed when the legions stormed across the Italian penin-sula. They had built excellent roads and traveled by foot or by horse. Now they were engaged in a massive campaign where the entire battlefield was on an island. They wisely saw the need for ships.

In their patented hard-driving manner, the Romans wanted the best—and the sooner the better. So they painstakingly copied the Phoenician ships and put a huge premium on launching as many of them as they could put in the water. Great naval skill was not their objective. The ships were basically transports for troops and supplies. But they had to be strong enough to withstand impact with another ship, and maneuverable enough to catch an enemy ship. The sturdy vessels they built were then outfitted with boarding ramps. These allowed Roman troops to scramble across onto the deck of enemy ships whenever they got close enough. The fighting was then by hand-to-hand combat, just as it would be on land.

In a twist of fate which was to prove regrettable for the Phoenicians, the more Carthage focused on land superiority, the more it lost its advantage at sea. It was gradually yielding what had been the mainstay of Phoenician strength and survival since the first days at Byblos when small cedar boats were put into the water.

As the unpredictable fortunes of combat ebbed and flowed through many bloody engagements during the war, large numbers of ships and troops were lost on both sides. Hamilcar and his men fought well, but the Romans rolled slowly and inexorably across Sicily. In 241 BC, a peace treaty was signed in which Carthage yielded the island to Rome. The First Punic War was over.

Sicily thus became Rome's first possession outside the Italian peninsula. The acquisition of this initial foreign province was in many ways the first step in creating the Roman empire.

With this, a formal state of peace existed between Carthage and Rome. But declaration and reality can often be two different things.

Carthage's resources were seriously depleted by the cost of war, rendering it unable to pay its mercenary soldiers for services they had provided.[86] So the mercenaries went into revolt. While Hamilcar was fully engaged in putting this down, the Romans took advantage and seized Sardinia and Corsica.[87] Wresting these two major islands from Carthage was a blatant breach of the peace. Even some in Rome had qualms about the repercussions which might come from this move. But it was done.

The people of Carthage were outraged, but unable to respond while still recovering from the recent riots and the previous war. However they began shoring up their resources against a day of reckoning. The inexhaustible Hamilcar moved his army to Carthage's colonies in Spain, where sufficient resources, people and land existed to raise and train a powerful army. After Hamilcar and his successor Hasdrubal passed away in the performance of their duties, the mantle of commander-of-the-army fell to Hamilcar's son: the twenty-one-year-old Hannibal Barca.

With this, something happened to the Phoenicians for the first time in their history. During all the millennia prior to the founding of Carthage, the Phoenicians had been peaceful by preference, and the

Fig. 93 Hannibal

people of Lebanon continued to act in that manner. As a result, they had never produced a great, conquering leader. Their leadership was by agreement, their power was economic, and their great wealth came from ships' voyages rather than charges across battlefields.

But when Carthage put its faith in land power and the fortunes of war, the way was opened for heroes to stand on bloody fields. Onto one such field now strode young Hannibal. In many ways he was a Phoenician counterpart to the young and brilliant Alexander the Great.

As the son of a highly capable general, Hannibal soon took on his father's planned campaign against the power of Rome. His opportunity came quickly. The city of Saguntum, deep within Carthage's lands in Spain, asked for and received promises of protection from Rome. When Hannibal heard reports that Saguntum was actively lobbying other Spanish cities to join it, he besieged Saguntum, tore open its walls, and sacked the city.[88] With this act in 218 BC, the Second Punic War began.

Hannibal quickly assembled a massive army and set out on a difficult march across Europe. This was the famous campaign in which he marched over the Alps with a vanguard of elephants girded for battle. In northern Italy, he met and defeated each of the Roman armies he encountered. Moving southward with the fifty thousand men who had survived the ordeals of war to that point, he was confronted by the main army from Rome numbering 80,000 strong. These were the Romans' best and finest troops. Shockingly, the Roman army was completely destroyed in what was believed to have been the worst defeat in Rome's long history.

Now Rome lay directly in front of Hannibal. But with so few men remaining in his ranks, he could not hope to successfully besiege the city. Even so, time seemed to be on his side. His incredible victories were bringing others to follow his standard, including Gauls who had no love for Rome. Emancipated Greeks and others who were being freed from Roman rule likewise came to him. But he needed many more to deliver the coup de grâce.[89] So he continued his far-ranging campaigns around the Italian peninsula, winning victory after victory. Everywhere he went, he stirred up the people previously conquered by Rome and urged them to join the fight against their former master.

To the Roman people, this became their defining moment. Their great army had been utterly defeated, their city exposed, their former possessions were in revolt, and the brilliant Hannibal marched freely across their land. There was no reasonable hope that Rome could survive. And yet it did. It found something deep within its character which enabled it to endure—and then flourish again. By so doing, the people of Rome came to believe they had a divine destiny for greatness. This was one of the central reasons why the Punic Wars became such an important part of their heritage. They never wanted to forget the moment they found this tremendous internal strength and began their march to greatness.

Since they could do nothing against Hannibal in Italy, the Roman leaders sought to carry the war to Carthage's empire. This would put some of the destruction upon Phoenician soil. They began to campaign fiercely in Spain. Borrowing a page from Hannibal's playbook, they provoked many uprisings there. After numerous difficult battles, the Romans won a great Spanish victory. The result was the total surrender of this large, rich and strategic colony to Rome. Carthage countered by immediately expanding the war to Sicily and provoking many uprisings there. But eventually, Rome regained the upper hand and managed to keep its grip on this essential possession. With momentum on its side, Rome ordered its navy and legions to carry the war to North Africa. When Rome won a major battle there, Carthage saw the writing on the wall.

While they still had some bargaining leverage left, the Phoenicians agreed to negotiate a treaty of peace. Hannibal was still undefeated in all his campaigns on the Italian peninsula, but he was now called home.

The two proud and unyielding forces that came to the bargaining table gave peace no chance. The negotiations fell through. Back on the bloody field once more to negotiate with swords, a pivotal, epic battle was fought in North Africa. The forces of Rome prevailed.

The resulting terms were exceedingly harsh. Carthage lost all of its overseas empire.[90] It had to make heavy payments to Rome as compensation for the war. It was stripped of all its warships except ten. It retained only its territory in North Africa and the right to live under its own laws.

With this, Rome formally claimed Sardinia, Corsica, and Spain as its foreign provinces. Along with Sicily, it now had provinces spanning a large expanse of the Mediterranean. Though they did it unwillingly, the Phoenicians had bequeathed upon Rome a great empire.

Over the next fifty-three years, Carthage was no longer a military power of any kind. That meant the city was able to devote all its energy to trade, allowing it to spring back quickly as an economic power. Carthage was able to do this despite having lost all those colonies because its trade relationships and networks spanning the Mediterranean were as good as ever. There was hope.

Unfortunately, the growing light of Carthage's success was seen clearly across the sea at Rome. Concerned about the Phoenicians' growing strength, some of the Roman leaders set about stirring up a Third Punic War. At their urging a demand was issued to Carthage that it move the entire city ten miles inland from the sea.[91] Of course the Romans were aware that the Phoenicians' life was sea-trading, and that the city would never comply. When Carthage refused, that became the pretext for war. Rome's navy began to rush battle-ready legions onto North African soil. After three years' siege, Carthage finally fell.

The Romans reportedly went door-to-door throughout the city slaughtering inhabitants in what was one of the largest executions of civilians in history until World War II. Any who were not killed were sold into slavery. The harbor was rendered unusable, and the city was so thoroughly destroyed that it was said no stone was left standing upon another.[92] The farmlands were reportedly sown with salt to render them desolate.

The scale of these actions revealed the incredible depth of Rome's feelings over having lived for centuries in Carthage's shadow. And for having endured the pain of defeat Hannibal inflicted upon their armies. All these things exploded across the North African coast in a ferocious display against this city that had not been a military threat for many years. When the destruction was complete, the Roman leaders who had sought that outcome were finally able to declare the famous words, "Carthago delenda est!" Carthage is destroyed.

The Romans had done their best to obliterate Carthage and all memory of the Phoenician people. With the city of Carthage, they succeeded, leaving only rubble behind.

With the Phoenician people, they were not quite as successful. Terrible things were said and written about these people they vanquished, in the apparent hope that making them less respectable and less worthy would cause them to be forgotten. Incredibly enough, some people continue to follow that example today.

Although it may seem hard to believe, an occasional book or article is still published these days by some academics who claim the Phoenicians never existed.

Fortunately, far too much evidence about the lives and deeds of the Phoenicians has been left for us over the many centuries of their existence. Too many records were written by Egyptians, Greeks, Hebrews and even some Romans. Too many archaeological finds have come to light across Lebanon and other Mediterranean countries for them to be forgotten now.

In fact, we come to know the Phoenicians better with each passing year. We know more about their lives, their society and even how they impacted other societies at the roots of our civilization. Some of the things the Phoenicians did still affect us today. Hopefully they will never be forgotten.

With the passing of Carthage, virtually all of the city's records were destroyed. That was not too surprising because whenever the Phoenicians gave up a city or outpost, they never left any significant records behind. Their principle of privacy and desire for secrecy to protect their society made this their reasonable and normal course of action. And it was implemented rigorously, even if arriving enemy troops did not do it for them. It has been regularly noted by historians and archaeologists how remarkably few traces were left behind.

At first, some people thought the Phoenicians had nothing to leave. Now it has become quite evident that they had extensive writings and detailed records. Could the people who gave the world the written alphabet have lived any other way? Their business records were described in detail during Wenamun's report on his trip to Byblos. Pieces of their writing were also physically seen in the great quantity of clay records found in the palaces of Minoan Crete.

Many works on other subjects were likewise written by Phoenician authors. We know this because Phoenician texts were quoted or cited by Greeks and Romans in their own writings, even though the originals became lost.[93]

As late as the fourth century AD, the well-read St. Augustine wrote in a letter to Maximus Madaurus, "On the word of many scholars, there was a great deal of virtue and wisdom in the Punic books."

At Carthage, an exception to the Phoenicians' "no records left behind" rule proved to be a spectacular one. A twenty-eight volume library of definitive writings on agricultural expertise had been compiled by a Carthaginian named Mago (no relation to the general). It was so valued by the Romans that they ordered it to be translated into Latin for the benefit of their own people. Even though the original translation was eventually lost, enough of Mago's master-work was cited by others that parts of it have been preserved down to the present day. Each entry was unique and showed something of value—even on a subject as simple as this recipe for raisin wine.

> Take bunches of grapes, quite ripe, and well boiled; take away the dry or faulty parts; form a frame of stakes or forks, spreading thereon a layer of reeds; spread the grapes upon these, and place them in the sun, covering them at night from the dew. When they are dry, pluck off the berries, throw them in a cask, and make of them the first must. If they have well drained, put them the sixth day in a vessel, press them, and take the (first) wine. After adding thereto must, quite cold, the berries must be again pounded and pressed. The second wine may then be placed in a pitched vessel lest it become sour. After twenty or thirty days, when it has fermented, clear it off into another vessel, whose cover must be im-mediately stopped close, and covered with a skin.
>
> Columella xii. 39, 1, 2

These stores of Phoenician writings existed when their cities were active and prospering, but what happened to them?

First and foremost, they seemed to have been held in close control even in the cities' heydays. While many acknowledged that the Phoenicians sailed by the stars and went to distant lands, no one ever reported seeing their charts and maps. As a result, many who wished to compete with these sea-traders were compelled to sail only within sight of land at first, and feared to go beyond the Strait of Gibraltar. Shipbuilding and sources of trade must likewise have been docu-mented by the Phoenicians. If the making of raisin wine was carefully recorded, what about the selection and curing of wood for the critical keel beam of a ship?

Strabo told us the lengths to which the Phoenicians would go to protect their secrets.

> The Cassiterides [islands just off England's southwest coast]…as they have mines of tin and lead, they give these metals and the hides from their cattle to the sea-traders in exchange for pottery, salt and copper utensils. Now in former times it was the Phoenicians alone who carried on this commerce (that is, from Gades), for they kept the voyage hidden from everyone else. And when once the Romans were closely following a certain ship-captain in order that they too might learn the markets in question, out of jealousy the ship-captain purposely drove his ship out of its course into shoal water; and after he had lured the followers into the same ruin, he himself escaped by a piece of wreckage and received from the State the value of the cargo he had lost.
>
> Strabo
>
> *Geography* iii.5.11

This was how dedicated the Phoenicians were to keeping secret the sources of their trade. Any written materials relating to their council deliberations, rules, and practices which made up Phoenician society were likewise kept concealed.

As a result, whenever a Phoenician city was in danger of being attacked, in addition to evacuating families and the richest wealth, the critical records seem to have been taken elsewhere as well. In all the sackings of Phoenician cities which happened over time, there was never a report of sensitive materials being captured.

The second protection of records applied when a city was not just in danger of attack but when its walls were breached and falling. This was to burn all records that were not essential enough to have been removed. Though it was not unusual for invaders to burn a city, there have been clear reports of Phoenicians burning a portion of their own city as the enemy came through the walls.[94]

For towns and outposts, those two actions seemed to have eliminated virtually all the records which existed. For extremely large lands and cities, the job appeared to have been too large and required some compromise. When the Phoenicians left Minoan Crete, the palaces were emptied of all essential records. But with Mycenaean forces approaching across the land, the massive piles of clay tablets recording individual business transactions were left behind. They were not really critical, and the volume of them was too huge.

Similarly for the metropolis of Carthage. No essential records were found by the Romans. Yet some of the noncritical material, which might usually have been burned, somehow managed to escape that fate and fall into their hands. The Roman author Pliny the Elder told us, "After the sack of Carthage, our Senate presented the libraries of the town to the African princes, with the sole exception of the twenty-eight books of Mago, which they decreed should be translated into Latin."[95]

The "African princes" referred to by Pliny are almost certainly the leaders of Utica, the Phoenician city twenty-five miles up the coast from Carthage. Given the Phoenician principles and practices, the people of that city would reasonably have requested any documents that survived the destruction of the city. Rome—in a manner similar to the invaders of Lebanon who wanted a share of its rich trade—sought cooperation from the surviving Phoenician cities, and would have given up the books if they were deemed to have no military value. As evidence of its desire to seek cooperation, after these wars Rome named Utica as the governing city of its new African province.

The bottom line is that no critical materials survived from the Phoenician cities. Believe it or not, some historians still insist these materials disappeared because they were written on papyrus and the sea air made them disintegrate. Since the Phoenicians and their writings survived until at least 146 BC when Carthage fell, those who harbor that belief would need to demonstrate why much older writings on papyrus—by people such as Plato, Herodotus, Thucydides, and others who wrote beside the same Mediterranean Sea—were able to survive while the Phoenician documents did not.

Nor would it have been necessary for the original documents to survive. Almost all of the widely-read Greek and Roman documents did not come down to us by virtue of the original document being saved in one place for everyone to read later. They came to us because they were laboriously copied by hand many times—then those copies were distributed and finally came to us.

The Phoenician records did not survive—for better or for worse — largely due to the Phoenician principle of privacy and desire for secrecy to preserve their society. They did not encourage copies of their documents to be made. Nor did they distribute the existing ones widely. And when no longer needed at that place, the documents were made to disappear.

What they created was theirs to do with as they thought best, of course. But even so, it was unfortunate how matters turned out. Think of all the things the Phoenicians knew. The art of navigation and countless annotated maps. The internal affairs of all the societies with whom they traded, from Egypt in 3200 BC to the Canaanites, Hittites, Cilicians, Mycenaeans, Greeks, Romans and many others. Those documents could have included the golden years of the Minoans with their palaces, society and beautiful arts. And the volumes on agriculture, science, literature and history that inspired the comment by St. Augustine on the "virtue and wisdom" of these books. All have been lost.

They are lost unless, of course, they have been preserved in some secure place out of sight. For centuries, the Phoenicians watched Egyptians carefully build secret chambers lined with stone and cedar, accompanied by extensive preparations to preserve mummies and possessions for eternity. It was certainly within the Phoenicians' ability to build a similar chamber of ashlar-cut stone blocks hermetically sealed against intrusion by air or moisture—a place to keep the things of value to them.

Why would they do such a thing? It was true they had an extraordinarily strong sense of privacy. But they also had a strong desire to pass down to later generations of their people the knowledge and practices that made them who they were. They conscientiously did this for over three thousand years, because it was important to them.

Did they create such a vault of their most secret and critical knowledge? There is every reason to believe they did.

If such a place is found, will the door be discovered broken open by grave robbers who left only shreds of papyrus and fragments of

Fig. 94   Phoenician underground vault found in Lebanon

clay tablets strewn across the floor? Or will the door be found sealed, the contents intact, and a treasure worth more than gold waiting inside?

Only time will tell.

On a hillside in North Africa, smoke from the charred remains of Carthage blew across the land and out to sea. From the moment of its birth almost seven hundred years earlier, Carthage had been the "bad boy" of the Phoenician family. Its determination to be a land power seemed to have been the cause and purpose of its existence ever since it was a gleam in the eye of Elissa and those who came with her from Tyre. That desire had raised it to great heights, and plunged it into terrible depths. Carthage's emphasis on being a land power drove Rome to such a fever pitch that it triggered the North African city's final, total destruction.

No doubt the remaining Phoenicians who were scattered across the Mediterranean shed a tear over the amount of death and devastation which took place in this once-mighty city. Yet they probably could not help but let out a small sigh of relief. Carthage had stretched—and perhaps torn—the fabric of Phoenician society. It became a lightning rod of anger from Rome over the course of many horrendous battles. And that stigma caused a clear and present danger to the individual Phoenicians who survived. The stigma also forever colored the way Roman and other writers of history viewed and portrayed the Phoenician people.

Traditionally, the destruction of Carthage marked the passing of the Phoenicians from the face of the earth. The first boot of this passing was dropped by Alexander in Tyre. The second was dropped by Rome at Carthage.

But were the Phoenicians really gone?

CHAPTER 23

ADONIS STILL LIVES

What actually happened to the Phoenicians?

To answer this question we return for a moment to the day after Alexander sacked Tyre. It was a terrible loss, with some Phoenicians being pressed into service and compelled to support Alexander's campaign. But surprisingly, they may not have been unwilling to do so.

Contrary to the image summoned up by what had just happened, Alexander was not normally a destroyer of cities. He had been able to move swiftly and conquer many lands because he was almost universally generous in victory. Traditionally, he spared the leaders of a conquered city, and often let them retain their titles. This was done on condition that they acknowledge his authority, agree to live under his viceroy for that region, and supply materials or soldiers to support his ongoing military efforts. Most cities were greatly relieved and even eager to accept his terms, since it left them alive, and in possession of their lands. This was the positive inducement he presented for city leaders to surrender to him.

The negative inducement, which was also powerful and persuasive, was the shocking force with which he had defeated them. There was no doubt in their minds that—should they be less than fully cooperative—he would return and do it again. And that he could be vicious when crossed.

He displayed both these traits—positive and negative—during his sojourn in Lebanon. The terrible price he exacted at Tyre had little to do with the killing of his emissaries. For that offense he is reported to have ordered the impaling of two thousand Phoenician youths along the coast—a sufficiently harsh punishment to insure the safety of his other emissaries to the cities who received them in the future.

Yet a second "crime" had been committed as well—one much more serious to him. This once-indomitable city of Tyre had held him up for nine months before being taken by force of arms. Alexander's quest, and in fact his destiny, was to quickly seize perhaps a thousand cities and create a great empire. If he stood nine months before each city, he would not live long enough to achieve his goal, even if he lived to be a white-haired and wizened one hundred years of age. No, there needed to be a sharp, crystal-clear message to every city he approached. The distinction between his generosity to those who threw open the city gates at his approach and his wrath to those who forced him into a siege had to be clearly drawn. He did that at Tyre. The larger punishment—six thousand killed in the city and thirty thousand sold into slavery—was the price for forcing him into a long and agonizing siege.

This word traveled before him, and appeared to have the desired effect. Many cities fell at his approach or in the turbulence caused by his passing on horseback. His battles were memorable, his sieges few, and the empire he desired took shape around him. Egypt fell quickly. He created there the city of Alexandria on its coast—at the site of a small village called Rhakotis and an "ancient harbor" on the island of Pharos just offshore. Returning through Palestine to Mesopotamia, he conquered that land and went on to take Persia, Afghanistan and part of India before returning to Babylon. There he died of a sudden illness at the age of thirty-three.

What happened to the Phoenician people in Lebanon during this time? Recall for a moment Alexander's generosity to cities that surrendered at his approach. Byblos, Arwad, Beirut, Sidon, and all the other Phoenician towns across Lebanon had done exactly that. True to his word and reputation, Alexander did them no harm. Even at Tyre, which had defied him and been severely punished, the leading citizens were spared and allowed to live. Alexander was justifiably respected for his surprising mercy, where others would have shown no quarter.

Alexander largely left these cities to their own affairs. This was subject to their recognizing his authority and supporting his campaigns. The contingent of Phoenicians required to travel with him almost certainly built and captained boats for the Macedonians on their long march of conquest. These services were especially valuable on the long return from India and Persia to Mesopotamia, which was accomplished largely by sea.

Nine years after the fall of Tyre, however, Alexander passed away and the ship-builders came home.

Just as quickly, his short-lived empire was divided into three parts by his able lieutenants. Ptolemy took Egypt, Seleucus took Asia, and Antigonus took Greece. Lebanon was among the lands apportioned to Seleucus. By paying Seleucus what they had to pay, and causing no trouble, the Phoenician cities wisely earned a great deal of independence and managed to thrive. This peaceful approach was greatly appreciated by Seleucus, the new leader of Asia, who was preoccupied with expanding his realm in India and fending off revolts around Afghanistan.

Left largely to their own devices, the Phoenicians went on with their lives. In many ways this was no different than living under any of their previous overseers. In fact it was better than some of those earlier experiences.

The Lebanese cities that had surrendered to Alexander and went undamaged now grew larger and flourished. Even Tyre, quickly rebuilt as was customary among the Phoenicians, joined its sister cities in the prosperity of these times. Sea trade continued as the cornerstone of Lebanese life, especially with their daughter city at Carthage. This was 300 BC, and the North African city was at the height of its power—the disaster of its Roman experience would come later. In short, the Lebanese people lived in the same places, did the same work and kept the same relationships they had before the time of Alexander. In the traditional Phoenician manner, they began to blend in with their new Greek-speaking overseers, and that relationship also grew.

Even before Alexander, the Phoenicians had started to appreciate Greek sculpture and other arts. One of the kings of Sidon, born with the name Abdashtart, began using the Greek-style name of Stratton. Now, living in the shadow of Alexander's Hellenic empire, all things Greek became fashionable.

Though the Lebanese successfully established good relations with Seleucus and the kings who came after him, it was never as strong as their relationship and influence with Carthage. And the sheer power, beauty and wealth of Carthage was on a par with the greatest cities of its day. All the incentives in the world seemed to draw the people of Lebanon forward to maintaining their Phoenician ties and life. Yet they did it quietly and privately, as was their way.

This Phoenician life "under the surface" in Lebanon emerged briefly after the Second Punic War. Hannibal had just achieved his great victories against the Romans, but then was forced to flee Carthage after the peace was made. He could have gone anywhere in the world, but followed his Phoenician connections to Lebanon. There he found an open channel to the successor of Seleucus: king Antiochus III. That king gave Hannibal command of a part of the Seleucid navy in the battles being fought around Anatolia. However Rome's long arm reached him even there, and he had to flee once more. Eventually he died at Libyssa near Byzantium, the city that would one day be known as Constantinople and then Istanbul.

Fifty years later, when Carthage was threatened with destruction, the traditional Phoenician practice called for evacuation of as many of its families and as much of its wealth as could possibly be arranged. Some of these would have gone to Utica and other colonies. Much of the rest would have come home to the ancient cities in Lebanon, which were safe havens well out of Rome's reach. At least for the moment.

The ferocity of Rome's attack on Carthage was shocking, especially since the North African city was no military threat by that time. It seemed clear that the people of the Tiber had incredibly strong feelings about the Phoenicians that could only be put to rest by fire and sword. The chilling reality of hundreds of thousands of people slaughtered in Carthage drove the message home.

This sobering experience gave the people in Lebanon pause as nothing else could have done.

Rome had already shown its strength by forcing Hannibal to leave the Mediterranean coast and pursuing him to the Black Sea. Its armies had marched eastward through Greece and Macedonia. It seemed only a matter of time until they would reach the Lebanese coast. In fact, a hundred years later Rome added Lebanon and Egypt to its empire, along with all of the eastern Mediterranean.

How could the Phoenicians prevent a repetition of Carthage's fate now that the Romans were arriving in Lebanon? The reasonable course of action would be to follow the usual Phoenician practice of blending in with the culture around them—in this case the Greek culture of the Seleucids. But this could not be a superficial blending. The Phoenicians would need to become invisible to the Romans, as if they did not exist. The risk, of course, was that they might actually cease to exist.

Was it really possible to drop the visible signs of Phoenician society, and yet manage to preserve it through family tradition, business arrangements, and social practices? There was no way to know. But the alternative was another possible feeding frenzy by the Roman army which left bloody stones at Carthage.

Without question, the distinctive Phoenician society became covered with a layer borrowed from Greek society at this time. The only question was whether that Greek layer was a thin veneer under which strong Phoenician principles of religious tolerance, peaceful resolution of differences, privacy, and all the rest still continued to drive their daily decisions. Or was the Greek layer as thick and final as some suggest, snuffing out the last breath of Phoenician life?

All we know is that the Phoenician desire to keep their affairs out of public view led Greek and Roman historians to conclude that these people no longer had any private affairs—and that what one saw was all there was.

Yet by now we clearly know there was always more to the Phoenicians than met the eye. And that they lived that way by choice.

The Phoenicians may well have been among the first to declare that their visible society had come to an end with the fall of Carthage. This was a wise course, since giving that impression seemed to have a salutary effect. With the passing of years, Roman hounds no longer bayed and barked on their trail. The hunt had ended.

Over the course of the next two thousand years, conquerors came one after another to add layers of culture on top of the Lebanese people. The Arab Conquest in 636 AD was followed by Crusaders, Mamluks and Ottoman Turks. That the original seven principles had become almost completely buried was demonstrated from 1975 to 1990 when terrible fighting and civil war raged within Lebanon. The times were so desperate that Syrian soldiers stood on Lebanese street corners to "keep the peace."

There would be no point in reliving the details of those disastrous fifteen years. Suffice it to say that religious tolerance and peaceful resolution of differences were nowhere to be seen. If the rest of the seven principles were not as close to oblivion as those two, they were at least heavily battered and reduced to a shadow of their former existence.

Yet sometimes the darkest night is followed by a brighter day. That truism applied not just to the long war but also to what subsequently happened in the year 2005.

Sometimes, it takes a terrible disaster to shake people out of the small things that preoccupy their days. It forces them to think about what is really important in their lives. For Lebanon, such a disaster happened on February 14, 2005. On that afternoon in downtown Beirut, Rafik Hariri and more than ten others were brutally killed when a massive bomb ripped apart his motorcade and left a huge crater in the middle of the street. It opened an even larger wound in the hearts of people the length and breadth of Lebanon, and of related people around the world. A leader who had been one of the hopes of Lebanese society was suddenly gone.

His value did not come solely from having been prime minister of the country, nor from having personally worked to rebuild much of war-damaged Beirut. His value was that he had started to reach across the dividing lines which had become engraved in Lebanese society. And because he wanted independence for his country.

In the days that followed his shocking murder, people's outpouring of emotion and demonstration of commitment to those same goals were incredible in magnitude. On March 14, one million people of all faiths, parties and parts of the country came together in the streets of Beirut. They came bearing only one mark of identification:

Fig. 95   One million people demonstrating in Beirut

the image of a cedar tree on a stripe of white, bordered by two broad lines of red—the flag of Lebanon. No matter how they had thought of themselves the day before that bomb blast, on March 14 and the days thereafter they saw themselves only as Lebanese. And the people they saw pouring into the streets were only Lebanese. That was all they needed to know to embrace, perhaps shed a tear or show a smile, and walk down the street together.

Around the world, people watched these events unfold on television and shared those same feelings. It conjured an irresistible pressure that pushed Syrian troops from their land, and Lebanon was free once more.

If there was any time in the past two thousand years when the early Lebanese principles were polished like ancient gold, and restored to a semblance of their former luster, this was the time. In the light of day, reflected on a million faces in the streets of Beirut was sincere religious tolerance, honest desire for peaceful resolution of differences, a powerful and hopeful partnership across all of Lebanese society, a feeling of equality, respect for women and men from every village and city, respect also for privacy that allowed people's beliefs or affiliation to be their own affair, and an embrace that was international in reach, including all who were touched by what was occurring.

As sometimes happens, however, the passage of time then began to obscure the beautiful things that had emerged in those days. The pressures of daily life and the habits of fighting that had been acquired over recent centuries seemed to intrude again on the peaceful and inclusive vision that had opened in that brief time.

Perhaps these occurrences—both terrible and wonderful—contain a message of some importance. It seems clear that the deeply-held principles of the early Lebanese people never went away entirely. When summoned up again they were powerful and uplifting, and enabled people in this land to move forward to freedom once more. But perhaps we also see how a temporary commitment to principles does not produce lasting value. For the result to be lasting, the commitment also needs to be lasting.

Yet at least we know peace, partnership, and all the other principles are still possible. Those heady days in early 2005, when a million people took to the streets in Beirut, clearly showed there is a little more magic left in those pieces of ancient gold today.

EPILOGUE

It was mentioned earlier that many professors of ancient history say the Phoenicians did not exist before 1200 or 1500 BC. That is particularly strange since, as we have seen, the overwhelming body of evidence shows the Phoenician people were active long before that time.

This situation seems to have arisen from an unfortunate belief that any acknowledgement or credit given to the Phoenicians will somehow diminish the honor and respect shown to Greeks and Romans. But there is no need to worry. The Greeks and Romans accomplished so many things that their reputations are safe and do not need further embellishment. Understanding the experiences of the Phoenicians before those dates simply serves the purpose of filling in more of the rich history of the ancient Mediterranean. In fact it makes the rise of the Greeks and Romans to great heights even more admirable.

So many students and readers of books such as this one now know Phoenician history well enough that continuing to deny it does not add luster to anyone's name. Students are not just aware of this history now, they are armed with conclusive evidence.

A hundred and fifty years ago the assumption that Sea Peoples destroyed all societies around the Mediterranean—including those in

Phoenicia—was understandable since we knew so little about early Mediterranean history. But when archaeologists showed in great detail that Phoenician cities were intact before, during and after the actions of the Sea Peoples in 1200 BC, it was time to acknowledge the continuity of Phoenician society.

Instead, a new story was created. It stated that even though the Phoenician cities existed before 1200 BC, they should only be called Phoenician from that date onward because their society was not distinguishable from others around them until this time.[96]

Clearly, however, that argument was not true.

In 2005 the original edition of this book demonstrated for the first time that the Phoenicians had established themselves as sea-traders through major exchanges with the Egyptians in 3200 BC. Their sea trade financed large public buildings, a new way of life and a city wall around Byblos by 3000 BC. Archaeologists have confirmed these developments.

In those days the neighbors of the Phoenicians were still shepherds, farmers and land-based traders with caravans of animals carrying goods. Phoenician society, on the other hand, was based on sea trade and all the other attributes we have seen—clearly distinguishable from their shepherd-and-caravan neighbors.

So the argument against the existence of the early Phoenicians had to shift. But it was moved only as far as 1500 BC. That concession was largely based on Egyptian letters to-and-from officials in Byblos and other Phoenician cities in that time frame. But it was still arbitrary.

Consider the Phoenician city of Tyre. It was founded in 2750 BC, as we have seen. And recall also the Phoenician-sourced boats made with cedar of Lebanon which were placed at the Great Pyramid in 2566 BC for the king's use in the afterlife.[97] One of those cedar boats is still on display there for everyone to see. History cannot really be erased.

So it is time to be reasonable. Let us set aside arbitrary dates such as 1200 or 1500 BC for the beginning of Phoenician history.

Why is that important? Because some of their most fascinating experiences happened before those dates.

Can you imagine being a Phoenician trader intimately involved with the island of Santorini[98] in the Aegean Sea around 1600 BC, when its smoking volcano began to erupt? Surrounded by multistory buildings decorated with artistic frescoes, you would have joined other people hurrying to ships leaving the island—perhaps feeling a sense of loss at the disaster happening to this beautiful city around you. And yet mixed with that might have been a measure of joy at having contributed some of the trade which made the magnificent palaces on Minoan Crete possible. What an amazing feeling that would have been.

The Phoenicians were a long-lived society.
The Greeks and Romans were great societies.
Those two statements are not mutually exclusive.
It is best to simply acknowledge that and move on.

S.H.
Los Angeles
December 12, 2021

APPENDIX

ART OF BOATBUILDING

Fortunate occurrences brought me to Tyre in Lebanon during May of 2004, just as the harbor's boatmaster was finishing a handmade Phoenician vessel he had created using the ancient methods. It was

Fig. 96   Newly built boat in Tyre of Phoenician design

the same boat that later appeared in *National Geographic* magazine's October 2004 article, "Who Were the Phoenicians?"

This particular vessel was built by Elijah Toufic Barbour. It had been under construction for about one-and-a-half years when I happened to stop by with my friend Joumana Medlej. The encounter could not possibly have been timed any better because he was just two days from completing it. In the first picture here, you can see that only the painting of the lower hull and some sealing remained to be done. As soon as the boatmaster finished, his son would take the craft out on its maiden voyage. Before continuing this story, let me share with you how those truly remarkable Phoenician boats—including this one—were actually built.

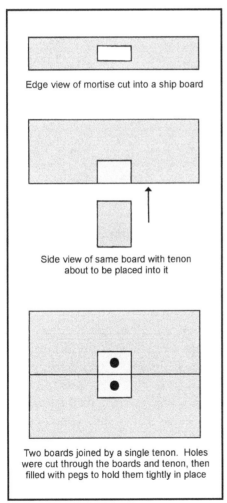

Edge view of mortise cut into a ship board

Side view of same board with tenon about to be placed into it

Two boards joined by a single tenon. Holes were cut through the boards and tenon, then filled with pegs to hold them tightly in place

Fig. 97 Ship boards joined by mortise and tenon

The entire vessel began in the boatyard using a single, massive piece of wood which formed the centerline at the lowest part of the boat called the keel. Built up from this was the hull and two sides of the boat, one board at a time, in an absolutely unique and fascinating manner. On one side of the keel where the first board would be attached, a series of small cutouts were made. These were spaced roughly a foot apart and continued the entire length of the piece. On the edge of the first board a series of identical incisions were made, at exactly the same spacing as on the keel. Small, flat pieces of wood called tenons were then placed halfway-down into the cutouts in the keel. This method was sometimes referred to as "mortise and tenon," with the mortise being the small hole into which the piece of wood was placed.

When the first board was laid beside the keel, every incision in the edge of the board had to line up perfectly with one of the tenons protruding from the keel. When the board was pushed toward the keel, all of the tenons disappeared into the openings in a perfectly tight fit.

The board was then secured in this position by carefully drilling a hole through the board and the tenon. A small peg, the exact size of the hole, was then hammered into the opening. When the peg was wedged tightly into place, it prevented the tenon

Fig. 98   Pegs holding together the Tyre boat

from ever being pulled out of the board again. Once the keel was pegged in the same manner, the board and keel could no longer be separated. This process was then repeated for every board in the boat, and formed the bottom—the hull—of the boat. Then it was continued smoothly upward to make the sides.

When all was done, a framework was added inside the body of the boat to stiffen the structure and provide places for the fishermen to sit while they rowed or cast their nets. It should be mentioned that non-Phoenician boats today are made in exactly the opposite way: the framework is built first, then boards are fastened to the framework. This is much faster, though not necessarily better. The ancient art of boatbuilding involved much intensive woodworking, but the vessels were watertight, stood up to punishment from the stormy sea, and lasted a long, long time.

Two days after I met with the boatmaster and was shown how these Phoenician boats were built, Antonia Kanaan and I were exploring the site of ancient Byblos about seventy miles north of

Fig. 99   Phoenician boat arrives in Byblos at the Fishing Club

Tyre. After an exhilarating but exhausting morning at the site, we walked to the town harbor where the famous Fishing Club was located. This destination had long been popular on the jet-set circuit, and photos of celebrity patrons covered several walls. The remarkable owner, Pepe Abed, was graciously treating us to lunch and several fascinating stories, when something fairly incredible happened. The Phoenician boat sailed into the harbor and tied up directly in front of our table! We congratulated its crew, who were as surprised as we were that the maiden voyage of this vessel had brought us together again.

Lebanon is a place of many magical encounters.

LEGEND OF THE PHOENIX

After all the other intriguing facts which have come to light about the Phoenicians, there should perhaps be little surprise that their epic adventures appear to have given rise to the legend of the Phoenix. The Greeks originally called the Phoenicians *phoinikes*. The singular form of that same word is *phoinix*. The Romans later spelled this as *phoenix*. Even so, those simple facts might have been written off as a coincidence, were it not for everything else that happened.

First, consider the legend: The mysterious bird known to us as the Phoenix was quite popular in ancient Egypt. Later, it was adopted in Greece as well. The legend told of a magnificent bird which lived for five hundred years. At the end of that time, it suddenly burst into flames and was consumed. Then, from its ashes, a new Phoenix would arise and live another five hundred years.

This story turns out to have remarkable parallels with the long history of the Phoenician people. Their thriving cities in Lebanon were attacked many times. Every few hundred years one of those cities would be completely destroyed. War-like people would descend upon the large town, burn it to the ground, and take away whatever spoils they could find. That was not too remarkable, since such destruction happened at one time or another to virtually every city in every land. It was the nature of war and life during those days.

The remarkable part of the story was what happened next. Often in history, a destroyed city would not be rebuilt at all, ending as scattered stones on an overgrown field. Other cities would be slowly patched back together by local people whose meager resources might require a hundred years or more to restore its buildings and liveli-hood. With the Phoenicians, this experience was completely different.

A destroyed Phoenician city would quickly spring back to life, often within five or ten years. And just as quickly it would flourish again, sometimes becoming even richer than before. This oft-repeated miracle by the Phoenicians was perhaps the eighth wonder of the ancient world. And it became legendary.

We saw Byblos sacked several times. And each time it rebuilt and prospered. We saw the city of Sidon burned to the ground by the Persians in 345 BC. Twelve years later, Alexander the Great marched into Lebanon and found Sidon not only back in operation but once again a major, prosperous center for gold coinage and shipping. At first blush this seemed impossible—but that was what actually happened.

We also saw how close the ties were between the Phoenicians and Egyptians. This extended even to the point of the Egyptians includ-ing Byblos and its people in their Osiris legend and other traditions. For several thousand years the people of the Nile had seen one Phoenician city after another be attacked and destroyed. Their ongoing amazement at the sudden and spectacular recovery of these cities was clearly the stuff of legend, and they recorded it that way.

Yet one of the most intriguing parts of this story was the reason behind these sudden resurrections of Phoenician cities. The most visible cause was the Phoenicians' traditional approach to impending attacks by war-like people. They responded by immediately saving the people and wealth of the city, carrying them away on boats before the attack. The rest of the city was just stones, and was left for the invader. After the attacker had burned the city and taken what little was left by way of spoils, those intruders went away. The Phoenicians then returned by boat with their people and their considerable wealth, and were able to quickly rebuild the city, often making it greater and more beautiful than before.

The other, less visible reason for these sudden restorations lay in the whole nature of Phoenician society. They were a peaceful people

Fig. 100   Phoenix Risen, by LaMarche

who sought to avoid conflict whenever possible, and were highly
skilled at negotiating to obtain that result. If negotiations failed, they
had no delusions about winning a war. They did not even have an
army. Instead they relied upon their mastery of the sea and the fact
that their major cities were on islands or promontories sticking out
into the sea. Failure of negotiations led to immediate evacuation of

the afflicted city to the fullest extent possible, using their many boats. After the invader left, it was a rich and vigorous society that returned to rebuild the city. They were well aware that the sooner the city was restored, the sooner the wealth from sea-trade would flow into it again. So they set to their work with a will, and small miracles were accomplished.

This wondrous rebirth after being consumed by fire made the Phoenician cities truly remarkable in their day. Even legendary.

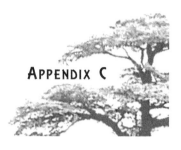

ACADEMIC PAPERS

The academic papers shown here explore several major milestone events covered in this book. These papers go into significant detail, presenting opposing arguments and citing numerous sources where specific material can be found to support the points made. While the general reader may find these papers to be laborious undertakings, for the scholar and researcher they are essential. Rather than include the forty-two pages of material in this work, the four central academic papers are incorporated by reference, and have been placed on the Internet for ready access.

Origin of the Phoenicians

Presented at Queen Mary College in London, England

This paper explores the major theories advanced by historians and scholars such as Herodotus, Maurice Dunand, Gerhard Herm and Sabatino Moscati on the origin of the Phoenicians. The year 1200 BC was a stumbling block for many years, due to the early assumption that the Sea Peoples destroyed *all* societies in the eastern Mediterranean at that time. Archaeological excavations have now shown the Phoenician cities were not destroyed then, and existed for many years prior to that date. Genetic research by Pierre Zalloua and Spencer Wells also indicates the long term existence of the Phoenicians in Lebanon. Details of the various theories, arguments, excavations and historical records are examined in this paper to determine the best-supported place and date of origin for the Phoenicians. The results are consistent with the material presented in this book.

> Retrieve from: https://phoenician.org/origin_of_phoenicians. Paper was presented on 29 June 2008 by Sanford Holst at Queen Mary College in London, England. 10 pages, 61 footnotes.

Fig. 101 Byblos

Minoans and Phoenicians

Presented at California State University, Long Beach, USA

Two opposing views on the origin of the Minoans and their palace-building society on Crete have been advocated by scholars such as Colin Renfrew and Sir Arthur Evans. The "indigenous development" theory, advanced by Renfrew and others, held that the Minoans achieved their society in relative isolation from the outside world. Evans and others found "Eastern influence" in Minoan society, referring to architecture, practices and other cultural elements from the Near East. Examination of additional evidence by scholars such as Keith Branigan, Saul Weinburg and James Walter Graham shows that the preponderance of archaeological and historical records now support the "Eastern influence" explanation.

> Retrieve from: https://phoenician.org/minoans_phoenicians_paper. This paper was presented on 24 June 2006 by Sanford Holst at California State University, Long Beach, USA. 12 pages, 70 notes.

Fig. 102   Knossos

Sea Peoples and the Phoenicians

Presented at Al Akhawayn University in Ifrane, Morocco

This paper explores the destructive passage of the Sea Peoples through the eastern Mediterranean around 1200 BC, and their serious impacts on the Mycenaean Greeks, Hittites, Phoenicians, Egyptians and other societies of that time. Scholars have advanced several theories regarding the origin and actions of the Sea Peoples, including those of Eliezer D. Oren, Shelley Wachsmann, R. D. Barnett and Eberhard Zangger. These are examined and compared to the factual record, resulting in reliable identification of the Sea Peoples and their specific effect on each of the other societies.

> Retrieve from: https://phoenician.org/sea_peoples. Paper was presented on 28 June 2005 by Sanford Holst at Al Akhawayn University in Ifrane, Morocco. 10 pages, 48 footnotes.

Fig. 103   Medinat Habu

War and Peace: Phoenician Society's Peaceful Foundation and the Deviation into War

Presented at Marquette University in Milwaukee, Wisconsin, USA

The descent of the Phoenicians' unusually peaceful society into one capable of fighting the Roman legions to a standstill is one of the paradoxes of antiquity. It is examined here in detail, with contributions by Thucydides, Herodotus, Diodorus and Polybius among others. This reveals rarely-studied aspects of Phoenician and Roman society, as well as additional impacts of their confrontation in the Punic Wars.

> Retrieve from: https://phoenician.org/punic_wars_and_peace.
> Paper was presented on 30 June 2007 by Sanford Holst at Marquette University in Milwaukee, Wisconsin. 10 pages, 55 footnotes.

Fig. 104 Zama

SEVEN PHOENICIAN PRINCIPLES

Over the course of thousands of years the Phoenicians remained committed to seven principles which gave their society its unique nature and contributed strongly to its longevity. Surprisingly enough, these principles are still practiced to greater or lesser degree by many members of Lebanese society today. It is a lasting link to their long and fascinating heritage.

Each of these principles is seen in this book in the context within which it developed in Phoenician society. And each of them has been exhibited numerous times during the Phoenicians' long history, showing they were an ongoing and integral part of the social fabric. They are:

1. Peaceful Resolution of Differences
2. International Trade
3. Religious Tolerance
4. Creating Partnerships
5. Respect for Women
6. Equality
7. Privacy

These seven principles were visible in the earliest days of the Phoenicians around 3200 BC when those sea-faring people began their international trade with Egypt. The Phoenician traders played down the differences between their cultures to such an extent that the people of Byblos became accepted into Egyptian lore. The Phoenicians not only respected women at that time, their primary deity was a woman known as Our Lady. Even so, they tolerated all the Egyptian gods. Their economic partnership with Egypt benefitted all the Phoenician people with a great degree of equality. Even their leader was more chairman-of-the-board than king. And the privacy with which they shrouded their affairs was reflected in the lack of graven images and stone-carved declarations common in other societies.

In recent years those principles suffered a setback during the fighting in Lebanon between 1975 and 1990. But they have been re-emerging into view again.

Among Lebanese ex-pats all around the world, those seven principles never really faded. Their social groups are notable for peacefully resolving any differences, and reflect much-desired religious tolerance. Many people of Lebanese heritage are still among the world's business leaders, yet this ex-pat society shows remarkable equality in choosing people to lead them. The strong role played by women in these active groups is immediately visible, as is the respect shown for them. Even the legendary Phoenician desire for privacy is still present, with all the things these people do to support Lebanon through her recent troubles being kept largely out of public view.

After all that has happened, the seven principles which guided the Phoenicians still seem to be felt to some degree and kept alive by those who share this ancient heritage.

ILLUSTRATIONS, ACKNOWLEDGMENTS

Fig. ────────────

1 Phoenician coins (Byblos: ship, Carthage: woman and horse)
2 Western Wall, Jerusalem (Holst)
3 Temple at Kition, Cyprus (Holst)
4 Cedars at Bcharré (Holst)
5 Byblos homes 4500 BC (Holst)
6 Steps up to Byblos (Holst)
7 Early cities around the Mediterranean^Map (Holst)
8 Newly built boat in Tyre of Phoenician design (Holst)
9 Egyptian reed riverboat (Holst)
10 Hierakonpolis (Courtesy of the Hierakonpolis Expedition)
11 Scorpion's macehead (Courtesy of Jon Bodsworth)
12 Narmer's Palette (Courtesy of the Egyptian Museum, Cairo)
13 Ivory label, Menes (Courtesy of the Egyptian Museum, Cairo)
14 Lebanese floor plan (Holst)
15 Baalat Gebal temple (Holst)
16 L-shaped temple (Holst)
17 Ancient Byblos^Map (Holst)
18 Trading house-Byblos (Holst)

Fig. ────────────

19 Lebanon in 2750 BC^Map (Holst)
20 Early Sidon^Map (Holst)
21 Early Tyre^Map (Holst)
22 Pharos Island^Map (Holst)
23 Pharos ancient harbor^Map (After E.M. Forster 1922)
24 Djoser's Step Pyramid (Courtesy of Jon Bodsworth)
25 Malta and Gozo^Map (Holst)
26 Ġgantija temple (Holst)
27 Hypogeum (Photo by Richard Ellis, 1910.)
28 Tarxien temple (Holst)
29 Great Pyramids of Egypt (Courtesy of Jon Bodsworth)
30 Cedar boat at Khufu's pyramid (Courtesy of Jon Bodsworth)
31 Egyptian boat (Courtesy of the Science Museum, London)
32 Aegean Sea, Crete^Map (Holst)
33 Mountains and valleys of Crete, from Phaistos (Holst)
34 Dia Island (Holst)
35 Double axes of Knossos (Holst)

Fig. ━━━━━━━━━━━━

36 Europa coming to Crete (Paolo Veronese, c. 1580, Palazzo Ducale, Venice)

37 Royal road at Knossos (Holst)

38 Outside king's chambers (Holst)

39 Light-well at palace (Holst)

40 North entrance, through the Trading House (Holst)

41 Throne room, Knossos (Holst)

42 The Procession fresco (Holst)

43 Bull Leaping fresco (Holst)

44 King's chambers (Holst)

45 Queen's chambers and Dolphin fresco (Holst)

46 Ladies in Blue fresco (original photo by cavorite/CC-BY-SA-2.0, enhanced by Holst)

47 Beirut on the coast^{Map} (Holst)

48 Beirut's settlement^{Map} (Holst)

49 Ancient, modern Beirut (Holst)

50-56: Enhancements of ancient frescoes from Akrotiri by Sanford Holst with reference to photographs by Jürgen Liepe (50), Serge Briez/ Art'Hist (51, 52-54) and H. Iossifides – G.

Fig. ━━━━━━━━━━━━

Moutevellis (49, 55) in *The Wallpaintings of Thera*, Kapon Editions, Copyright © 1992, The Thera Foundation – Petros M. Nomikos

50 Flotilla fresco part 1 (ack. above)

51 Adorant fresco (ack. above)

52 Naked Boys fresco (ack. above)

53 Mistress of Animals fresco (ack. above)

54 Antelope fresco (ack. above)

55 Fisherman fresco (ack. above)

56 Flotilla fresco part 2 (ack. above)

57 Aegean Sea and Santorini at 1628 BC^{Map} (Holst)

58 Santorini volcano surrounded by lagoon today (Holst)

59 Queen Hatshepsut's boats (After A. Mariette, *Deir-el-Bahari,* Leipzig 1877, pl.6)

60 Levant ca. 1400 BC^{Map} (Holst)

61 Sidon Sea Castle (Holst)

62 Old harbor in Tyre (Holst)

63 Black Sea, Aegean, Eastern Mediterranean^{Map} (Holst)

ANNOTATIONS

[1] Homer. *The Iliad of Homer*. Samuel Butler trans. (London: Longmans, Green and Co., 1898).

[2] Schliemann's excavations at Troy began in 1870 at the suggestion of Frank Calvert, and produced a trove of golden objects in 1873 which cemented this discovery. His findings were published in 1874.

[3] Gore, Rick "Who Were the Phoenicians?" *National Geographic*. Vol. 206:4 (October, 2004), pp.26-49.

[4] Flavius Josephus, who wrote in the first century AD, quoted Menander the Ephesian as saying, "Upon the death of Abibalus, his son Hirom took the Kingdom. He lived fifty three years, and reigned thirty four." So Hiram was nineteen when he became king, succeeding his father Abibaal. Whiston, William *The Genuine Works of Flavius Josephus the Jewish Historian* Greek translated into English by Syvert Havercamp (London: William Whiston, 1737), *Contra Apionem* 1:18.

[5] The Bible is apparently not the only source of these letters between Hiram and Solomon. In the first century AD, Josephus wrote, "And many of the epistles that passed between them are still preserved among the Tyrians." *Contra Apionem* 1:17. While it is unlikely the original documents were still in existence at that time, copies of them might have survived.

[6] 1 Kings 5:17, King James Version.

[7] Josephus cited Dius and Menander as sources on Hiram's construction works at Tyre. *Contra Apionem* 1:17-18.

[8] These temples and the roles of the Mycenaeans, Anatolians and Phoenicians on Cyprus are discussed in later chapters.

[9] Meyers, Eric ed. *Oxford Encyclopedia of Archaeology in the Near East* (Oxford: Oxford University Press, 1997), Vol. 1, p. 391.

[10] Casson, Lionel *Ships and Seamanship in the Ancient World* (Baltimore: Johns Hopkins University Press, 1995), pp. 7-8.

[11] Dunand, Maurice *Byblos* H. Tabet trans. (Paris: Librairie Adrien-maisonnueve, 1973), p. 15. He points out that the visible home foundations were built during 5000-3800 BC.

[12] Grant, Michael *The Ancient Mediterranean* (New York: Meridian, 1969), p. 18.

[13] Çamurcuoğlu, Duygu Seçil *The Wall Paintings of Çatalhöyük (Turkey): Materials, Technologies and Artists* (Thesis, University College London, September 2015). Retrieved on Jan. 17, 2021 from discovery.ucl.ac.uk/id/eprint/1471163/1/Camurcuoglu_compressed.pdf.%20COMPLETE.pdf

[14] Bass, George F. "A Bronze Age Shipwreck at Ulu Burun (Kas): 1984 Campaign" *American Journal of Archaeology* (1986) 90 (3): 269–296.

[15] See Appendix A, the Art of Boatbuilding, which shows the ingenious way these boats were crafted.

[16] Casson *Ships and Seamanship in the Ancient World* pp. 11-12.

[17] Herodotus *The Histories* 2:96.

[18] Davies, Vivian and Renee Friedman *Egypt Uncovered* (New York: Stewart, Tabori & Chang, 1998), p. 27-28.

[19] Friedman, Renee "The Ceremonial Centre at Hierakonpolis, Locality HK29A" *Aspects of Early Egypt* A.J. Spencer, ed. (London: British Museum Press, 1996), pp.16-35.

[20] Dunand *Byblos* pp. 18-19.

[21] Translated from Greek to English by C.W. King in Plutarch "On Isis and Osiris." *Morals.* (London: George Bell and Sons, 1882).

[22] Bikai, Patricia. *The Pottery of Tyre.* Warminster, UK: Aris & Phillips, 1978

[23] The reports provided by Dr. Fattah were contained in the "Workshop on Status of the Pilot Project for the Sustainable Development of the Submarine Archaeological Sites at Qayet Bey Citadel and Eastern Harbour, Alexandria, Egypt, 20-21 November, 1999. Published by the Ministry of Culture, Supreme Council of Antiquities, Department of Underwater Archaeology.

[24] Verner, Miroslav *The Pyramids* Steven Rendall, trans. (New York: Grove Press, 2001), pp. 208-209.

[25] Casson *Ships and Seamanship in the Ancient World* p. 20.

[26] Jidejian, Nina *Byblos Through the Ages* (Beirut: Dar el-Machreq, 1968), p. 21.

[27] This island was known as Thera in antiquity but is now recognized as Santorini.

[28] Herodotus noted the Phoenicians' long association with Santorini—also known as Thera and as Calliste—in his *Histories* 4:147.

[29] Explorations on Dia Island by Jacques Cousteau and others have shown evidence of the ancient port there, but it remains largely unstudied.

[30] Only a few names of Minoan kings have come down to us through Greek mythology, so there is no way to know if the first king of this dynasty was in fact named Minos. But that is the tradition, so it is followed here.

[31] Dimopoulou-Rethemiotaki, Nota; David Wilson and Peter M Day "The earlier Prepalatial settlement of Poros-Katsambas: craft production and exchange at the harbour town of Knossos" *Sheffield Studies in Aegean Archaeology* (Sheffield, UK) January 1, 2007.

[32] Fitton, J. Lesley *Minoans* (London: British Museum Press, 2002), p. 29

[33] Watrous, L. Vance "The Role of the Near East in the Rise of the Cretan Palaces," in R. Hägg and N. Marinatos, eds., *The Function of the Minoan Palaces* (Stockholm 1987), p. 67.

[34] Renfrew, Colin *The Emergence of Civilisation: The Cyclades and the Aegean in the Third Millennium BC* (London: Methuen, 1972), pp. xxv-547.

[35] See Appendix C for the paper presented by Sanford Holst at California State University, Long Beach on June 24, 2006, titled *Minoans and Phoenicians: Indigenous Development versus Eastern Influence.*

[36] Bikai, Patricia *The Pottery of Tyre* p. 72.

[37] Bikai *The Pottery of Tyre* p. 65. It should be noted that "visits" preceded the permanent resettlement at Tyre, beginning in 1600 BC just after the volcano eruption at Santorini

[38] For example, Thucydides 1:4.

[39] Bentley, Jerry and Herbert Ziegler *Traditions & Encounters* (New York: McGraw Hill, 2000), p. 51.

[40] Dr. Nota Dimopoulou, Director of the Iraklion Archaeological Museum on Crete, shared with me her many years of research regarding Poros and Knossos, much of which is still unpublished.

[41] If the king did not serve personally, the high priest could be drawn from his immediate family, see Markoe *Peoples of the Past: Phoenicians* p. 120.

[42] After the Knossos courtyard became paved, it would have been necessary for a layer of dirt to be spread over the yard, allowing traction for the bull and the leapers to perform.

[43] Graham, James Walter *The Palaces of Crete* (Princeton, NJ: Princeton University Press, 1962), pp. 231-2.

[44] Casson, Lionel *The Ancient Mariners, Second Edition* (Princeton, New Jersey: Princeton University Press, 1991), p. 6.

[45] The Linear A script used by the Minoans is still an enigma as of this writing. Linear B, which was subsequently used by the Greeks, has been deciphered.

[46] Doumas, Christos *The Wall-Paintings of Thera* (Athens: The Thera Foundation, 1999), p. 176.

[47] Manning, Sturt *A Test of Time: The Volcano of Thera and the Chronology and History of the Aegean and East Mediterranean in the Mid Second Millennium BC* (Oxford: Oxbow Books, 1999), pp. 1-419.

[48] Grimal, Nicolas *A History of Ancient Egypt* French translated into English by Ian Shaw. (Oxford: Blackwell, 1988), p. 215.

[49] Bryce, Trevor *The Kingdom of the Hittites* (Oxford: Clerendon Press, 1998), p. 306.

[50] Bryce, *The Kingdom of the Hittites* p. 320.

---

[51] Betancourt, Philip P. "The Aegean and the Origin of the Sea Peoples" *The Sea Peoples and Their World: A Reassessment* (Philadelphia: University of Pennsylvania Museum, 2000), pp. 298-300.

[52] Freeman, Charles *Egypt, Grece and Rome* (New York: Oxford University Press, 2004), p. 74.

[53] Singer, Itamar "New Evidence on the End of the Hittite Empire" *The Sea Peoples and Their World: A Reassessment* (Philadelphia: University of Pennsylvania Museum, 2000), pp. 24-25.

[54] Wood, Michael *In Search of the Trojan War* (Berkeley: University of California Press, 1998), p. 219.

[55] Barnett, R. D. "The Sea Peoples" *Cambridge Ancient History* (Cambridge: Cambridge University Press, 1975), Vol. II, Part 2, p. 366.

[56] Van Soldt, W.H. "Ugarit: A Second-Millennium Kingdom on the Mediterranean Coast" *Civilizations of the Ancient Near East* (New York: Charles Scribner's Sons, 1995), p. 1265.

[57] Murnane, William J. "The History of Ancient Egypt: An Overview" *Civilizations of the Ancient Near East* (New York: Charles Scribner's Sons, 1995), p. 708.

[58] Finkelstein, Israel "The Philistine Settlements: When, Where and How Many?" *The Sea Peoples and Their World: A Reassessment* (Philadelphia: University of Pennsylvania Museum, 2000), p. 159.

[59] Breasted, J. H. *Ancient Records of Egypt* (Chicago: University of Illinois Press, 2001/1906), vol. 4, pp. 37-39.

[60] Dothan, Trude "The 'Sea Peoples' and the Philistines of Ancient Palestine" *Civilizations of the Ancient Near East* (New York: Charles Scribner's Sons, 1995), pp. 1267-1279.

[61] Barnett, "The Sea Peoples" pp. 367-368.

[62] Bikai, Patricia *The Pottery of Tyre* pp. 73-74.

[63] Markoe, Glenn *Peoples of the Past: Phoenicians* p. 24.

[64] Thucydides *History of the Peloponnesian War* Translated from the Greek by Rex Warner (New York: Penguin Group, 1972), 6:2

65 Translated by Miriam Lichtheim in: *Ancient Egyptian Literature: Volume II: The New Kingdom.* Berkeley: University of California Press, 1976.

66 Lagassé *The Columbia Encyclopedia, Sixth Edition* p.7.

67 1 Chronicles 28:3

68 Markoe *Peoples of the Past: Phoenicians* p. 196.

69 Strabo *Geography* 16:23.

70 See Chapter 14 for the previous trades that were read to Wenamun from a Phoenician ledger at Byblos.

71 Markoe *Peoples of the Past: Phoenicians* p. 49.

72 See Appendix B, the Legend of the Phoenix, which explores the origin of this legend.

73 Markoe *Peoples of the Past: Phoenicians* pp. 178-179.

74 Heeren, A. H. L. *Historical Researches into the Politics, Intercourse and Trade of the Carthaginians, Ethiopians and Egyptians.* London: Henry G. Bohn, 1850.

75 Polybius *Histories* 3.22.

76 Herodotus *The Histories* 3:19.

77 Herodotus *The Histories* 7:165-166.

78 Diodorus *Diodorus Siculus: Books 11-12.37.1: Greek History 480-431 B.C.* 11:1, 11:20-22.

79 Schwartz JH, Houghton F, Macchiarelli R, Bondioli L (2010) *Skeletal Remains from Punic Carthage Do Not Support Systematic Sacrifice of Infants.* PLoS ONE 5(2): e9177. Retrieved on Feb. 5, 2021 from https://doi.org/10.1371/journal.pone.0009177

80 Smith P, Stager L, Greene J, Avishai G (2013) *Cemetery or sacrifice? Infant burials at the Carthage Tophet: Age estimations attest to infant sacrifice at the Carthage Tophet.* Retrieved on Feb. 5, 2021 from https://www.cambridge.org/core/journals/antiquity/article/abs/cemetery-or-sacrifice-infant-burials-at-the-carthage-tophet/EA2F96A8FD7229800391B766C95ECBE1

81 The people of Carthage could have come up with this "substitution" idea by themselves. But since the Phoenicians helped their Jewish neighbors build

Solomon's Temple, and then lived beside them for hundreds of years, they may actually have known the story of Abraham and his deferred sacrifice.

[82] Hornblower, Simon *The Greek World: 470-323 BC* (London: Routledge, 2002) pp. 293-295.

[83] Lancel, Serge *Carthage: A History* Antonia Nevill trans. (Oxford: Blackwell, 1995) pp. 269-270.

[84] Lazenby, J.F. *The First Punic War* (London: University College London Press, 1996) p. 36.

[85] Polybius *Histories* 1:20.

[86] Bagnall, Nigel *The Punic Wars* (London: Hutchinson, 1990) pp. 111-114.

[87] Livy *The War with Hannibal: Books XXI-XXX of The History of Rome from its Foundation* 21:1.

[88] Hoyos, B.D. *Unplanned Wars: The Origins of the First and Second Punic Wars* (Berlin: Walter de Gruyter, 1997) pp. 254-259.

[89] Caven, Brian *The Punic Wars* (London: Weidenfeld and Nicolson, 1980) p. 228.

[90] Polybius *Histories* 15:18-19.

[91] Polybius *Histories* 36:2-7.

[92] Grant, Michael *History of Rome* (New York: Charles Scribner's Sons, 1978) pp. 144-145.

[93] For example, Pomponius Mela 1:56 "The Phoenicians...were outstanding in literature and other arts...."

[94] See the self-set fires reported by Diodorus during the sack of Sidon by the Persians.

[95] Pliny the Elder *Natural History* 18:22.

[96] Moscati, Sabatino "Who Were the Phoenicians?" *The Phoenicians* (New York: Rizzoli International, 1999), pp. 18-19.

[97] Jenkins, Nancy "The Smell of Time" *Saudi Aramco World* (Houston, TX: January/February, 1980) pp. 12-17.

[98] The ancient name for the island of Santorini is Thera.

BIBLIOGRAPHY

Alsop, Joseph. *From the Silent Earth: A Report on the Greek Bronze Age.* New York: Harper & Row, 1964.

Appian. *Wars of the Romans in Iberia.* (Greek, translated into English by J.S. Richardson.) Warminster, UK: Aris & Phillips, 2000.

Aristotle. *The Politics.* (Greek, translated into English by B. Jowett). Oxford: Clarendon Press, 1885.

Arrian. *The Campaigns of Alexander.* (Greek, translated into English by Aubrey de Sélincourt.) London: Penguin Books, 1958.

Aubet, Maria Eugenia. *The Phoenicians and the West.* (Spanish, translated into English by Mary Turton.) Cambridge: Cambridge University Press, 2001.

Bagnall, Nigel *The Punic Wars.* London: Hutchinson, 1990.

Baramki, Dimitri. *Phoenicia and the Phoenicians.* Beirut: Khayats, 1961.

Bard, Kathryn A. *Encyclopedia of the Archaeology of Ancient Egypt.* London: Routledge, 1999.

Barnett, R. D. "The Sea Peoples" *Cambridge Ancient History.* Cambridge: Cambridge University Press, 1975, Vol. II, Part 2, pp. 359-378.

Bengtson, Hermann *History of Greece* (Edmund F. Bloedow trans.) Ottawa: University of Ottawa Press, 1988.

Bentley, Jerry and Herbert Ziegler *Traditions & Encounters.* New York: McGraw Hill, 2000.

Bernal, Martin. *Black Athena, Volume I.* New Jersey: Rutgers University Press, 1987.

_____ *Black Athena, Volume II.* New Jersey: Rutgers Uni-versity Press, 1991.

Betancourt, Philip P. "High chronology and low chronology: Thera archaeo-logical evidence" in *Thera and the Aegean World III: Papers to Be Presented at the Third International Congress at Santorini, Greece, 3-9 September 1989.* Thera Foundation, pp. 9-17.

_____ *Kommos II.* (Joseph W. Shaw and Maria C. Shaw, editors.) Princeton, New Jersey: Princeton University Press, 1990.

_____ "The Aegean and the Origin of the Sea Peoples" *The Sea Peoples and Their World: A Reassessment* Philadelphia: University of Pennsylvania Museum, 2000, pp. 298-300.

Bierling, Marilyn R., ed. *The Phoenicians in Spain.* (Spanish, translated into English by Marilyn R. Bierling.) Winona Lake, Indiana: Eisenbrauns, 2002.

Bikai, Patricia. *The Pottery of Tyre.* Warminster, UK: Aris & Phillips, 1978.

_____ *The Phoenician Pottery of Cyprus.* Nicosia, Cyprus: A. G. Leventis Foundation, 1987.

_____ "The Phoenicians." *Archaeology Magazine.* 43:2 (1990): 22-35.

Blegen, Carl W. *The Mycenaean Age.* Cincinnati, Ohio: The University of Cincinnati, 1962.

Boardman, John et al, eds. *The Oxford History of the Roman World.* Oxford: Oxford University Press, 1986.

_____ *Cambridge Ancient History.* Cambridge: Cambridge University Press, 1991.

Bradford, Ernle. *Hannibal.* New York: McGraw-Hill, 1981.

Branigan, Keith *The Foundations of Palatial Crete.* London: Duckworth, 1970.

Braudel, Fernand. *Memory and the Mediterranean.* (French, translated into English by Siân Reynolds.) New York: Random House, 2002.

Breasted, J. H. *Ancient Records of Egypt.* Chicago: University of Chicago Press, 1906.

Broodbank, Cyprian. "Minoanisation." *Proceedings of the Cambridge Philological Society* Vol.50 (2004): 46-91.

Bryce, Trevor. *The Kingdom of the Hittites.* Oxford: Clerendon Press, 1998.

Bunnens, Guy. *L'Expansion Phénicienne en Méditerranée.* (In French.) Bruxelles, Belgium: Institut Historique Belge de Rome, 1979.

Camps, Gabriel, ed. *Encyclopédie Berbére.* (In French.) Aix-en-Provence, France: Edisud, 1984.

Cancik, Hubert and Helmuth Schneider, eds. *Brill's New Pauly Encyclopedia of the Ancient World.* Leiden, The Netherlands: Brill, 2002.

Casson, Lionel. *The Ancient Mariners.* Princeton, New Jersey: Princeton University Press, 1991.

_____ *Ships and Seamanship in the Ancient World.* Baltimore, Maryland: John Hopkins University Press, 1995.

Castro, María Cruz Fernández *Iberia in Prehistory.* Oxford: Blackwell, 1995.

Caven, Brian *The Punic Wars.* London: Weidenfeld and Nicolson, 1980.

Chadwick, John. *The Mycenaean World.* Cambridge: Cambridge University Press, 1976.

Cherry, John "Evolution, Revolution, and the Origins of Complex Society in Minoan Crete," in O. Krzyszkowska and L. Nixon, eds., *Minoan Society* Bristol: Bristol Classical Press, 1983, p. 33.

Clark, J. Desmond, ed. *The Cambridge History of Africa.* Cambridge: Cambridge University Press, 1982.

Cline, Eric H. *1177 B.C.* Princeton: Princeton University Press, 2014.

Coldstream, J.N. *Geometric Greece.* London: Ernest Benn Limited, 1977.

Corm, Charles. *La montagne inspiree: trois etapes de la vie du Liban: chansons de geste.* (In French) Beirut: Editions de la Revue phenicienne, 1964.

Cullen Tracey, ed. *Aegean Prehistory.* Boston: Archaeological Institute of America, 2001.

Davies, Vivian and Renee Friedman. *Egypt Uncovered.* New York: Stewart, Tabori & Chang, 1998.

de Beer, Sir Gavin. *Hannibal.* New York: The Viking Press, 1969.

Desborough, V.R.d'A. *The Greek Dark Ages.* London: Ernest Benn Limited, 1972.

Dickinson, Oliver. *The Aegean Bronze Age.* Cambridge: Cambridge University Press, 1994.

Diodorus. *Diodorus of Sicily.* (Greek, translated into English by Charles L. Sherman). Cambridge, Massachusetts: Harvard University Press, 1952.

Dodge, Theodore Ayrault. *Hannibal.* Boston: Da Capo Press, 1891.

Dothan, Trude. "The 'Sea Peoples' and the Philistines of Ancient Palestine" *Civilizations of the Ancient Near East.* New York: Charles Scribner's Sons, 1995.

Doumas, Christos. *The Wall-paintings of Thera.* (Greek, translated into English by Alex Doumas.) Athens: The Thera Foundation - Petros M. Nomikos, 1999.

Dueck, Daniela. *Strabo of Amasia.* London: Routledge, 2000.

Dunand, Maurice. *Byblos.* (French, translated into English by H. Tabet.) Paris: Librairie Adrien-Maisonneuve, 1973.

_____ *Fouilles de Byblos: 1926-1932.* (In French.) Paris: P. Geuthner, 1937-1939.

_____ *Fouilles de Byblos: 1933-1938.* (In French.) Paris: A. Maisonneuve, 1954-1958.

Fage, J.D. *A History of Africa* London: Routledge, 1995.

Finkelstein, Israel "The Philistine Settlements: When, Where and How Many?" *The Sea Peoples and Their World: A Reassessment* Philadelphia: University of Pennsylvania Museum, 2000, p. 159.

Fitton, J. Lesley. *Minoans.* London: British Museum Press, 2002.

Flexner, Stuart Berg et al (ed.) *The Random House Dictionary of the English Language, Second Edition Unabridged.* New York: Random House, 1987.

Forster, E.M. *Alexandria: a History and a Guide.* Woodstock, New York: Overlook Press, 1974/1922.

Freeman, Charles. *Egypt, Greece and Rome.* New York: Oxford Univeristy Press, 2004.

Friedman, Renee "The Ceremonial Centre at Hierakonpolis, Locality HK29A" *Aspects of Early Egypt* A.J. Spencer, ed. London: British Museum Press, 1996.

Friedrich, Walter L. *Fire in the Sea: the Santorini Volcano.* (German, translated into English by Alexander R. McBirney.) Cambridge: Cambridge University Press, 2000.

Gamble, Clive "Surplus and Self-Sufficiency in the Cycladic Subsistence Economy," in J. L. Davis and J. F. Cherry (eds.), *Papers in Cycladic Prehistory* Los Angeles 1979, pp. 122-134.

Garraty, John and Peter Gay, eds. *The Columbia History of the World.* New York: Harper& Row, 1972.

Gibran, Kahlil. *The Prophet.* New York: Alfred A. Knopf, 2003.

Gore, Rick. "Who Were the Phoenicians?" *National Geographic Magazine.* 206:4 (2004): 26-49.

Graham, James Walter *The Palaces of Crete* Princeton, NJ: Princeton University Press, 1962.

Grant, Michael. *The Ancient Mediterranean.* New York: Charles Scribner's Sons, 1969.

_____ *History of Rome.* New York: Charles Scribner's Sons, 1978.

_____ and Rachel Kitzinger (ed.) *Civilization of the Ancient Mediterranean.* New York: Charles Scribner's Sons, 1988.

Gras, M., P. Rouillard and J. Teixidor. *L'Univers Phenicien.* (In French.) Paris: Arthaud, 1989.

Grimal, Nicolas. *A History of Ancient Egypt.* (French, translated into English by Ian Shaw). Oxford: Blackwell, 1988.

Hägg, Robin And Nanno Marinatos, eds. *The Minoan Thalassocracy Myth and Reality.* Stockholm: Swedish Institute in Athens, 1984.

Halstead, Paul "From Determinism to Uncertainty: Social Storage and the Rise of the Minoan Palace," in A. Sheridan and G. Bailey (eds.), *Economic Archaeology.* Oxford 1981, pp. 187-213.

Harden, Donald. *The Phoenicians.* London: Thames and Hudson, 1962.

Harrison, Richard J. *Spain at the Dawn of History: Iberians, Phoenicians and Greeks.* London: Thames and Hudson, 1988.

Heeren, A. H. L. *Historical Researches into the Politics, Intercourse and Trade of the Carthaginians, Ethiopians and Egyptians.* London: Henry G. Bohn, 1850.

Herm, Gerhard *The Phoenicians: The Purple Empire of the Ancient World.* New York: William Morrow, 1975.

Herodotus. *The History* (Greek, translated into English by George Rawlinson.) New York: Tandy Thomas Co., 1909.

Hesiod. *Theogony.* (Greek, translated into English by Dorothea Wender). Harmondsworth, England: Penguin Books, 1976.

Holst, Sanford. *Phoenicians: Lebanon's Epic Heritage.* Los Angeles: Cambridge & Boston Press, 2005.

Homer. *The Iliad.* (Greek, translated by Samuel Butler.) Berkeley: University of California Press, 1925.

_____ *The Odyssey.* (Greek, translated by Robert Fitzgerald.) New York: Farrar, Straus and Giroux, 1998.

Hornblower, Simon *The Greek World: 470-323 BC.* London: Routledge, 2002.

Hoyos, B.D. *Unplanned Wars: The Origins of the First and Second Punic Wars.* Berlin: Walter de Gruyter, 1997.

Ioannides, G.C. *Studies in Honour of Vassos Karageorghis.* Nicosia, Cyprus: Society of Cypriot Studies, 1992.

Jidejian, Nina. *Tyre through the Ages.* Beirut: Dar El-Machreq, 1969.

_____ *Sidon through the Ages.* Beirut: Dar El-Machreq, 1971.

Karageorghis, Vassos. *Cyprus.* London: Thames and Hudson, 1982.

_____ et al. *The Relations Between Cyprus and Crete ca. 2000-500 BC.* Nicosia, Cyprus: Cyprus Department of Antiquities, 1979.

Kemp, B.J. and R.S. Merrillees *Minoan Pottery in Second Millennium Egypt.* Deutches archäologisches institut, Abteilung Kairo. Mainz am Rhein: Philipp von Zabern, 1980.

Krzyszkowska, O. and L. Nixon, eds. *Minoan Society: Proceedings of the Cambridge Colloquium 1981.* Bristol, UK: Bristol Classical Press, 1983.

Lagassé, Paul et al, eds. *The Columbia Encyclopedia, Sixth Edition.* New York: Columbia University Press, 2001-04.

Lancel, Serge *Carthage: A History.* Antonia Nevill trans. Oxford: Blackwell, 1995.

Lazenby, J.F. *The First Punic War.* London: University College London Press, 1996 .

Lefkowitz, Mary and Guy Rogers, eds., *Black Athena Revisited.* Chapel Hill: University of North Carolina, 1996,

Lichtheim, Miriam. *Ancient Egyptian Literature: Volume II: The New Kingdom.* Berkeley: University of California Press, 1976.

Livy. *The Early History of Rome.* (First books of *The History of Rome from Its Foundation.* (Latin, translated by Aubrey de Sélincourt.) London: Penguin Books, 1960.

_____ *The War with Hannibal.* (Books XXI-XXX of *The History of Rome from Its Foundation.* Latin, translated by Aubrey de Sélincourt.) London: Penguin Books, 1965.

Lopez-Ruiz, Carolina and Brian R. Doak, ed. *The Oxford Handbook of the Phoenician and Punic Mediterranean.* New York: Oxford Univrsity Press, 2019.

Manning, Sturt W. *A Test of Time: The Volcano of Thera and the Chronology and History of the Aegean and East Mediterranean in the Mid Second Millennium BC.* Oxford: Oxbow Books, 1999.

Markoe, Glenn. *Phoenician Bronze and Silver Bowls from Cyprus and the Mediterranean.* Berkeley: University of California Press, 1985.

_____ *Phoenicians.* Berkeley: University of California Press, 2000.

Matyszak, Philip. *The Enemies of Rome.* London: Thames and Hud-son, 2004.

McDonald, William A. and Carol G. Thomas. *Progress into the Past: The Rediscovery of Mycenaean Civilization.* Indianapolis: Indiana University Press, 1990.

Mellor, Ronald, ed. *The Historians of Ancient Rome.* New York: Routledge, 2004

Meyers, Eric, ed. *Oxford Encyclopedia of Archaeology in the Near East.* New York: Oxford University Press, 1997.

Miles, Richard   *Carthage Must be Destroyed.*   London: Allen Lane/Penguin Group, 2010.

Mokhtar, G., ed.   *General History of Africa, Volume II, Ancient Civilizations.*   London: Heinemann, 1981

Montet, Pierre.   *Byblos et L'Egypte.*   (In French.)   Paris: P. Geuthner, 1928-29.

Moran, William L.   *The Amarna Letters.*   Baltimore, Maryland: John Hopkins Press, 1992.

Moscati, Sabatino.   *The World of the Phoenicians.*   (Italian, translated into English by Alastair Hamilton.)   London: Weidenfeld & Nicolson, 1968.

_____ (ed.)   *The Phoenicians.*   New York: Rizzoli International, 1999.

Murnane, William J.   "The History of Ancient Egypt: An Overview"   *Civilizations of the Ancient Near East.*   New York: Charles Scribner's Sons, 1995.

Nilsson, Martin   *The Mycenaean Origin of Greek Mythology* (Berkeley: University of California Press, 1972 [1932]).

Not Applicable.   *The Holy Bible, King James Version.*   1987.

Olmstead, A.T.   *History of the Persian Empire.*   Chicago: The Univeristy of Chicago Press, 1948.

Oren, Eliezer D.   "Introduction"   *The Sea Peoples and Their World: A Reassessment.*   Philadelphia: University of Pennsylvania Museum, 2000.

Oxford Staff, eds.   *Atlas of the World, Seventh Edition.*   New York: Oxford University Press, 1999.

Pliny.   *Natural History.*   (Latin, translated into English by John Bostock and H. T. Riley).   London: Henry G. Bohn, 1855.

Plutarch.   "On Isis and Osiris."   *Morals.*   (Greek, translated into English by C. W. King).   London: George Bell and Sons, 1882.

Polybius.   *Histories.*   (Greek, translated by Evelyn S. Shuckburgh)   London: Macmillan, 1889.

Powell, Barry B.   *Homer and the Origin of the Greek Alphabet.*   Cambridge: Cambridge University Press, 1991.

Pritchard, James Bennett. *Recovering Sarepta, a Phoenician City: Excavations at Sarafand, Lebanon, 1969-1974, by the University Museum of the University of Pennsylvania.* Princeton, New Jersey: Princeton University Press, 1978.

Quinn, Josephine. *In Search of the Phoenicians.* Princeton: Prinston University Press, 2018.

Redford, Donald, ed. *The Oxford Encyclopedia of Ancient Egypt.* New York: Oxford University Press, 2001.

Renfrew, Colin *The Emergence of Civilisation: The Cyclades and the Aegean in the Third Millennium BC.* London: Methuen, 1972.

Rufus, Quintus Curtius. *The History of Alexander.* (Latin, translated into English by John Yardley.) London: Penguin Books, 2001.

Sacks, David *Language Visible.* New York: Broadway Books, 2003.

Sanders, Nancy K. *The Sea Peoples.* London: Thames and Hudson, 1978.

Sasson, Jack M., ed. *Civilizations of the Ancient Near East.* New York: Charles Scribner's Sons, 1995.

Singer, Itamar. "New Evidence on the End of the Hittite Empire" *The Sea Peoples and Their World: A Reassessment.* Philadelphia: University of Pennsylvania Museum, 2000.

Speake, Jennifer et al, eds. *The Hutchinson Dictionary of World History.* Oxford: Helicon Publishing, 1993.

Strong, Anthony. *The Phoenicians in History and Legend.* Bloomington, Indiana: 1st Books Library, 2002.

Thucydides. *History of the Peloponnesian War.* (Greek, translated into English by Richard Crawley.) London: Longmans, Green and Co., 1874.

Tubb, Jonathan N. *Canaanites.* Norman, Oklahoma: University of Oklahoma Press, 1998.

Van Andel, Tjeerd and Curtis Runnels "An Essay on the 'Emergence of Civilization' in the Aegean World," *Antiquity* 62(1988), pp. 234-247.

Van Soldt, W. H. "Ugarit: A Second-Millennium Kingdom on the Mediterranean Coast" *Civilizations of the Ancient Near East.* New York: Charles Scribner's Sons, 1995.

Verner, Miroslav *The Pyramids* Steven Rendall, trans. New York: Grove Press, 2001.

Virgil. *The Aeneid.* (Latin, translated into English by Harlan Hoge Ballard). New York: Charles Scribner's Sons, 1930.

Wachsmann, Shelley. "To the Sea of the Philistines" *The Sea Peoples and Their World: A Reassessment.* Philadelphia: University of Pennsylvania Museum, 2000.

Walbank, F.W. ed. *Cambridge Ancient History.* Cambridge: Cambridge University Press, 1989.

Ward, William A., ed. *The Role of the Phoenicians in the Interaction of Mediterranean Civilizations.* Beirut: The American University of Beirut, 1968.

_____ *Egypt and the East Mediterranean World 2200 – 1900 BC: Studies in Egyptian Foreign Relations During the First Intermediate Period.* Beirut: American University of Beirut, 1971.

Warren, Peter and Vronwy Hankey. *Aegean Bronze Age Chronology.* Bristol, UK: Bristol Classical Press, 1989.

Watrous, L. Vance "The Role of the Near East in the Rise of the Cretan Palaces," in R. Hägg and N. Marinatos, eds., *The Function of the Minoan Palaces.* Stockholm 1987, p. 67

_____ "Egypt and Crete in the Early Middle Bronze Age: A Case of Trade and Cultural Diffusion," in E. H. Cline and D. Harris-Cline, eds., *The Aegean and the Orient in the Second Millennium* [*Aegaeum* 18] (Liège/Austin 1998), p. 24.

Weinberg, Saul "The relative chronology of the Aegean in the Neolithic period and the Early Bronze Age," in R.W. Ehrich, ed., *Relative Chronologies in Old World Archaeology.* Chicago: University of Chicago Press, 1954, p. 95.

Wood, Michael. *In Search of the Trojan War.* Berkeley: University of California Press, 1998.

Zangger, Eberhard. "Who Were the Sea People?" *Saudi Aramco World.* 46:3 (1995): 20-31.

INDEX

CPSIA information can be obtained
at www.ICGtesting.com
Printed in the USA
BVHW071421261222
654959BV00014B/546/J